MOUSEJUNKIES!

MORE Tips, Tales, and Tricks for a Disney World Fix

all you need to know for a perfect vacation

Bill Burke

TRAVELERS' TALES
AN IMPRINT OF SOLAS HOUSE, INC.
PALO ALTO

Travelers' Tales is a trademark of Travelers' Tales/Solas House, Inc., 2320 Bowdoin Street, Palo Alto, California 94306. www.travelerstales.com

Art Direction: Kimberly Nelson Coombs
Photo Credit: © Blaine Harrington
Author Photo Credit: © Katherine Burke
Interior Design and Page Layout: Howie Severson
Production Director: Susan Brady

Library of Congress Cataloging-in-Publication Data

Burke, Bill.
  Mousejunkies! : more tips, tales, and tricks for a Disney World fix : all you need to know for a perfect vacation / Bill Burke.
     pages cm
  ISBN 978-1-60952-101-1 (paperback)
  1. Walt Disney World (Fla.)--Guidebooks. 2. Orlando (Fla.)--Guidebooks. I. Title.
  GV1853.3.F62B87 2015
  917.59'2404--dc23

Third Edition
Printed in the United States
10 9 8 7 6 5 4 3 2 1

To the Mousejunkies:

Amy, Katie, Randy, Carol, J, Deb,

Jenna, Ryan, Walt, and Barry.

Thank you for the invaluable help,

endless patience and support.

Table of Contents

Foreword

The traditional gift for a 17th anniversary is furniture or a watch, according to time-honored customs. I've been dragging my friends and family to Walt Disney World, every year, for just about that long.

By my estimation, then, Disney can ship me one of those great leather rocking chairs from the Carolwood Pacific Room in the Wilderness Lodge Resort, because another watch at this point would seem excessive. But then, that's what being a Mousejunkie is all about.

One Mickey watch is nice. Amassing an unnecessarily massive and jumbled pile of timepieces is something a Mousejunkie does. It's an apt metaphor for stringing together endless trips to central Florida. After all, this book isn't called *Mousemildlyinterested*. This is what we do, this is who we've become, and this is why you're holding the third edition of *Mousejunkies* in your hands—or more likely these days, downloading it onto your tablet. (If you're reading the preview file, just spring for the whole thing. Spoiler alert: there's a section about someone throwing up all over a Disney boat.) If that doesn't entice you to delve deeper into this book, then maybe you need to make sure you wouldn't

be better off spending your vacation time in a sensory depri-
vation tank and crafting haikus. Not that I have anything
against haikus.

You have a problem
You should move to Orlando
And marry Mickey

Anyone afflicted with our particular malady has heard
versions of this before. And it is a fair, if uninformed, question. I've been to Walt Disney World scores of times over the
past 17 years. Why don't I just move there?

Well, I'll tell you...

If this was a Disney movie, this is where music would
begin to swell and I'd break into song and explain all there is
to know about visiting Walt Disney World again and again.
There would be a verse about discovering the place and how
it exceeded all my expectations. The chorus would have
something to do with how I love having it as an escape from
reality, and how if I lived there it would become the reality
I sometimes need a break from. There would probably be a
final verse about how the constant, frenetic pace of change
on the property keeps it forever evolving. At the end, I'd turn
dramatically from the camera, my dress flowing in the warm
breeze. Wait, no, I didn't say dress. (Note to publisher: We
can edit that out, right?)

I'd also make sure there was a mind-melting bass solo in the
middle of it, because, well, it's my name on the front cover and
if you can't blast a bass solo in your own book, then why do it?

The point is, there's a third edition of *Mousejunkies* because our World—our favorite vacation destination above all others—never stops moving. Keeping up with the changes is very difficult: From what to do and where to stay to deciding where to eat and how to get around, things are rarely the same from trip to trip. Even planning a vacation to Walt Disney World is dramatically different than it was just a year ago.

Over the next few hundred pages, we'll talk about what's so great about Walt Disney World and what's different and new. There is, however, a minor challenge. As soon as I attach this to an email, hit "send" and the book is transported through the tubes across the country to Traveler's Tales, my publisher, Disney is going to announce a new project, restaurant, hotel, or theme park alteration. To Disney, I say: Stop it. Just for a few months, so I don't look dumb. Or at least a little less-so.

I love sharing our adventures and helping people experience as much of the Florida Project as possible. If any of the information herein helps that to happen, then great. If you laugh, even better.

It's my hope that through this book, you'll untangle the sometimes arcane process of planning a Walt Disney World vacation. I hope you'll come to discover, or rediscover, the joy that can be found there, and hopefully, just when you need a fix the most, you'll be transported there and you'll be reminded about what it means to be a Mousejunkie.

While you do that, I'm going to go wait at the mailbox for my leather rocking chair.

Mousejunkie
Return And Return. And Return.

To the casual observer, I might seem rather normal. For that matter, you might as well—but you and I know better. We are just like everyone else—just Disneyer.

Like Normal People, Just Disneyer

Scratch the surface and a new truth emerges. We are Disney addicts. Take a look around my house and it becomes clear quickly. There are far too many ear hats scattered about my office, a jumbled pile of metal that I like to call my Disney watch collection sits in a twisted heap right next to my computer, framed pin sets decorate the walls, and there's even a big fig of Mickey and Minnie holding hands and taking up way too much room next to the TV. It's all pretty much routine for someone living the life of a Mousejunkie. And the great thing about reveling in the throes of this obsession is that before too long, you'll learn that you're not alone. Disney has built a vacation destination that people feel compelled to return to again and again.

There's a reason Mousejunkies exist. People visit Walt Disney World and they (the royal "they" that is, meaning me and possibly you) return again and again—which means that Disney is doing something right. And when it all comes together, it can form a potent concoction that turns a seemingly normal individual into an unabashed, wide-eyed fanatic. It's that heady fusion that breeds Mousejunkies.

More often than not, it all starts with a lightning bolt moment. Weather, crowd levels, company, and circumstances combine into a synchronous mash that converts even the most apathetic vacationer. I know this to be fact because to what else can I attribute my compulsion to sit in a giant honey pot and ride through the Hundred Acre Wood like a child?

Mousejunkies also know that when you're not at Walt Disney World, you're doing your best to recreate that feeling anywhere and everywhere. Facebook groups and online forums eat up billable hours, attraction ride-throughs on YouTube completely remove us from mundane reality, and theme park music playlists pipe atmosphere-completing audio into our world.

If you do not yet count yourself among us, fair warning: You soon will. You've picked this book up for one of three reasons:

1. You're a confirmed Mousejunkie. You love Walt Disney World and everything about it, and you need to get your Disney fix. You saw a picture of Cinderella Castle on the cover and fell into a pixie-dust infused haze. You awoke to the sound of the cash register with this book in your hands.

2. You thought the cover said, "Mouthjunkies," and you're studying dentistry.
3. You're planning a Walt Disney World vacation and can use some advice.

If you're already an addict, then I welcome you with the secret handshake. (Hint for the uninitiated: It involves a big, white glove with four fingers.)

If you're about to embark on your first Walt Disney World vacation, I envy you. A Walt Disney World vacation is not just a week away at an amusement park. It's a potentially life-changing event. I realize that sounds a bit overly dramatic, but I speak from experience.

I first visited Walt Disney World on June 7, 1981. Sure, it blew my mind, but I was also twelve. My next visit wouldn't be for another eighteen years. I was knocking on thirty and needed to pick a vacation destination. For a variety of reasons—most of which turned out to be invalid—Walt Disney World was not at the top of my list. However, after a little debate between my wife and I, that's where we ended up. I booked the trip and left our home with zero expectations—and I think that's why I would be transformed into a Mousejunkie in less time than it takes to say "our travel agent was on crack."

Everyone has their own story about how they became a Mousejunkie. Here's mine:

We had been on the ground in Orlando for less than an hour, and we were already rethinking our plan to vacation at Walt Disney World. My wife and I had just battled an unruly mob while checking in to our non-Disney-owned hotel somewhere on a patch of oily, sun-softened asphalt in Kissimmee.

Then we discovered that our travel agent had dramatically misrepresented our accommodations. My travel partner/wife Amy was succumbing to what was shaping up to be a disaster of a week ahead of us. There was no kitchenette, as was promised by our travel agent. There was no shuttle ready to take us to Walt Disney World, which allegedly lay just to our west. Perhaps it lay strategically hidden behind the fried chicken shack or the crappy t-shirt shop.

There were flies. And all around us was an absolutely crushing, all-enveloping, relentless heat. It is memorable only because where there was once an air conditioner in our room was now a large metal box that conditioned approximately no cubic feet of air whatsoever.

In a quiet voice shaking with regret, she summed up our vacation thus far.

"I can't do this," she said.

If, at that moment, I had grabbed a taxi back to the Orlando International Airport and hopped the next flight home, this would be a very short book, perhaps called *Laying on the Couch All Weekjunkies*. We certainly would have saved a lot of money. And we definitely would have avoided curious stares from people when they learned we'd be returning to central Florida. Again.

But then we would have missed so many things. Like the overwhelming nostalgia that made it feel like we were traveling back in time, watching *Wonderful World of Disney* as a youngster in the '70s (he said, revealing his age). Or the tangible high that accompanied being completely immersed in an admittedly manufactured world where everything exceeded my expectations. What I would've missed most, without even knowing it, would have been the relationships.

Mousejunkies are a fraternity of like-minded Disney enthusiasts that speak a shared language, and have experienced similar things at a fixed location. It's almost impossible to not forge new bonds with people who have also been moved by what started out as nothing more than a simple trip to a theme park resort.

It also could have been the bread pudding at 'Ohana. Either way, our lives would be dramatically different right now if it wasn't for that decision to see our planned vacation through.

It all truly began with a change in venue. Refusing to stay at our pre-arranged hotel, we fled for Disney property. It's there that we were welcomed into the world of Disney obsession. When I first walked through the front doors of the All-Star Music Resort, it was if I had been smashed in the face by a sledgehammer. An animated, comically oversized sledgehammer that didn't really hurt, but a sledgehammer nonetheless. It was probably because we were coming from a completely underwhelming and frankly kind of scary hotel, and stepping into a colorful, impossibly happy environment. That transformative experience was much more than just upgrading to a nicer accommodation. I had all my expectations exceeded during that week at Walt Disney World. We saw great shows, ate at fantastic restaurants, heard amazing music, shared a million laughs, experienced top-notch thrills and attractions and got away from reality for a while.

It was, in retrospect, something to write home about.

So I'm glad we decided to change hotels, brave the heat and the crowds and embark on what would become a life-changing seven days. It wasn't exactly a religious experience, but it did open up a whole new world and provide an all-encompassing hobby/lifestyle.

Here's an example of what being beaten by the magic stick will do to you: One of my favorite attractions is Peter Pan's Flight in Fantasyland at the Magic Kingdom. On the surface that might not seem like much, but consider that the target audience is probably seven years old. Such is my shameless love for all things Disney now that I have fallen under its spell.

Never in a million years did I suspect that I'd stand in line to hug a sweaty stranger in a bear suit and gasp at water fountains. It all happened during those first few days at the resort. I arrived a fairly normal guy. I left a Mousejunkie.

What occurred next can be summed up fairly succinctly: We embarked on roughly 17 bajillion trips to central Florida and spent far too much money at my favorite vacation destination.

Why? The short answer might mention the food, the world-class customer service or the obsessive attention to detail. But it's more than that. Walt Disney World makes you feel things. There's a Disney high that comes along with visiting. Everything about the place has a story or a history to it. You get wrapped up and inexorably involved. The atmosphere, the music, the lighting—it all goes into creating a world that becomes very real.

Over time I got pretty good at navigating this massive world. Its size alone, however, meant that while I could effortlessly skip from one attraction to the next in one small portion of the property, I'd bungle some other part of our experience. (Like not even knowing there were nighttime shows until our second trip. Feel free to mock me.)

That's where the Mousejunkies came in. We are all Mousejunkies, but the originals—a group of friends who, it turned out, were Walt Disney World fanatics—could help navigate the ins and outs of visiting Walt Disney World. They were the like-minded friends I could turn to in times of Disney-related calamity.

Meet the Mousejunkies

What's the difference between a satisfied Walt Disney World guest and a hopelessly addicted Mousejunkie?

For Mousejunkies, Disney is a lifestyle. A satisfied guest might feel they got a good value for their vacation dollar. A Mousejunkie has a great time and leaves no vacation dollar unspent. And if there are a few meager funds left at the end of the week, they are spent planning the next trip—which has already been booked.

In the simplest terms, a Mousejunkie is an admitted Walt Disney World fanatic. I think of it like this: If you go on Twitter and look at what topics are trending, you'll often find hashtags followed by one form of the following phrases:

Justin Bieber, One Direction, Harry Styles, and a whole bunch of other stuff that I don't get because I'm not a fifteen-year-old, nor a girl. But I don't expect other people to understand the life of a Disney freak either. To those people, I'm sure we look like screeching Bieber fans, except we're brawling over the best way to meet Anna and Elsa.

Conduct a little self-examination and see if any of this sounds familiar: A Mousejunkie has Dole Whip running through his or her veins. A Mousejunkie has more than one Disney trip planned and booked at any time. A Mousejunkie can tell you what day is 180 days away from any given date. It's all part of a lifestyle that makes picking a Mousejunkie out from a crowd quite easy.

Here's a quick litmus test to gauge whether or not you might be a Mousejunkie: Take a look at your browser's bookmarks. Do you see your child's school, your bank, a search engine? Well then, ZZZZZZZZZZZZZZZZZZZZZZZZZZZ.

Oh, I'm sorry, I fell asleep while writing this book because I got to a part where I had to write about people who aren't addicted to Walt Disney World. (And to be completely honest, I've never known anyone who made a "Z" sound while sleeping.)

Check that list of browser bookmarks. Do you see a Disney Dining link, Mickeyxtreme.com, the Parks Blog, the WDW Today Podcast site or the DIS Boards? Well then, pull up a Mickey Premium Bar and let's talk.

Say you're on the road and you think you may be stuck in traffic behind a Mousejunkie. Take this quick visual inventory: Are there Disney antennae toppers or license plate frames? Bumper stickers are a dead giveaway: "Honk if you want my Soarin' FastPass."

Be aware of these subtle clues, and you'll see that Mousejunkies in the wild are actually quite common.

Crowdsourcing the Mouse

Mousejunkies are, of course, Disney fanatics—the label people sometimes assign to themselves when explaining their love for Disney. But they're also my panel of personal experts—the people I turn to when I need to know something about Walt Disney World.

Here's the strange thing—each of these people found their way to Walt Disney World separately. None of us traveled together when we were first inducted into this fraternity of fantasy. It only emerged that we were wrestling with internal Disney needs at weddings, cookouts and gatherings. Each person traveled their own road to Disney addiction, but as time passed and our habitual vacation patterns emerged, we connected on another level.

In the following pages I'll rely on the sage advice of these people. These are the leisure ninjas who have embraced this lifestyle. Each possesses a black belt in Disney trip planning, and each has their own particular area of expertise. Ask about what time of year to go, what park to visit or which restaurant to eat at, and they'll slap a little Mickey jujitsu on you. They're each capable of throwing a magical submission hold that'll have you flailing about in the happiest tap-out on Earth.

There are a million Disney experts, but below are the dossiers on the Special Forces of this army. (Assembled mainly because I know them and can bother them endlessly for tips and information.)

I've said it before: I'm an enthusiast, but these people are true experts. All I know is I came back from that first trip to Walt Disney World, sat down in front of my computer and started typing. These people helped me make sense of it all.

Think of this roster as a Walt Disney World jury. My opinion is no more valid than the next guest's. So if there's a mob of Disney freaks and if we can reach a quorum on whether or not Citrico's is great or the ABC Commissary is awful, or whether it's smarter to use cash on a weekend rather than using Disney Vacation Club points for your room, then I'd say we've hit upon something.

These are the Mousejunkies:

Name: Mousejunkie Randy
AKA: Disney King
Profile: Randy once worked as a cast member in The Disney Store one night a week. By day he'd help design defense systems for the U.S. Government, and by night he'd help design Disney vacation plans for store customers. He pioneered pin trading at the store, and was instrumental in launching scores of first-time ventures to the vacation kingdom.

His claim to the throne of Disney King didn't come lightly. Randy took his role at the store seriously. His enthusiasm for anything Disney was contagious. I admire his ability to approach trip planning with the eye of a detached analyst. He can weigh financial concerns against cost-per-hour and come up with best practices in a matter of seconds.

I suspect there's something more nefarious at work with Randy, however. Legend has it that Randy's house is exactly 1971.00 miles from Cinderella Castle in the Magic Kingdom—a number that reflects the same year the resort opened. It's sort of like a pixie-dust-laden version of *Poltergeist*.

Expertise: Name it. The man's brain is constantly scanning options, plans, prices and new information to formulate the most efficient Disney vacation possible. He doesn't answer to "Disney King" for nothing. Try this experiment: The next time you're at Walt Disney World, look for a guy with broad shoulders, very short hair, a New England Patriots or Boston Red Sox jersey, and a backwards baseball hat on. That will be Randy. Just walk up behind him and say "Disney King." Trust me, he'll answer.

Name: Mousejunkie Carol
AKA: Mousejunkie Mathlete
Profile: Carol is an executive financial officer at a bank. But even in the suit-and-tie world of high finance, Carol's sharp eye can spot a potential Mousejunkie from across a desk.

"It's like a secret society for adults," she said. "I don't mention a word about it unless I see something from Disney in a person's office. And then it's like we have a different nature toward one another. It's like we've been friends for years. We speak the same language."

Expertise: Carol is a connoisseur of Walt Disney World's resorts. Sure, the attractions are fun, the restaurants are nice and the shows are great, but for this discerning woman, it's all about where you lay your head. Carol and her husband Mousejunkie Randy have stayed at all but one of the Disney-owned resorts. And with literally scores upon scores of nights spent in resorts ranging from luxury to bargain-level, she knows her stuff.

Just one note of advice: Don't stand between Carol and a zebra-dome dessert at Boma in the Animal Kingdom Lodge. She may be slight in stature, but she packs a wallop.

 Name: Mousejunkie Amy
AKA: The Reluctant Mousejunkie
Profile: For someone categorized as a Mousejunkie, Amy is pretty tough on my addiction. I suppose someone has to be.

In the interest of full disclosure, Amy also answers to the name "Mrs. Burke." We've been married for twenty years, so of all the Mousejunkies, I know her best. She might be small, but she has the heart of a cornered badger that ate a bad-tempered wolverine. Just try adding a little debt to our family's finances, you'll see it emerge. Her eyes take on a suspicious, and some might say violent stare whenever she sees me with a credit card in one hand and the phone in the other. That tableaux of irresponsibility can mean only one thing: I'm booking a Disney trip, and she's going to be the one to arrange payment. In our family, I'm the camp counselor, as it were. She's the CFO.

Don't get me wrong. She's not heartless. Far from it. The minute we're in our seats on the flight to Orlando, she becomes as Mickey-addicted as any of us. I think that's what makes her so great: She'll go along for the ride, but she's also the reason I'm writing this on a laptop in our own home, instead of using a crayon on a cardboard box in an alley. She's the responsible adult to my eternally tweaked adolescent.

Expertise: Amy is fairly laid back and affable about things. Aside from her passion for playing hockey. She's pretty intense about her hockey. But get her on Disney property, and she'll start trying to figure out a way to get the most for our dollar while not missing anything. Nothing scares that woman. Except when I get that telltale Disney itch.

Name: Mousejunkie Barry
AKA: The Blindside
Profile: Barry never expected to fall in love with Walt Disney World. He was sucker-punched with a white, four-fingered glove. He was unexpectedly battered with a switch ripped off the Tree of Life.

"I was fifteen years old and touring Disney World for the first time when it happened," he said. "When you're fifteen, you're perhaps both too old and too young to really appreciate the Magic Kingdom—the naiveté of youth is gone and you haven't experienced enough of the world yet to truly appreciate the escapism. I was wandering through the park looking for something interesting to do when I came upon the entrance to the Pirates of the Caribbean ride. There's no cutesy cartoons involved, right? Okay—off we go, then. As I made my way through the dungeon queue, I was being steadily wowed by the little touches; the skeletons, the dankness, the anticipation of what's to come. By the time I made it to the boat loading area, I was thoroughly enthused. The lightning bolt moment—that one moment where your spine tingles and you are at a loss for words—came when the boat shot down the falls and out into the harbor.

"As we slowly made our way past the side of the ship lobbing cannon balls across and into the water in front of us, I would have sworn that I had actually been shot out of the humid 2 P.M. sunlight of Florida and into 14th century at 2 A.M. I was completely blown away by the Inside-Outside— the feeling that you're actually outdoors in another world when in reality you're putting around inside a building in interesting-smelling water with convincing fake fire and robots chasing each other around. I went on Pirates no less than five more times that day and it remains my favorite ride of all time."

Expertise: A father of two Disney-loving girls, Barry has become an expert on traveling to Walt Disney World with kids. In his enthusiasm for all things Disney, Barry immediately jumped in and started using the Walt Disney World shorthand. He's also been known to make up his own: "I love my new BGSMM t-shirt." (Biscuit-and-Gravy Stained Mickey Mouse T-Shirt.)

Name: Mousejunkie Ryan
AKA: Betrothedjunkie
Profile: Ryan made her debut in the *Mousejunkies* series of books at a fairly young age. Once known as the Teen Mousejunkie, she has been promoted—partly because she's not a teen anymore. It's not polite to ask a woman her age, but let's just say she's twenty-four. Because I'm not always polite.

Ryan has continued her string of Walt Disney World trips, and has even indoctrinated her fiancee. That's right, our young Ryan is betrothed, and the man who will be Mr. Mousejunkie Ryan loves Disney. We approve.

When Ryan was but a teen, her favorite attraction in all of Walt Disney World was "The Italian boys scooping gelato at the Italy pavilion at Epcot." But now she brings a new perspective to the game—that of a young, newly-married couple.

Expertise: Ryan knows that the characters aren't just for kids. "Alice is my obsession, and during my last trip, I made her my number one priority," she said. "I scheduled my days and coordinated my outfits around meeting my favorite Wonderland chick (the best shirts to show off my Alice tattoos, of course), and I was not disappointed. I met her three times in one trip, and twice she recognized me immediately.

Our interactions by far were the most magical moments of the vacation, from her excitement at remembering me and my tattoos, to her declarations to onlookers that we were special friends. Meeting your favorite character can be just as magical as meeting a celebrity or your idol. Don't pass up the opportunity. Trust me, it's worth it."

She's also the loudest to mock my stubborn refusal to experience anything more thrilling than, say, Small World.

Ryan keeps forgetting that she hates crème brulee.

 Name: Mousejunkie J
AKA: Just J
Profile: A mechanical engineer at a nuclear power plant, J is smart, successful, and just as addicted to Walt Disney World as the rest of us.

Around the office, he's the guy people turn to when there are questions regarding a Walt Disney World vacation. Above his desk is a huge digital clock that is always counting down. The Doomsday Clock perhaps? Nothing so serious. The clock is forever marking time toward J's next Disney vacation.

Also, I've known J for about thirty-five years. His name is J. It says so on his license plate: "JustJ." He's not hiding his identity. I think.

Expertise: For J, Walt Disney World is all about the food. An expert in touring theme parks and planning meals at Disney's table service restaurants, J has an uncanny way of recalling menus, describing flavors and maximizing dining options.

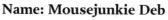

Name: Mousejunkie Deb
AKA: Just Deb
Profile: In the real world, Deb leads a Project Management Office for information systems within Boston's world-renowned healthcare industry. She seems to exude an endless capacity for vacation fun, and has put into words perhaps my favorite quote for why we are repeat visitors: "I like to think my favorite Disney memory hasn't happened yet."

Her Disney enthusiasm is catchy. However, if you are ever lucky enough to travel to Walt Disney World with Deb, don't let her tiny frame and big smile fool you. As one of the creators of the "Cote Pace"—a speedy way of traversing Disney property—she may kill you. Must be special sneakers or something.

The Cote Pace has become such a well-known and infamous part of our trips together that I've come up with a plan to combat the side effects of Deb's blinding gait.

It's a studied, highly-scientific response, and I'd like to share it with you now: Try to be skinny. It's just a theory at this point, since I can't actually put it to the test, but I think it'll probably work.

Expertise: Deb possesses a ruthless Disney efficiency. From money-saving tips to mapping out travel routes, she's got it down. Deb can map out the best route for getting from any spot on Disney property to another, and do so in record time.

Name: Mousejunkie Jenna
AKA: The Librarian
Profile: As one who flies her Mousejunkie flag proudly, Jenna's interest in Disney World is readily apparent. Disney mementos dot her entire home. Wander into her cubicle at work, and if it wasn't for the bitter Michigan cold freezing your nose hairs, or someone laughing at you because the Red Wings have won about two dozen Stanley Cups and your team has only won one in about forty years, you'd swear you were somehow transported to the Emporium shop on Main Street USA. When she goes golfing, she has a Mickey Mouse pouch on her bag. She has a Disney Vacation Club sticker on her car. She's a walking, talking Disney convention.

Expertise: Jenna is a Walt Disney World trip-planning guru. As a writer, Jenna is a virtual library of Disney knowledge with an encyclopedic ability to recall even the most minor Disney detail.

And that's where Jenna's inner-librarian removes her glasses and shakes out the bun in her hair in slow motion. Trip planning is where Jenna truly comes alive.

"I have always been a planner and a list-maker, and my interests in subjects often turn into obsessions," she said. "I don't do things in half measures. When a friend and I made plans to meet for a vacation in 1999—my first trip in thirteen years—she soon let me take over the planning because I immediately began poring over books and the internet to find out everything I could. Over the years, I've continued following those resources and adding new books, sites, and experts and try not to let any new information slip by unnoticed."

"Think of me as a sort of Walt Disney World reference desk—I know a little bit about a wide range of subjects, but more importantly, if I don't know the answer to a question, I know where and how to find it."

 Name: Mousejunkie Walt
AKA: The Mayor
Profile: Walt lives his life with flair. Traveling around the country while working on the finance side of the restaurant business, Walt has friends in every corner of the map.

If there's ever anyone in our group likely to run into an acquaintance while on vacation at Walt Disney World, it's Walt. He knows, and seems to be known, by everyone.

Expertise: Doing Disney deluxe is Walt's trademark. A Disney Vacation Club member, he and his family have nearly six hundred points between them. There may be Mousejunkies who go more often, but there may not be any that go with more style.

"I only go once or twice a year," he said. "So I stay at the BoardWalk, I get the BoardWalk view—I do it right. When I'm there I want to treat myself to the best I can afford."

Name: Mousejunkie Katie
AKA: The Kid
Profile: The newest Mousejunkie to join our jury,
Katie will answer to Kate, Katherine, Kathringo or
even just, "Hey." That's because she is my daughter. Since I
started writing books about Walt Disney World, she'd always
ask: "Daddy, when can I be a Mousejunkie?" Truth be told,
she's been a Mousejunkie pretty much since birth. But over
the years she's developed her own likes and dislikes and her
own personality and sense of humor. So I guess the answer
is "now."

Expertise: Katie brings the perspective of someone much
younger than the rest of our group. She's twelve now, which
is the same age I was when I first visited Walt Disney World.
She got a much earlier start on her addiction than I did,
though. Her first trip was taken at three years old. Since then,
she's been traversing Disney property in a stroller and atop
my shoulders. Her favorite princess has always been Jasmine,
and though she was a bit shy about attractions in the beginning, she's totally on board now. Well, except for the more
thrilling rides like Expedition Everest or the Aerosmith Rock
'n' Roller Coaster—but then again, she is my kid.

"When I was born into a Mousejunkie family, I had no
idea. Mainly because I was an infant," Katie says. "But once
I figured it out, it was pretty fabulous. I was really excited
to go to Disney for the first time—and that was before my
dad wrote the first *Mousejunkies* book. The first time I went

with my parents, I felt like it was something I wouldn't forget—even though I did forget because I was three. But get
this (plot twist)—I got to go back. And I loved returning to
Orlando again and again. I was really glad I was a part of a
Mousejunkie family, even if sometimes my dad goes without
me, leaving me to fend for myself and survive in the woods.

"My mom can be kind of unenthusiastic, if you will, about
Disney sometimes. When I or my dad say that we *have* to go
back to Disney, she'll usually just talk about money. Luckily,
I'm just like my father. I really like being a part of a Disney
family because I know how lucky I am to have gone to Walt
Disney World so many times. Something I don't like is when
my dad gets invited to Disney but doesn't go, or when he
goes—but he's the only one going. Ah, the struggles of being
a Mousejunkie.

"I was really happy when my dad asked if I would be a
Mousejunkie in the third book (O.K., I was the one who
asked), because I've been wanting to write in his books. Now
I have another reason to be glad to be a Mousejunkie."

When someone books a trip to Walt Disney World, they realize fairly quickly that it takes a little more planning and
expertise than a similar vacation to Six Flags
might. And that's when the questions begin:
When should I go? Where should I stay?
Should we get the Disney Dining Plan? Where
are your pants? Where can I get a massage?
Where can I watch the football game on Sunday?

The Mousejunkies have, at one time or another posed these questions themselves. And they've learned the answers by trial-and-error. They've lived the answers and they're more than happy to share their Disney knowledge.

And then, of course, there's me. I've made huge mistakes, and I'm happy to tell you about them. Learn from me. Don't take a Disney cruise during hurricane season. Don't get bronchitis just before a Disney trip. Remember to wear pants.

There are a few things I can do well though. I can tell you what it feels like to hug strangers dressed in furry costumes in 100-degree heat, and I can tell you what it feels like to be "That Guy" at the Monsters Inc. Laugh Floor.

Mainly, I'm just a guy with an addiction and a need to get it all down.

What You'll Find In This Book

Mousejunkies is a travel guide with a sense of humor. My opinion might not match up precisely with yours, but the way you opt to go about your Walt Disney World vacation is just as valid as mine. As long as you have a plan. This book will provide you with information you need to formulate a strategy—because you'll need one. The cautionary tales about families who arrive on Mickey's doorstep, suitcase in hand with little prior preparation are chilling.

You'll find **"What's New"**—Disney is constantly changing and "plussing" itself—looking for ways to improve and challenge how it engages and entertains. What was new two years ago may be old hat now. Things never stop moving at the Florida property, which is part of what makes it so fun to return. There are new lands, attractions, restaurants, hotels, shows, food and parades.

You'll find **"The Straight Dope"**—these are tips you may be able to use on your own trip. They've come about as a result of scores of trips by the Mousejunkies in this book. Experience breeds knowledge, and at least in my case, a load of mistakes.

You'll find **"Mousejunkie U"**—tidbits of trivia any self-respecting student of the Mouse would want to know.

"Mousejunkies Choice"—a favorite, can't-miss attraction, resort, or experience chosen after countless trips to the World.

There are comments, tips, anecdotes, and advice from a group of people collectively known as **the Mousejunkies**. They're a friendly, fun group who love Walt Disney World and are excited to share their experiences with anyone from first-time travelers to fellow addicts.

And you'll see **"Awesome/Stupid Disney Ideas"**—these are the things that pop into my head while I'm staring out the window daydreaming about my favorite vacation destination. They might be awesome ideas, but there's an equal chance that they're stupid. It's been said that there's a fine line between clever and stupid. I walk that line pretty much every day.

I hope you laugh and maybe learn something about Walt Disney World. Most of all, I hope this book transports you there. Because every Mousejunkie needs a fix now and then.

Mousejunkie Rising

When the first edition of *Mousejunkies* was released, I hoped it would strike a chord with small pockets of Disney fanatics. I thought it might find its way into the hands of people like me who can't get enough of Walt Disney World.

I had no idea that there was such a vast Mousejunkie army—a fifth column of enthusiasts, as it were, ready to mobilize the minute Annual Passholder room rates are released. What I learned is that we are legion. Geeky, maybe, and strangely obsessed, but we've got numbers. And opinions. With the release of *Mousejunkies* came a torrent of encouragement, shared experiences and questions. And it's all helped, because the only thing that remains consistent at Walt Disney World is change.

At times I get particularly attached to an attraction or show and then it disappears. I still miss the Tapestry of Nations parade and the Hunchback of Notre Dame stage show. Get off my lawn. And now that the brilliant a cappella group Four for a Dollar has been excised from the Beauty and the Beast pre-show, Sunset Boulevard is just a bit less bright.

Yet somehow all that anguish is mitigated by the fact that you can get a cronut at Epcot now. For every time I feel kicked in the pants by an oversized yellow shoe, there's something new that grabs my attention. The Mouse giveth and the Mouse taketh away.

At the same time, some things never change. It's an addiction that has no signs of abating. I have yet to discover some sort of methadone that keeps my pulse from racing every time I hear the theme from IllumiNations: Reflections of Earth. I wonder if one day there will be a convenient wearable patch that'll make Dole Whips taste like paste or make me want to vacation somewhere that's not in central Florida. Maybe something that'll help keep my meager earnings in the bank and out of Mickey's purse.

Even if there was something that'd break the spell Walt Disney World has on me—or something that would make me act a bit more responsibly—I don't think I'd sign up for it. Besides, I like to think the profits Disney scored off of my many trips to its vacation kingdom went into developing a new attraction or subsidized the cost of humongous turkey legs in Frontierland.

It may sound crazy to the uninitiated, but there are others out there with a habit much worse than mine. I am most definitely not alone.

In fact, I know that many other seemingly well-adjusted adults go to Walt Disney World as often—or more often—than I do. I can't get through a day without running into a fellow Mousejunkie. They're scattered everywhere throughout my life. They're my poker buddies, coworkers, family members, my UPS driver, online acquaintances and longtime friends. I even sleep with one.

I feel better knowing that I'm not alone, but it doesn't completely kill the inkling that I'm somehow seen as a social oddity since my love of all things Disney has been outed. I don't mind. For every person who thinks I've been blinded by Disney's skilled marketing gurus, there's someone else calculating how an order of pot roast mac-and-cheese at the

Magic Kingdom fits into his Dining Plan allotment. That person understands.

Our paths cross on Main Street USA—he's wearing an inexplicably stupid souvenir Goofy hat, I'm wearing a hopelessly outdated fanny pack and proudly sporting a lanyard with unnecessarily expensive collectible pins on it. We make eye contact and think nothing of our otherwise regrettable fashion choices. These things are part of the dress code at Walt Disney World, and we revel in it.

I don't have to convince a Walt Disney World guidebook reader. Chances are you're already planning a trip, have been there several times or are suffering the inevitable withdrawal that comes with the end of every Disney vacation, and you want to experience that magic again. Face it, you're either a Mousejunkie, or you're a potential Mousejunkie. There's a reason you're holding this book and not flipping through something from a more respectable section of the bookstore.

But I know not everyone shares our love for the place. All Disney addicts face the same quizzical looks and opinionated replies when coworkers or friends learn we'll be returning to Walt Disney World on vacation.

To combat this, we've prepared a brief, two-page worksheet suitable for distribution.

Simply fill out the form on the following two pages, make copies, and hand it out to any naysayers, party poopers or mundane-loving coots around your workplace.

Mousejunkie

Two cubicles over
The one with all the Disney junk everywhere
Your office

Dear _____,

Yes, I am going to Walt Disney World on vacation. Again. Before you
A. Roll your eyes
B. Snort
C. Offer your unsolicited opinion

Let me try to explain to you why I have decided to visit WDW for
the ____th time.

I love the magical atmosphere, incredible attractions, Broadway-
caliber shows, unmatched customer service and value for my
vacation dollar.

There is nothing quite like
A. Seeing the wonder in my child's eyes when his/her dreams come
    true
B. Seeing the wonder in my spouse's eyes when his/her dreams
    come true
C. Seeing my dreams come true
D. Having a Dole Whip in one hand and your My Disney Experience
    app in the other

Since you choose not to visit Walt Disney World, I can only assume
A.   You will not be in line in front of me at Expedition Everest
B.   It'll be that much easier to get an ADR at Be Our Guest
C.   You won't mind covering my shift/responsibilities while I'm at
     IllumiNations: Reflections of Earth

Remember, you'll be stuck back here sitting in a conference room
while I hug:
A.   The lovely Princess Jasmine
B.   The rugged, if slightly tipsy, Jack Sparrow

Sincerely,

_____

Your Walt Disney World-bound co-worker

P.S. Plplpblbbblblllblllll

Or, alternately, if you don't really like your co-workers or
care for their opinion on your love of Walt Disney World,
we've prepared a secondary worksheet:

Mousejunkie

Two cubicles over
The one with all the Disney junk everywhere
Your office

Dear _____,

Yes, I am going to Walt Disney World on vacation. Again.

Shut up. Shut up.

Sincerely,

_____

Your Walt Disney World-bound co-worker

P.S. Plplpblbbblblllblllll. Shut up.

2 Mousejunkies Travel

EVERYTHING SEEMED FINE. Mousejunkie Amy and I were up early and on a Disney bus headed for the Magic Kingdom.

It was sunny, not too humid and complete Disney indulgence was seemingly just minutes away. Little did I know I was about to get a bustle in my hedgerow in a big way.

Cinderella Castle popped into view in the distance and a sense of happiness had begun to settle in. We were just minutes away from passing through the main gates and entering a world where we'd forget—at least for a little while—that this was our last day at Walt Disney World.

That detail gnawed at the edges of the Disney-induced haze that was fighting for a better toehold in the celebraccio lobe of my brain. The last day is always a little bittersweet. No matter how great everything seems to be going, a tiny, nagging voice reminds you that by this time tomorrow, you'll be home. It's not great.

Yet with the complete sensory overload that is Walt Disney World, it's possible to go hours without thinking about the end of your trip. It was this state I was fighting to enter as we disembarked and headed for the turnstiles. Sure, it would soon all be over, but we still had a full day of attractions, parades, food and shows. It would be these elements that would help stave off the inevitable.

Or so I thought.

We stepped up, ran our park tickets through and prepared to step into the Magic Kingdom proper.

An angry, red "X" appeared on the readout to our right and a mighty peel of thunder smashed through my Mickey-loving soul. The metal arm in front of me refused to budge.

Instead of the welcoming green arrow that would signify our passage into daylong happiness, we were met with an entirely different signal. The red "X" mocked us silently, and the arm of the turnstile barred entry with inhuman, metal authority. Stupid machine. I looked at the cast member in confusion. She took my ticket and ran it through the machine again. This gave me enough time to calm the inner freakout and realize that there had been a temporary glitch that would now be remedied.

Again, the big red "X" blazed angrily. I began to panic. Just beyond this obstinate and obviously evil machinery was a world of swelling music, hours of entertainment, and a perfect, gleaming castle. Yet I could not pass.

"There aren't any days left on your park pass, it seems," the cast member told me.

I looked at the ticket as if staring at it for a few more seconds would change this fact. It didn't. We had cobbled together a few tickets with spare days on them and simply counted wrong. We were out of time and suddenly it was all over.

I stepped aside so other guests who had the ability to count to five were able to pass. Meanwhile, the full weight of the situation slammed into me. Everything I loved about Walt Disney World was literally at the end of my fingertips—yet it might as well have been on the other side of the planet. I wouldn't be distributing hugs to random, costumed strangers this day.

Note: This incident occurred before I was gripped by a total and incurable urge to abandon all financial responsibility in the face of the Mouse. Even now, though, a one-day pass to the Magic Kingdom is an expensive item. Racking up nearly $200 more in debt just so I could ride the Carousel of Progress for the ninth time this week really wasn't an option.

I continued to glare at the offending park pass, hoping it would somehow morph into a valid form of entry. This method continued to fail me, however, as family after family passed by and gained entry into the world I desperately wanted to be a part of.

There was nothing left to do, really, but begin the interminable march back to the bus stop—where motor coaches filled with people who knew how to complete the most basic of Disney planning processes would empty into the promise-filled morning. I avoided eye contact with these people as we swam upstream against the constant flow.

We were the only people heading away from the Magic Kingdom at this time of day, because who in the world would be leaving just as the place was opening? Just dumb people. And here we were.

The bus driver didn't seem surprised as we stepped aboard to be shuttled back to our hotel. Alone. The entire ride back I worked on not losing what was left of my mind. I could literally feel every inch of the distance being put between us and Main Street USA as we passed by the Contemporary Resort, under the water bridge and then out onto World Drive.

Amy made an effort to console me. She's much more reasonable that I am, but she knew exactly what was going on inside my head. Visions of a Main Street Bakery chocolate croissant, which should've been in my face at that very moment, were instead taunting me. Meanwhile, she formulated a plan to make the best of our last day. Because she's an adult who can think rationally.

Thankfully, since one of us can function emotionally beyond the level of a twelve-year-old, the day was salvaged. Or, I survived it, anyway. I got beyond the idea that the Magic Kingdom would have to wait until our next trip, and we instead assuaged my wounded psyche at various Downtown Disney restaurants and shops. It was the only way.

I did learn a valuable lesson, though: Be aware of how you're going to get into a Walt Disney World theme park. These days, doing so has changed dramatically. Where there was once a plastic card or a paper pass, there is now a wearable piece of RFID technology that tracks pretty much everything you do.

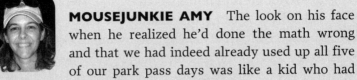

MOUSEJUNKIE AMY The look on his face when he realized he'd done the math wrong and that we had indeed already used up all five of our park pass days was like a kid who had dropped his ice cream cone on the ground. The sheer horror and disbelief was a bit amusing, but I knew his head would explode if I tried to joke and cheer him up. I knew it wasn't the end of the world. It just put a crimp in our plans. Now I could happily relax at the pool perhaps, or shop at Downtown Disney. It was nice to actually have a day of vacation doing nothing so I wouldn't need to recover from all the walking. We actually made the best of the situation and had a great day of spontaneous exploration at Downtown Disney.

What's New About Traveling to Walt Disney World

Disney never sits still. Walt Disney himself always said the original Disneyland would never be finished—it would continue to grow as long as there is imagination in the world—and operating budgets.

O.K., maybe he didn't mention that last thing, but realistically, things are always changing and evolving at Disney theme parks. In fact, I recently caught myself griping about doing Walt Disney World "back in the day." Then I whipped my walker against the wall, nearly choked on my loose bridge and told someone I had diabeetus.

If you take six months off, Disney's constantly moving machine will pass you by. At one time, you'd return to the World to find a refurbished attraction or a new dining option. Now the entire experience is undergoing a revolution.

MyMagic+

Gone are the days of making dining reservations mere weeks in advance, and your Key to the World card is fast becoming a relic.

That's because the entire overarching guest experience is changing. Most of these efforts fall under the MyMagic+ umbrella—something that connects many elements of your vacation, including the My Disney Experience mobile app and website; Disney's MagicBand, FastPass+ and Photopass Memory Maker.

The My Disney Experience (disneyworld.disney.go.com/plan/my-disney-experience) website and mobile app enables guests to get more information about resorts, attractions and restaurants, allows them to take part in shaping and customizing their vacation, make dining reservations and FastPass+ selections and even connect with friends and family members and share photos.

It might sound like a lot, because it is. Here's a look at the new MyMagic+ way of doing things:

➤ Step one: You make your vacation reservations.
➤ Step two: You wait. People will offer advice. Some will overwhelm you with information and tales of their

Disney vacation, and still others will question your sanity. It's at this point that reading this book would probably be helpful. At the very least it might give you a few laughs before the avalanche of planning information hits. The planalanche, as it were.

➤ Step three: As soon as you link your reservation to your My Disney Experience account, you can choose a color and assign a name for each of your MagicBands. It certainly sounds like a small, simple step, but don't underestimate the agita this can cause. Picking a color can take up a lot of time and effort.

It all starts to get exciting when your MagicBands arrive in the mail. These colorful wristbands connect the choices you made online. It acts as your park pass, credit card, room key, keeps track of your FastPass+ selections and connects you to Disney's PhotoPass.

Now, your MagicBands can even link you to on-ride photos, including Buzz Lightyear's Space Ranger Spin, Space Mountain and Splash Mountain at the Magic Kingdom; Test Track at Epcot; Rock 'n' Roller Coaster and the Tower of Terror at Disney's Hollywood Studios; and Dinosaur and Expedition Everest at Disney's Animal Kingdom. So thanks to the technological sorcery Imagineers are bring to bear, you can access and purchase that image of you looking like you're going to puke on the Tower of Terror—all from the comfort of your own home. Those images will be linked to your My Disney Experience account, as long as you've purchased a photo package ahead of time.

FastPass+

If that sounds good, you're going to actually have to make sure you can get on those attractions. That's where FastPass+ comes into play. In ancient times (prior to 1999), guests would walk to whatever attraction they wanted to experience, get in line and wait. Then came FastPass—a way of making an appointment with a ride so that there was less time spent standing in a long queue.

Now that's all morphed into FastPass+. Where once you could hoof it to an attraction and get yourself a FastPass, you can now make some of those selections before you even leave your home for central Florida.

FastPass+ is the next step in the evolution of appointment theme park touring. Guests can use the My Disney Experience site to make FastPass+ selections—ride appointments, essentially—on must-do attractions or make seating area reservations for shows, parades and fireworks, or even make appointments to meet some of their favorite Disney characters at meet-and-greets.

FastPass+ is included with your ticket or package. There is no charge for it. Just buy your ticket and then log on to My Disney Experience thirty days prior to your arrival and choose up to three FastPass+ experiences per day at one park. If you're staying at a Disney resort, you can do all this sixty days prior to check-in, and you get a MagicBand to tie it all together. (To summarize: Stay off-site and you get the bare minimum. Stay on-site and enjoy the whole MagicBand experience.)

After you've used those three FastPass+ experiences on that particular day, you can select another FastPass+ experience. Each time you use the latest one, you can choose a new one. Additional FastPass+ experiences can be selected at kiosks within the park.

There are FastPass+ kiosks at several locations throughout the Magic Kingdom:

➤ In Tomorrowland across from the Monsters Inc., Laugh Floor
➤ In New Fantasyland near the train station
➤ In Fantasyland next to Mickey's Philharmagic
➤ In Liberty Square near Sleepy Hollow

In Epcot, you will find FastPass+ kiosks at the following locations:

➤ Innoventions West near the Character Spot
➤ Innoventions East near the Electric Umbrella
➤ The Tip Board
➤ The International Gateway (located between the UK and France in the World Showcase)

There are also several FastPass+ kiosks located near these attractions and shops in the Animal Kingdom theme park:

➤ Disney Outfitters
➤ Dinosaur
➤ Expedition Everest
➤ Kali River Rapids
➤ Kilimanjaro Safaris

➤ Island Mercantile
➤ Primeval Whirl

Here's where the FastPass+ kiosks are in Disney's Hollywood Studios:

➤ Pixar Place
➤ At the corner of Hollywood and Sunset Boulevard
➤ At the end of Sunset near the Tower of Terror
➤ The entrance to Muppet*Vision 3D

I Can't Believe How Hot/ Cold/Humid/Rainy It Is

On yet another visit, there were no issues with our passes. The unexpected element this time around was the weather.

All the familiar pieces were in place: people shuffling through wallets to find theme park passes, cast members wrangling guests already worn out from a week of traipsing through queues and keeping to schedules, and people trying to put any body part *but* a finger into the biometric scanner at the turnstiles, thus delaying our entry.

And everywhere was the crush of humanity. The smell of sunscreen mixed with impatience. But finally the throng began to move forward. The rope was dropping and we were about to head into the park.

I was standing outside the main gates at Disney's Hollywood Studios, just minutes away from starting another day of our Walt Disney World vacation, and yet something was amiss. A completely unexpected feeling was enveloping me. My Mousejunkie senses were in full-on alarm mode. As we moved closer to the cast member waving people through the gates and into the park beyond, I started to put my finger on it.

I believe the sensation was...Cold.

Not a slight chill that might send locals scrambling for warmer gear, but a full-on arctic bite that was sinking its teeth into my obstinate bones.

It was mid-January. The dead of winter. And shockingly, I was freezing. This would not have been unusual back at my home in the northeast, where ice storms paralyze daily life and gray, gritty slush lines the roadways nine months out of the year. But this was Florida—the Sunshine State: land of orange groves and palm trees and very strange infomercials about appliances. And yet I was standing there with my Annual Pass clutched in my numb fist, shivering.

I had no one to blame but myself. As we were packing for this particular vacation, Mousejunkie Amy reminded me that since this was actually winter, it might be prudent to prepare. It was going to be cooler in central Florida during our trip, according to the weather forecast.

"Perhaps packing a pair of pants would make sense," she said.

Since I don't wear pants, I declined. Before you recoil in horror, by "I don't wear pants," I mean "I wear shorts." All the time. Every day. Even back home in the depths of one of those aforementioned winters. I'll head out in mid-February to get my newspaper, coffee and scratch tickets—because I am a born-and-bred New Englander and this is what we must do—clad in shorts.

"It's going to be cold in Florida?" I scoffed. "So it'll be what...70 degrees?"

Oh, how I laughed. I probably made a disparaging remark about being hearty and having much thicker blood than my Floridian counterparts, and then I packed my shorts.

I relived those rather dumb words as I scanned the mass of people around me. Every single guest was bundled up in jackets, in some cases hats, and in every case pants. Wonderful, element-deflecting pants. I refused to admit the folly of my ways, primarily because I was a Mousjunkie—a supposed Walt Disney World expert. I don't make mistakes in the confines of my favorite forty-seven square miles. My rime-encrusted Disney ego was telling me otherwise, however. There was also the telltale shade of purple my skin was turning that announced to the world that I was stubborn, dumb, and obviously had no idea what it meant to tour Walt Disney World in the winter.

I started visualizing odd scenarios: Perhaps I could tear the pages out of my first Walt Disney World book and tape them around my chilled appendages in an effort to stave off frostbite. Surely my warm, humorous words would comfort me. Alas, it was not to be. I didn't have any tape.

In a moment of triumphant "I-told-you-so" celebration, Amy suggested I use staples.

It was rather cold in central Florida that winter. On two nights during our ten-day vacation the temperatures dipped to 24 degrees and 29 degrees. The weather was the big news every night as citrus farmers fought to save their crops from the biting cold and for the first time ever a dim tourist from New Hampshire actually missed the crushing heat normally associated with a Disney vacation.

As a constant complainer when it comes to the Florida heat, I just assumed that a much cooler January vacation would be heavenly. On this particular trip, I could not have been more wrong.

Ask anyone who has ever traveled to Walt Disney World with me: I will whine at any given chance about how the Florida heat can be unforgiving and even dangerous. It can get so humid that you may be able to swim back to your hotel. The rain can be relentless and fall sideways. Unexpected freezes can catch guests completely unprepared.

And that's all in one day.

Chances are you won't encounter all of Florida's extremes in a twenty-four-hour period, but it's not entirely unheard of.

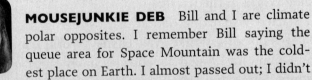

MOUSEJUNKIE DEB   Bill and I are climate polar opposites. I remember Bill saying the queue area for Space Mountain was the coldest place on Earth. I almost passed out; I didn't think Bill considered anywhere cold. Like Mousejunkie Carol, I bring a sweatshirt and roll it up in my bag, constantly pulling it out for every ridiculously air-conditioned building. Hey, instead of raising park pass prices to save money, why doesn't Disney raise the air-conditioner setting from sub-arctic to just arctic? I love coming *out* of the buildings to warm up!

An interesting thing about the weather in central Florida: Just because it's raining at Disney's Animal Kingdom doesn't mean it's raining at Epcot. In fact, while it might be soaking in Frontierland, Tomorrowland may be sunny and dry.

Rainstorms are frequent and often fast moving. While there may be days that are complete washouts, quite often the rainfall is predictable and temporary. And a prepared guest can take advantage of this. Grab a poncho and press onward.

The Straight Dope *If you have a rain poncho at home, bring it. The ponchos they sell in the theme parks all look the same, so it's easy to lose your traveling mates in the crowd of identical slickers.*

Here's a look at the monthly temperature averages, according to Intellicast.com:

Month	Average Temperature
January	71 degrees
February	74 degrees
March	78 degrees
April	83 degrees
May	88 degrees
June	91 degrees
July	92 degrees
August	1 billion degrees (aka 92 degrees and humid)
September	90 degrees
October	85 degrees
November	79 degrees
December	73 degrees

The heat can often be bearable until the summer months when the humidity arrives. Even then, most of the theme park queues are covered or are inside and air-conditioned. While the heat and humidity were a one-time anathema to me, I've come to prefer it over the cold snaps we've experienced in January and February.

For visitors coming from cooler climates where it's not as hot or humid, just remember to hydrate and keep an eye on your sunscreen. Overheating can lead to meltdowns and crazy, unexpected mood swings, and that's not fun for anyone.

The Straight Dope *Feeling a bit dehydrated? Get a free cup of ice water at counter service restaurants. Or, plan ahead and grab a bottle of frozen water as you head out. As you sip some off the top, refill it. The unmelted ice will keep your water cold for a good portion of the day.*

If you're staying on Disney property, take advantage of your location to visit the parks early in the day before the real heat sets in. Hit the pool during the midday heat or put your room's air conditioner to the test while you grab a quick nap.

The Straight Dope *If you find yourself overheating in the middle of the Magic Kingdom, try Splash Mountain for an instant cool-down. If you're in Animal Kingdom, the Kali River Rapids attraction is guaranteed to submerge you in cool water, providing head-to-toe relief.*

If you're not interested in taking part in a Disney baptism, try one of the indoor attractions that provide a nice chance to get off your feet and out of the sun: The American Adventure and Ellen's Energy Adventure in Epcot; the Hall of Presidents, Mickey's Philharmagic, and Carousel of Progress in the Magic Kingdom; Voyage of the Little Mermaid and the Great Movie Ride at the Studios; and It's Tough to Be a Bug and Festival of the Lion King at Disney's Animal Kingdom.

Then there's the rain. It's possible to go an entire vacation without seeing a drop of precipitation. But into every life a little rain must fall.

In the summer you can set your Mickey Mouse watch by the twenty-minute showers every afternoon between 3 and 4 P.M. Yet in the winter it's a lot dryer. Here's a look at the average rainfall in the Orlando area in inches:

Jan.	Feb.	March	April	May	June
2.35"	2.47"	3.77"	2.68"	3.45"	7.58"
July	Aug.	Sept.	Oct.	Nov.	Dec.
7.27"	7.13"	6.06"	3.31"	2.17"	2.5"

Crowd Levels

When I'm outed as a Disney fanatic, the first question is as inevitable as it is predictable: "When should I go?" Which, translated from the common tongue means "When won't I have to wait in line?" But it's not as simple as asking, "When should I go?" There are many details to take into account: not the least among them crowd levels.

When will Walt Disney World be virtually line-free? Probably never. But occasionally the planets align and the path is clear. As Disney freaks know, there are times when lines will be non-existent; it's just something that doesn't happen too often. But there is no simple answer to solving the crowd-level conundrum. Historically, there were times when there were fewer people in the parks than others. These times have shifted a bit, and let's face it—if crowd levels are down, then Disney is going to do something to fix that. That's where seasonal special events have come in. Autumn was once a great time to visit. It still is. But the once sparse crowds have been replaced by larger groups of people visiting the annual Halloween celebration or the Epcot International Food and Wine Festival. When the buses are standing room only and the entry turnstiles are whirring with wave after wave of paying guests, Disney is happy.

"When should I go?" is best answered with a little vacation quiz:

➤ "Is cost a concern?"
➤ "Is weather a concern?"
➤ "Do you want to experience special events?"
➤ "Do you have issues standing in a fellow guest's armpit? Because the parks can be that crowded.

But rather than duck the question, I'll answer it directly: You'll find me at Walt Disney World two times during the year for sure—late January and in early October. January will be cooler (sometimes quite chilly) and less crowded, and October offers Halloween festivities and additional food choices at the Epcot International Food and Wine Festival.

Any time after that is cake. I'll take a Disney trip any chance I get. I've topped out at six times in one year. Mousejunkie Randy, on the other hand, set foot in a Walt Disney World theme park more than 150 days in one year. A Florida resident might not be impressed, but since he lives nearly 2,000 miles away from the place, I admire his persistence and his unflagging enthusiasm.

But even he will tell you, after all those trips, just slow down. And above all, open your eyes and ears. It's the small things that make Walt Disney World such an addictive place.

Deciding when to travel to Walt Disney World is obviously a very important aspect of planning your trip. Almost every time of year has its benefits and drawbacks. For every report of walking on to an E-ticket attraction, there's inevitably a woeful tale of protracted wait times. When it gets crowded, it can become uncomfortable and difficult to get around. The bottom line is that no one wants to wait in one.

According to figures provided by Disney, you'll want to avoid these dates if large crowds make you break out in the happiest hives on earth:

1. Marathon weekend in January
2. Presidents' week in February
3. Spring Break (St. Patrick's Day through the end of April)
4. Easter
5. Memorial Day weekend
6. The summer months: June through Labor Day

7. Columbus Day
8. Thanksgiving Day and the two to three days following
9. Christmas week through New Year's Day

To some, however, crowd levels are not something to get worked up about. After all, the busiest days of the year— New Year's, the Fourth of July, Christmas—also offer the longest park hours. Navigating the ocean of newly-minted Mousejunkies shoe-horned into the theme parks on such days is something Mousejunkie Randy has perfected, and actually prefers.

MOUSEJUNKIE RANDY   It is true the crowd levels at the parks are at their highest during the holidays, but it is for a good reason. It's not just that everyone has days off from work. There are things to see and do that you can't see or do any other time of the year. Carol and I go often enough that if we don't get a chance to hit some of the rides, its O.K. People-watching is our second favorite activity at the parks next to riding attractions, and during these times there are some great people-safari opportunities. But that's not the only reason we battle the crowds. On July 4th there's a fireworks display that's unmatched in its scope and beauty. Christmastime is Disney World dressed in the splendor of a winter wonderland, and on New Years Eve—let's just say six months later I can still feel the concussions from the New Years Eve special finale of IllumiNations: Reflections of Earth at Epcot. And the festive crowds just add to the magic.

So you're still not convinced. Here are the recommended times of year to visit Walt Disney World when the crowd levels will likely be lighter. The scientists down at Mousejunkie Labs have spared no expense in uncovering these recommended dates:

➤ Mid to late January: Guests staying for the New Year's holiday have gone home, and it'll be too early for students with February school vacations on the horizon. (Avoid New Year's Day, because that's just insane and only crazy people and Mousejunkies Carol and Randy go then.) It stays slow until Presidents' week, at which point it gets very busy again.

➤ Late August: Schools in the southern states are back in session.

➤ September: Disney has offered the Free Dining promotion this time of year recently, but all American kids are back in school at this point and the temperatures are still blazing. This keeps a percentage of youngsters away, and the blast furnace-like heat tends to keep the weaker of the species at bay.

➤ From just after Thanksgiving until just before Christmas. Historically, the closer you get to Christmas, the busier it gets.

The Straight Dope *Extra Magic Evening Hours (EMEH) allow resort guests to spend more time in a theme park after normal closing times. Either get to the EMEH park early, or plan to avoid it entirely. The EMEH park will be the*

*most crowded of the four Walt Disney World theme parks
that day, but an early start is a great advantage.*

Extra Magic Morning Hours (EMMH) allow resort guest
to enter the EMMH park prior to published opening times
and before non-resort guests. This is one of the best opportunities to see the shortest lines at your favorite attractions.
The downside: you and the entire family need to get up early
on your vacation.

Even within the ups and downs of the calendar year,
there are days where certain parks are busier than others.
According to numbers Disney has made available, here are the
days of the week and which parks are busiest:

Day	Busiest Theme Park(s)
Sunday	Magic Kingdom; Hollywood Studios
Monday	Animal Kingdom
Tuesday	Animal Kingdom; Epcot
Wednesday	Animal Kingdom, Hollywood Studios
Thursday	Magic Kingdom
Friday	Epcot
Saturday	Magic Kingdom

Another important consideration to take into account when
deciding travel dates is what will be going on during your stay.
From officially sanctioned events like Star Wars Weekends to
unofficial events that still draw larger crowds, like Gay Days in
June, there's usually a special event on the horizon.

MOUSEJUNKIE AMY Believe it or not, the crowds are part of the fun. You miss the people when they're not there. When you see the look on a little kid's face when a parade passes by, that makes your experience more enjoyable. You're all sharing this great experience.

The Seasons of Disney

Defining an "off-season" for Walt Disney World has gotten fairly tricky in recent years, so deciding on when to go is a question of whether you want to eat too much, drink too much, or sweat too much.

Travel in October and you'll arrive in time for the Epcot International Food and Wine Festival. Spend New Year's at the World and you'll be toasting with more people than at any other time of the year. Go in July for Independence Day, and you'll get to see special fireworks displays, but you may come away charred by the searing heat.

Disney Vacation Club members take advantage of dates in the fall and winter, since the point cost per room is quite low for the months of September and December. The past few years, Disney has offered a "Free Dining" period for the month of September to boost attendance. And now, RunDisney has people skedaddling all over the property at all times of the year.

While the crowds during those times may not rival summer levels, the parks are much busier than in previous years.

There are better times to visit. Not necessarily ideal, but certainly better.

Special Events

Disney has a peculiar way of marking time that carries over to almost all of its promotional seasons. Halloween at Walt Disney World starts in early September. Christmas at Walt Disney World starts at the beginning of November. The "Year of a Million Dreams" promotion was twenty-two months long, but "Almost Two Years of a Million Dreams" doesn't have quite the same ring to it.

As a guest, this method of scheduling provides plenty of opportunity to enjoy holidays and special events year-round.

Here's a look at the different "seasons" and special events at Walt Disney World:

January

New Year's Eve: For the bravest and most committed vacationers, New Year's Eve offers a unique experience. The parks are packed—often closing the front gates and refusing entrance when they're filled to capacity. Epcot, in particular, provides the most festive and diverse celebrations. Each country in the World Showcase is at its most celebratory, and as a park that serves countless alcoholic offerings, it tends to be the most wild.

Its reputation is now well publicized, with one of the best-known Disney websites advising guests: "Arrive early in the morning and be prepared to spend the entire day."

MOUSEJUNKIE CAROL I like to go in October. Hands down it's the best time of year to go. Don't even give a second thought to any other time of year. It's not that busy, it's not that blasted hot and it's usually pretty dry so you won't get rained out every day. Plus, that's when the two best celebrations are taking place: the Food and Wine Festival and Halloween.

MOUSEJUNKIE RANDY I like to go to Walt Disney World for New Year's, regardless of the crowd levels. I enjoy going to Epcot where there are parties in the streets. There are special fireworks and everyone is living it up all night long. At the same time, it's not like doing the same thing in Times Square where you are forced to freeze with six billion drunks.

It's the busiest night of the year, bar none. But realistically you're not there to ride the attractions. You're there to see the different DJs and dance and see the special New Year's IllumiNations display.

A special version of IllumiNations: Reflections of Earth is presented twice during the night, and Disney's Hollywood Studios features three Fantasmic! performances.

Walt Disney World Marathon: This annual 26.2-mile jaunt held every January brings crazy people—or "runners" in the athletic parlance—to the resort to race through all four theme parks. A half-marathon and 5k are also included during marathon weekend.

I have a hard enough time speed-waddling from my bus to Soarin' without getting lightheaded and developing blisters, so my hat is off to the people who accomplish such an admirable accomplishment.

Walt Disney World Marathon Weekend is held the first weekend following New Year's every year.

February

Spring Training: The Atlanta Braves hold Spring Training at ESPN's Wide World of Sports complex each February/March.

Previously, I hadn't had much reason to visit ESPN's Wide World of Sports. When I did head over (begrudgingly, since this was taking away from potential buffet time), I came away quite impressed. The facilities are top-notch, the grounds are typically eye-catching, and the architecture is pure Disney— classic, huge and utilizing stunning promenades and plazas to blow away any vision of a sports facility I've ever had. Think Big Time Sports mixed with the fast-paced excitement of ESPN run through the Imagineers' filter.

March

The Epcot International Flower and Garden Festival: Epcot blossoms anew every spring during this celebration of creative horticulture. Gardening experts drop in and out through the nearly three-month run. Weekends include free horticulture seminars at the old Wonders of Life pavilion. Make sure you get there early; the word "free"—which is rarely spoken on-property—attracts crowds.

May

Star Wars Weekends: You'll know things are different when you see a pair of armed Stormtroopers looming over the entry gates at Disney's Hollywood Studios. Guests can meet and greet characters from the Star Wars universe on weekends running from May through June. Star Wars Weekends, which are essentially a giant Star Wars convention, also includes parades, music and interactive experiences. Star Wars celebrities are on hand for autographs and parades. And now that Disney owns Star Wars, don't expect this to go away. In fact, rumors abound that a Star Wars land—most likely at Disney's Hollywood Studios—is inevitable. At this point, the rumors are just that—unsubstantiated and founded in fans' hope and speculation.

The Expedition Everest Challenge: A road race/obstacle course/scavenger hunt that takes entrants through the exotically themed world of Disney's Animal Kingdom, the Expedition Everest Challenge tests athlete's endurance and smarts. As with many RunDisney events, this sells-out quickly.

June

Sounds Like Summer Concert Series: Epcot's America Gardens Theatre hosts a rotating roster of tribute bands who play cover versions of songs made popular by the original artists. In the past, the schedule has included bands who pay homage to U2, Bon Jovi, the Eagles, Boston, Journey and the Bee Gees. There are normally three shows every night.

July

Independence Day: Special fireworks over the Magic Kingdom and dense packs of sweaty tourists mark the American Fourth of July celebration.

September

Night of Joy: Contemporary Christian performers headline an annual concert held throughout the Magic Kingdom. This is a hard-ticket event that runs from 7:30 P.M. to 1 A.M. over the course of two nights. Tickets are $59 for one night, and $108 for a two-night pass.

"That's why we go every September—so we can go to Night of Joy," multiple Night of Joy-attendee Christopher Lamb said. "That's our big thing. Ever since we saw our first Night of Joy, that's all we listen to is contemporary Christian music."

Some of the more notable artists that have performed over the years include Skillet, Casting Crowns, Mercy Me, Mandisa and the Jars of Clay.

MOUSEJUNKIE RANDY Disney puts on the best show. When you're looking for 4th of July fireworks, where else would you go? Even though the parks are a little busy those days, you get to see the greatest spectacle of national pride this side of Washington D.C.

I like to visit The American Adventure at Epcot, and then head over to the Hall of Presidents at the Magic Kingdom, followed by the "Celebrating America Fireworks" also at the Magic Kingdom. Watch from the beach of the Polynesian Resort across the Seven Seas Lagoon. It doesn't get any more patriotic. Besides, at Disney you can have two 4th of July celebrations. The Magic Kingdom does the "Celebrate America Fireworks" on both the 3rd and the 4th. So if you want you want to head over to Epcot on the 4th, you can see IllumiNations: Reflections of Earth, which features dazzling special effects, colorful lasers, brilliant fireworks and fiery torches all choreographed to a musical score, which becomes even more dynamic on July 4 as the normal show is supplemented with a patriotic finale.

Also, Epcot has two characters that only appear on the 4th of July: Betsy Ross, who tells stories in the American Pavilion, and Ben Franklin who also makes appearances there.

If Epcot is not your thing, you can go to Disney's Hollywood Studios for a special fireworks show set to a rock 'n' roll sound track.

October

Mickey's Not-So-Scary Halloween Party: Trick-or-treat through all the lands of the Magic Kingdom. Guests—many of whom get into the festive atmosphere by donning costumes—are given a candy bag to fill with goodies at spots all over the park. It's a family fun event that's fine for even the most timid youngster, topped by perhaps the best parade of the year. The "Boo-to-You" parade is kicked off by a live headless horseman riding through the streets of the Magic Kingdom, holding a lit jack o' lantern high over his head. (Or, more accurately, where his head would be.)

A special Halloween-themed fireworks display, "Happy HalloWishes" is also part of the celebration. This hard-ticket event actually kicks off in September, and runs from 7 P.M. to

MOUSEJUNKIE AMY It's all about the Horseman. You have to be waiting for the Headless Horseman with your camera, and if you miss him, that's it until next year. Be there early. When the lights go down get your camera ready. If you're taking a movie, start it early and just let it run. It's something you don't want to miss. The "Boo to You" parade is also great. Not so much for the floats, but for the performers. The undertaker drill team, with their sparking shovels, is incredible. And the ballroom dancing ghosts recreate a scene from the Haunted Mansion right in front of you.

midnight several nights a week through the end of October. Tickets range from $62 for adults and $57 for children, to a high of $77 for Oct. 30 and 31.

Epcot International Food and Wine Festival: Now running from mid-September to early November, this culinary celebration is a food and wine lover's Super Bowl. Guests can try delicious sample-sized food from countries not normally found in the World Showcase. Representative samples and price ranges from past Food and Wine Festivals included the rock shrimp ceviche for $4.75 from Chile or the $5 kielbasa and potato pierogie from Poland, to mealie soup with crabmeat and chili oil for $3.25 from South Africa and the Moroccan tangerine mimosa royale for $6. Snack credits on the Disney Dining Plan can be used to purchase certain items.

The Epcot International Food and Wine Festival is an epicurean orgy of tiny food and many drinks that makes a trip during this time of year a foodie's heaven. The Festival runs during World Showcase hours. A valid park pass is needed to enter. Other than the price of the food samples, there is no additional fee.

November

Festival of the Masters: More than 200 award-winning artists showcase their wares throughout Downtown Disney. The three-day festival, held in mid-November, features sculpture, jewelry, photography and painting, among other mediums. There is no cost associated with attending the outdoor event.

December

Candlelight Processional: First performed at Disneyland in 1958, the Candlelight Processional and Massed Choir is a nightly event that runs from late November through New Year's Eve. More than 400 performers take the stage to perform classic Christmas music and to back a celebrity guest narrator who reads the story of the Nativity. It is a moving and powerful performance and a can't-miss during the holiday season.

The orchestra is made up of fifty-one musicians, while hundreds of choir members dress in colored robes to create a visual Christmas tree on a multi-tiered stage. Performers in red and black make up the base of the tree, while cast members from all departments dress in green to make up the tree itself. One performer, stationed at the top, acts as the star atop the tree.

At the beginning of the show, the lights are dimmed and members of the choir file in holding candles. As they take their place, trumpeters herald the arrival of the guest narrator (Edward James Olmos is a perennial favorite) and the performance begins.

The celebrity narrator reads passages from the Christmas story, punctuated by traditional Christmas music.

Until recently, it all culminated with a reading of "One Solitary Life," by Dr. James A. Francis. It was excised from the performance in 2013. Disney said it was cut for time. Others speculate it was for content:

"He was born in an obscure village, the child of a peasant woman. He grew up in still another village, where he worked in a carpenter shop until he was thirty. Then for three years he was an itinerant preacher.

He never wrote a book. He never held an office. He never had a family or owned a house. He didn't go to college.

He never visited a big city. He never traveled two hundred miles from the place where he was born. He did none of the things one usually associates with greatness. He had no credentials but himself.

He was only thirty-three when the tide of public opinion turned against him. His friends ran away. He was turned over to his enemies and went through the mockery of a trial.

He was nailed to a cross between two thieves. While he was dying, his executioners gambled for his clothing, the only property he had on earth.

When he was dead, he was laid in a borrowed grave through the pity of a friend.

Nineteen centuries have come and gone, and today he is the central figure of the human race and the leader of mankind's progress.

All the armies that ever marched, all the navies that ever sailed, all the parliaments that ever sat, all the kings that ever reigned, put together, have not affected the life of man on this earth as much as that One Solitary Life."

Normally the high point of the performance, it was certainly missed. There is no word if the decision will be reversed.

Guests wishing to see the Candlelight Processional must arrive quite early, or purchase a Candlelight Dinner Package guaranteeing a seat in the America Gardens Theatre. The show runs about forty minutes, and three performances are put on nightly.

Each pavilion in the World Showcase in Epcot also celebrates **Holidays Around the World**. Storytellers in each country tell tales of holiday celebrations, often acting out fantastic skits that illustrate cultural observances.

Mickey's Very Merry Christmas Party: Christmas—on the extended Disney calendar—runs from the beginning of November through New Year's. Guests take part in a festive extravaganza, sipping hot chocolate and munching cookies as snow falls gently onto Main Street USA. A special parade

MOUSEJUNKIE RYAN I was really moved by the story and the atmosphere. It was very deep, and probably the most moving experience I had during any Christmas trip to Walt Disney World. (Even though halfway through I started counting how many performers were fainting and being carried off stage. Don't worry, they're fine. I think it's a combination of the heat and cutting off blood flow by standing on stage so long with their legs straight.)

MOUSEJUNKIE AMY The Christmas tradition that is a "don't miss" for me is the Osborne Family Festival of Dancing Lights at Disney's Hollywood Studios. It's a display of literally millions of Christmas lights and decorations strung up and down the Streets of America. It's a massive and breathtaking thing to see. When the majority of the people are watching Fantasmic!, make your way to the Streets of America to experience the incredible Christmas light show. The music is choreographed with the lights, the faux snow puts you in the mood, and hot chocolate is plentiful as you wander around. My Mousejunkie Hubby was far too tired after Fantasmic! and stumbled his way out of the park along with the throngs, while Mousejunkie Carol and I made our way to the lights. We spent a good amount of time hunting down hidden Mickey's in the lights (I think we counted almost forty.) Even though the park was closing, cast members weren't quick to boot us out. It was so relaxing and peaceful, and it really puts you in the Christmas spirit.

(Mickey's Once Upon a Christmastime Parade) steps off twice nightly, and a "Holiday Wishes: Celebrate the Spirit of the Season" fireworks display is featured each night of the party. Guests must purchase a separate entrance ticket for the event. *(The party runs from 7 P.M. to midnight. Tickets range from $67 to $72.)*

Cost Concerns

Another consideration when deciding on travel dates is how much it's going to cost. Different times of the year are more expensive than others, and a sharp-eyed traveler will know when to plunk down the cash to confirm a reservation.

Disney divides the calendar up into their own five seasons. From the least expensive to the most expensive, they are: **Adventure, Choice, Dream, Magic**, and **Premier**. In the King's English, those terms don't really mean much. They're fairly interchangeable and they don't signify any kind of cost increase or decrease. But naming them "**Expensive, More Expensive, Wicked Expensive, You're Joking** and **Left Arm**" doesn't carry the same sense of fun. The easiest way to look at it is this: Adventure Season is the cheapest time of the year to visit, while Premier is the most expensive.

A room at a value-level resort, Pop Century, during Adventure Season will cost $92 a night during the week, and $125 for weekend nights. That same room during Premier Season goes as high as $210 a night.

The seasons are divided up based on historical crowd size. The busier it is, the more expensive it is.

Here's a look at the most up-to-date seasonal categories:

➤ Adventure Season—The months of January and September, and December 1-14.
➤ Choice Season—The month of October and November 1-23, November 27-30 and December 15-23.

➤ Dream Season—February 1-15, the month of May, June 1-10 and August 16-31.
➤ Magic Season: February 16-28, March 1-27, April 11-30, June 11-30, the month of July, August 1-15 and November 24-26.
➤ Premier Season: March 28-31, April 1-10 (Spring Break) and December 24-31 (Christmas).

Disney On the Cheap

There are ways to get yourself a Walt Disney World vacation without breaking the bank. There are five primary elements: Flight, transfers, hotel, food, and park passes.

Flight: Booking early can save some money, and it's always less expensive than booking within days of your planned travel dates. Airlines like JetBlue, Southwest and Allegiant sometimes offer quite reasonable rates. Of course, the further away you are from central Florida, the more it's going to cost.

Transfers: Take advantage of Disney's Magical Express. If you're staying at a Disney-owned hotel, it's a free service. The Disney buses pick you up at the airport and deposit you right at your resort. When it's time to leave you'll get picked up at your resort and brought right to Orlando International Airport. Attach the pre-mailed Magical Express tags to your luggage, and you can even skip baggage claim. Disney will deliver your things right to your room. It might take a few hours, but if you don't need anything in your checked bags, it's a great service. It's a very simple process: When you arrive, go to Terminal B, level 1. Show them your paperwork and you're directed to the first line of your vacation. Minutes later, you're on your way—for free.

Resort: Travel during Adventure Season and choose a value-level hotel. The least-expensive resorts on Disney property are the All-Star Music, All-Star Sports, All-Star Movies, and Pop Century resorts. Guests get all the perks of staying on-site at a fraction of the cost of a deluxe-level resort.

Park passes: The longer you stay, the cheaper it gets. A one-day ticket to the Magic Kingdom is $99. But a four-day pass is $294, bringing it down to $73 a day. Add a fifth day and you're only paying $60 a day.

Food: Eating at Walt Disney World is expensive. Table service restaurants cost the most, while counter service can save some cash. When saving money is an issue, we'll pack small breakfast treats to eat in our room before we leave. The Disney Dining Plan is sometimes offered for free, but it means you pay rack-rate for your room.

Prices listed below are based on Disney-provided information as of press time.

Magic Your Way Base Ticket		
Days	**Adults, 10 or older**	**Children 3—9**
1-Day	$94 ($99@the MK)	$88 ($93@MK)
2-Day	$188 ($94 per day)	$175 ($85 per day)
3-Day	$274 ($91.34 per day)	$255 ($67.33 per day)
4-Day	$294 ($73.50 per day)	$274 ($68.50 per day)
5-Day	$304 ($60.80 per day)	$284 ($56.80 per day)
6-Day	$314 ($52.34 per day)	$294 ($49 per day)
7-Day	$324 ($46.29 per day)	$304 ($43.43 per day)

Note that the longer you stay, the cheaper it gets (an excuse I use with the family CFO to extend our stays for as long as possible.) For example, the difference between a six-day and a seven-day pass is just about $6.

If you add the **Park Hopper option** for an additional fee, you can leave one park and go to another any time you want. Jump between all four theme parks all day long with no worries, outside heat stroke, exhaustion, and an overdose of awesomeness.

The Park Hopping option can be extremely useful. I'm a big believer in being flexible, and the ability to run from one park to another—whether it's to avoid large crowds, make dinner reservations, or to see a specific parade or show—can be invaluable.

If you find yourself standing in the shadow of the Tree of Life in Animal Kingdom and you've made a dinner reservation for the Biergarten in Epcot's Germany pavilion, you're going to need that park hopping option to get there. Add $60 for the Park Hopper option.

Add the **Water Park Fun and More option**, and you can hit the Typhoon Lagoon or Blizzard Beach water parks, DisneyQuest, or the Wide World of Sports complex. If you're big on water parks or interested in the virtual games at DisneyQuest, it might be worth it. But I've never known anyone to pick this option so they could visit ESPN's Wide World of Sports complex—where many youth sports tournaments are held—unless they had a child competing there.

One thing to note if you're considering adding this option to visit DisneyQuest at Downtown Disney: DisneyQuest is essentially a large video game arcade. There are several interactive games such as the Virtual Jungle Cruise, where guests board a raft and paddle for their lives, or Pirates of the Caribbean: Battle for Buccaneer Gold, where you fire cannons from the deck of a pirate ship to capture treasure, that are billed as "state of the art" experiences. I'd agree if this was the 1999 edition of *Mousejunkies*. Since it isn't, I feel comfortable saying that most of DisneyQuest feels rather like ten years ago. On the other hand, DisneyQuest still has a dose of Disney's storytelling touch. You enter through a Ventureport (a gussied-up elevator) that dumps you out into a hub where you choose your next destination: the Explore Zone, the Create Zone, the Score Zone or the Replay Zone. It's a great place to spend a few hours on a rainy day, but I would not recommend adding the Water Park Fun and More Option just to visit this five-story arcade. Add $60.

Get both the Park Hopper and the Water Park Fun and More option for $86.

MOUSEJUNKIE WALT That is something I would not do again. I thought everything in DisneyQuest seemed a little dated. Maybe it was neat five or ten years ago, but it's not state of the art now. Not even close. If it was raining and I was with some kids that wanted to see it, then maybe. But even then I might find something else to do.

Guests can also opt to add the **Memory Maker option** to their passes now. With Memory Maker, guests have their photos taken throughout their vacation and get to take them all home when it's over. Disney's PhotoPass photographers get everyone in the picture at scores of locations throughout the parks and at dining experiences and attractions. There's no need to choose individual images and buy they separately—with Memory Maker you get digital copies of them all. Order Memory Maker in advance and save $50, paying $149. Otherwise, the cost is $199.

Being Mousejunkies, however, we tend to opt for the **Annual Pass.** This accomplishes two things: It allows us to park hop and not worry about the number of days we should buy tickets for, and it ensures we'll return to Walt Disney World at least one more time in the calendar year.

An Annual Pass costs $634 for anyone three years old and up. (Disney Vacation Club members enjoy a $100 Annual Pass discount.) You can purchase the Annual Pass at any time before your trip, and activate it when you get to a theme park. From that moment, you have one calendar year to come and go as you please. The rule of thumb is this: If you're going to be going to theme parks for eleven days or more in one year, it makes financial sense to get an Annual Pass.

It also allows special access to sneak previews and special events held throughout the year. Annual Passholders often get to check out new attractions before others. It gives Disney a chance to soft launch something new, and offers a little extra value to Annual Passholders.

Passholders can also take advantage of discounted room rates, which vary from resort to resort, and have limited availability. Annual Pass room discount rates are usually ferreted out and posted online by sharp-eyed Mousejunkies, giving you a bit of a head start on getting that cheaper room. Also, calling 407-WDISNEY can put you in touch with someone who can provide availability information. Rates and dates often change.

Moving Forward

A few questions that come up from time to time:

How do I buy a FastPass+? FastPasses are part of the ticket price structure. You reserve them as part of your MyDisneyExperience.

If I am in the Magic Kingdom and use my third FastPass+, can I select one for another park, like Epcot? You would have to go to Epcot (or whatever park you'd like the FastPass+ for) to choose a FastPass+ at Epcot. The FastPass+ kiosks are park-specific.

Can you save money by purchasing discounted Magic Your Way tickets? If you take one piece of advice from this book, it is this: Try the extra-spicy bloody Mary at the ESPN Club at the BoardWalk.

If you take a second piece of advice, it's this: Do not, under any circumstances, buy Walt Disney World park passes from ebay, Craigslist or roadside shacks.

Stories of families arriving at the theme park gate with counterfeit, expired, or used-up tickets are legion, and there is no recourse. Don't buy partially used tickets. Stick to reliable ticket brokers like Undercover Tourist or the Kissimmee Wal-Mart (4444 W. Vine, Kissimmee, or 3250 Vineland Rd., Kissimmee), which offer slightly discounted passes. They won't mail them to you, so if you want to take advantage you'll have to show up in person. They also don't have every ticket option at all times. While the ticket you want may not be available, a trip to neighboring Kissimmee might be worth it to save a few dollars.

Discounts can also be had for active or retired military, AAA members, Florida residents and Disney Vacation Club members.

"The best part about all the parks, after you've done them all so often, isn't seeing Philharmagic again, or riding Tower of Terror again," Mousejunkie Deb offers. "Although they're fun, the best part is taking in all the theming details and nuances of the Imagineers. Disney World is a creative, innovative, marketing marvel. The entire operation is nothing less than impressive."

Travel Checklist

Before You Leave Home

☐ Advanced Dining Reservations made (407-WDW-DINE or MyDisneyExperience app)
☐ Online airline check-in 24-hours ahead (if applicable)
☐ MagicBands packed
☐ Digital camera/phone
☐ Sun block
☐ Bodyglide
☐ Chargers for cell phone/laptop/iPad/various gadgets
☐ Comfortable shoes
☐ Sunglasses
☐ Stroller

Before You Leave the Room

☐ MagicBand on your wrist
☐ Room key/Key to the World card in-hand (skip if MagicBand is in use, as above)
☐ Sunblock applied
☐ Bodyglide applied
☐ Weather checked—poncho in-hand if necessary
☐ Advanced Dining Reservation confirmation numbers available on My Disney Experience
☐ Digital camera/phone with charged batteries
☐ Fully-charged cell phone
☐ Cash and/or credit cards
☐ Fanny pack ready to go

Yes, I did say fanny pack. That waist-enhancing fashion mistake has been part of our touring kit from the beginning. As Amy clips that pleather beauty on just before we leave our resort room every morning, I just look the other way and pretend I'm somewhere else.

MOUSEJUNKIE AMY   I don't care what the reputation of the fanny pack is. It's the most useful way to carry your money, park tickets, and small camera that I've found. My mom is always toting her giant pocketbook around, lugging it along in the parks. I like the hands-free approach, and the fanny pack is the best option for that.

I know many people prefer a backpack, but after a few hours in the sun, my shoulders are aching and the last thing I want is to be carrying everyone's extra stuff they don't want to carry. With my tried-and-true fanny pack (it's got three different zipper pockets-all with broken zippers at this point), I feel safe knowing my ID, cash and park tickets are within quick reach.

If you feel shame to be seen with it slung in front around your waist, you can always unclip it and sling it over your shoulder as well. I like that it's small, but it also has enough room to fit a digital camera. I've had the same fanny pack for every trip, and its a little worse for wear, but I'm always hunting for a new one. I have yet to find one that fits the bill.

Mousejunkies Sleep

I ONCE STAYED OFF-SITE during a Walt Disney World vacation.

I also stepped on a piece of glass once and took about thirty stitches. I am in no hurry to do either again.

I'm not exactly equating staying off-site to the searing pain that rips through you after having a shard of glass plunged into your foot.

Actually, yes I am. That's exactly what it's like.

This is where a lot of people will question my judgment. I'll admit that there are plenty of fine off-site resorts in the Orlando area. However, there are also a number of less-than-desirable accommodations. I found one of them. It was an experience that helped create an on-site adherent.

I'm nothing if not irrational about certain things. As a Mousejunkie, I want to be completely immersed in all-things Disney from the moment I step off the plane at Orlando International Airport. Bright colors, Disney music, exceptional service, and unparalleled convenience get me whistling Zip-a-Dee-Doo-Dah out of my navel and making jazz hands as I prance from attraction to attraction—both of which are deeply disturbing visual images. But when I'm in the depths of my fix, I don't care. Staying on-site allows that to happen.

(Author's note: I don't really prance. It's more of a hobble by mid-week.)

Secondly, I'm really strange when it comes to Florida's unfamiliar fauna. Where I live, there aren't too many things that want to bite you. Yet in my vacation destination of choice, I'm told there are plenty. Someone told me there are things known as fire ants in Florida. To an unstable tourist, this conjures horrific visual images of an insect shooting flames out of its eyeballs at anyone with a northern accent. This doesn't seem to bother the people that live there. But when I'm told to assume there are alligators wherever you find a body of water, my irrational side emerges. This is where I began my—up to this point—lifelong fear of the legendary Orlando Jumping Snake.

I had the opportunity to stay for several nights at an assumedly snake/fire ant/biting critter-free International Drive hotel during a business conference. The room was fine, but I noticed light streaming into the room from the gap between the bottom of the door and the ground. Daylight clearly shone through. And if sunlight could get in, then snakes could get in. I was convinced that if I drifted off to sleep, I would be attacked by one of the famous Jumping Snakes of Orlando during the night. (Jumping, because that's how they'd get up on the bed to bite me. Also, this is a breed of my own creation, since I am nothing less than irrational when it comes to snakes, as well.)

I stuffed a towel under the door (because what do snakes fear more than a freshly-laundered bath towel?) and spent much of the night listening for snakes. Which begs the question: How does one listen for snakes?

Regardless, I was convinced that if I were laying my head in a Disney resort not five minutes away, the Jumping Snakes of Orlando would not be a concern.

There are also quite a few not-so-irrational reasons for staying on-site. Among them:

➤ Location—Midday naps (otherwise known as "let's watch Stacey on the in-room channel and get out of this heat" time) can be a life saver.

➤ Theming—Remain immersed in the magic 24/7. You're an addict. Start acting like one.

➤ Kids' stuff—All on-site resorts offer in-room child care for ages six months to twelve years in partnership with independent childcare provider Kids Nite Out. Add the kiddie pools and playgrounds and we're set.

➤ Online check-in—Save a step during check-in.

➤ Concierge—Need tickets? ADRs? Tee times? Stop by the concierge desk in the lobby for some of that legendary Disney customer service.

➤ MagicBands—It's a hotel room key. It's a credit card. It's your park pass. It's a way for me to purchase more Disney stuff without drawing too much attention from our family's CFO until the bill arrives. Be careful who you grant charging access to—it's as good as cash.

➤ Merchandise delivery—Purchases at shops throughout Walt Disney World Resort can be delivered to the guest's resort at no charge. Got your eye on an oversized Big

Figure but don't want to lug it around all day? No problem. Just have it sent to your resort. Try that at an off-site hotel.

➤ Free parking at the theme parks—Don't underestimate the value of reducing this hidden expense.

➤ Refillable mugs—Guests can buy a mug they can continually refill with sweet, sweet, life-giving soda at their resort during the length of their stay.

➤ Preferred tee times—Guests get preferred tee times for Disney's four championship golf courses.

➤ Transportation to the tees—On-site guests get complimentary door-to-door transportation between their resort and Disney's four golf courses.

What's New at Walt Disney World's Resorts

Disney has re-imagined 512 rooms at its **Port Orleans Riverside** resort, turning them into a detail-packed ode to fairy tales. The Royal Rooms at Port Orleans Riverside have been refurbished and redecorated to tell a story: Princess Tiana of *The Princess and the Frog* has invited her Disney princess friends over for a visit. Each has left behind a memento to mark the visit. This is where the famous Disney eye for detail comes in. A rug in front of the bureau bears a striking resemblance to the flying carpet from *Aladdin*; the bathroom holds cleverly integrated images from *The Little Mermaid,* and "candid photos" of the princesses enjoying the resort hang on the walls. Gold accents drip from every conceivable corner, a letter from Tiana is left on the table, and a fiberoptic fireworks display lights up the headboard. And while the description screams "girls," the room isn't overly princessed. The re-imagining has given it a feel of luxury that any child—or adult, for that matter—would be comfortable in.

Similarly, the **Caribbean Beach Resort** has plundered some of its rooms and left them feeling as if they belong in Pirates of the Caribbean. Beds are made to look like ships, furnishings have a bit of a maritime feel, the rug is made to look like the planks of a ship and the bathroom curtain bears an instantly recognizable skull and crossed sabers.

The Polynesian Village Resort is undergoing several changes, including its name. Formerly known as The Polynesian Resort, it has returned to a version of its roots by squeezing the "Village" back into the title. As an opening-day resort, it opened with eight longhouses, 492 rooms, and the name, The Polynesian Village.

The lobby at the Poly is being dramatically refurbished. The large, lush centerpiece, complete with a scene-setting water feature, is being completely excised. In its place, a newly re-imagined lobby will greet guests. And out over the waters of the Seven Seas Lagoon, Disney Vacation Club Villas are taking shape. With direct views of the Magic Kingdom, these accommodations will no doubt be among the most sought-after on Disney property.

Right next door, the **Villas at the Grand Floridian Resort and Spa** have opened their doors. This Disney Vacation Club option includes 147 villas located near the wedding pavilion.

Disney's new **Art of Animation Resort**—a massive campus of buildings celebrating everything Disney/Pixar— offers a new option for families or groups who want to stay together. The hotel features 1,120 family suites that sleep up to six people, as well as 864 studio rooms that fall into Disney's value-level pricing structure.

The family suites sleep six with a master bedroom, a pull-out couch in the living room area and a pull-down bed that also doubles as a small dining table. The suites also include two bathrooms, a microwave, small refrigerator and counter space for preparing small meals.

The suites certainly are colorful, if a bit thin. The room with the pull-down bed/dining table feels like a kindergarten classroom—which is fine if you've got younger children along who fit into the tiny, plastic chairs. The lack of closet space is made up for in an open hangar space in the living room. The living room area is comfortable, but the walls are a bit cold with very little in the way of décor, though tertiary colors in a complimentary scheme give the suite life. But as always, there's more to this resort than just a room count and a list of amenities.

At Disney World, it's all about story, staging and immersion. For example, go for a swim at the Art of Animation Resort, and you'll hear characters from the Disney/Pixar film *Finding Nemo* talking to you—under the water.

The submerged sound system is just one of the details the Imagineers at Disney have added to this newest resort to make it as immersive as possible.

The story starts in Animation Hall—a lobby festooned with giant reproductions of early concept drawings of Disney/Pixar characters. Move further down the wall of sketches and the characters start to take on more detail and emotion. The theme moves forward to the Ink and Paint Shop (the ever-present gift shop) just to the side of the main lobby. When it's time to add background, walk through the Landscape of Flavors restaurant. Head through the doors into the resort-proper and you're looking at the medium shot—the scene where all the action happens. In this case it's a massive courtyard surrounded by oversized props and hand-painted murals on the resort buildings that recreate the East Australian Current from *Finding Nemo*. Finally, walk into the guest room and into your close-up—a chance for kids to feel as if they're part of the movie itself.

Cast members wear paint-spattered vests, representing the artist's creative process. The *Finding Nemo*-themed pool—Disney's largest outside of its water parks—sits directly in front of you, and is designed to make guests feel as if they're living in the undersea world of Nemo, Dory and friends. The props that line the inner buildings are scaled to make visitors feel like they are the size of the short-finned little clown fish from the film.

The *Finding Nemo* buildings were the first to open, followed by the *Cars*-themed buildings, which recreate the

Route-66 inspired Radiator Springs perfectly. The *Lion King* opened next, and it all wrapped up with *The Little Mermaid.*

Most standard Disney hotel rooms sleep four, so the option of a suite allows families to stay together, and isn't too far outside the cost of renting two adjoining rooms per night.

Mousejunkie Choice *The Cars suites at the Art of Animation Resort are among the best themed on property. If you're part of a group who would do well in a suite, do not hesitate to plant your flag in Radiator Springs. The rooms are fine, but it's what's just outside that makes it perfect. The pool area is lit up by neon after dark, which recreates the feel of the movie and is utterly immersive. The rooms are comfortable, bright, clean and the whole environment is a complete success in terms of artistic design and functionality.*

The bottom line: Choose your hotel wisely. I've stayed at each level of Disney's hotels, from Pop Century to The BoardWalk Resort. Each person's needs and requirements are different, which makes a blanket recommendation impossible.

While the deluxe resorts are certainly top-notch in every respect, the amount of time you spend in your room may not equal the amount of money you might spend for the little extras. The rooms in Disney's value resorts—Pop Century and the All-Star Movies, Music and Sports Resorts—are a bit smaller, but the hotels retain the characteristic Disney theming, cleanliness and service.

MOUSEJUNKIE JENNA Since I'm single and tend to want to spend my time and money in the theme parks, I always picked a value resort. I couldn't see the need to spend more money on my resort and room because I wasn't going to spend much time there. Instead, I put my vacation budget toward things like spa visits and tours.

The Straight Dope *If you are staying at an on-site resort, take advantage of the package delivery service. Purchase anything at any of the four theme parks or Downtown Disney, and you can have your packages sent to your resort. The packages normally arrive at your home resort 24 hours after the purchase.*

Even after dozens of trips I still find myself back at a value-level resort from time to time, and I never find myself grousing about it. That said, there are a few hard-and-fast rules that apply universally: the more you pay, the more you get.

The biggest perk associated with the costlier resorts is location. Something on the monorail line—The Contemporary Resort, the Polynesian Resort or the Grand Floridian—will set you back several hundred dollars a night, but offer easily the best access to the Magic Kingdom.

Awesome/Stupid Disney Idea *A Monorail Din-ing Car. Think about it—a high-priced dining option where guests could enjoy dinner while circling the Magic Kingdom resort route. A cast member could ride along while guests order from one of the restaurants along the route. The atten-dant would see to the guests' needs. Mousejunkie Randy has mocked this concept, pointing out two very obvious shortcom-ings: The goat smell that seems to permeate every monorail car; and the fact that the monorail is running at full capacity most of the time. Pulling an entire car out of rotation would make the crush even worse. Randy's probably right.*

The BoardWalk, Disney's Beach Club Resort and the Yacht Club Resort all offer walking-distance access to Epcot's International Gateway (the back door into the park.) Disney's Hollywood Studios is also a quick boat ride away from the Epcot area resorts. Crazy people like Mousejunkie Amy prefer to walk from the BoardWalk area resorts to Disney's Hollywood Studios. I'd rather wait for a Friendship.

MOUSEJUNKIE AMY   It's not a long walk at all, and it's beautiful along the water. Depending on where the boats are in their route, you can get to the park more quickly by just walking.

Mousejunkie U *Friendships are Disney's flotilla of boats used to ferry guests to and from Epcot area resorts, Epcot and Disney's Hollywood Studios. They were built in the shops behind the Magic Kingdom, and represent the ninth largest fleet of boats in the world.*

As you might guess, Disney's Animal Kingdom Lodge offers the most convenient access to Disney's Animal Kingdom, but don't be fooled into thinking you can walk there. Transport to the theme park still requires a quick bus ride.

If money is an issue, stay at the value level resorts off-season. Annual pass holders enjoy more savings, as do AAA members.

The Straight Dope *As soon as you know the dates of your vacation, call Disney central reservations (1-407-WDISNEY) and request the AAA room-only rate. Depending on season and class of resort, you can expect a 10-20 percent discount on rooms as a AAA member. When the vacation date gets closer, deeper discounts sometimes crop up. Annual Passholders sometimes also enjoy additional discounts. Using every edge, guests can sometimes score up to 45 percent off rack rate, so the savings can be fantastic. However, the discounts fluctuate and aren't always available. Persistence is the key.*

Sometimes, however, saving a little extra money doesn't matter.

MOUSEJUNKIE WALT Beyond trying to save Disney Vacation Club points (a time share-like lodging option where guests purchase a real estate interest), I don't really care about saving money. I'm not very good at trying to save money anyway. When I go, I want to go as big as I can while still being able to afford it. Sometimes people will ask, 'Why do you splurge on the BoardWalk view when it costs so much more than a normal view room?' The answer is because I like it! I say if you like it, go for it.

One way Disney categorizes its resorts is by location: Magic Kingdom area resorts, Epcot area resorts, Disney's Hollywood Studios area resorts, Animal Kingdom area resorts and Downtown Disney resorts.

The Resorts of Walt Disney World

Here's a closer look at each resort, by location:

Magic Kingdom

The Contemporary Resort
Theming: Sleek and modern
Facts: One of Walt Disney World's originals, this deluxe-level resort has 655 rooms and suites and a concierge floor in a 14-story, A-frame structure. The resort is divided into two sections: The tower and the garden wing. It's located between

the Seven Seas Lagoon and Bay Lake, and is within sight of the Magic Kingdom. Great views and an enviable location on the monorail line are two of the primary reasons to consider this resort.

★**Mousejunkie U** *The Contemporary Resort was built using some of the most forward-thinking techniques of the time. Individual rooms were built off-site—including all the plumbing and electrical work, carpeting, doors and windows—and then lifted by crane into the A-frame structure. This was one of the first major builds to use modular construction. The rooms could theoretically be replaced the same way, if it wasn't for the naturally swampy Florida ground beneath it. The entire resort has settled a bit since construction, locking all the rooms in place for good.*

Feed me: Table service restaurants include The California Grill, The Wave, The Contempo Café and Chef Mickey's—a character buffet. The Contempo Café is the new deluxe version of counter service at the resort. There are also three lounges, two snack bars and, as always, room service.

Feels like: Classic Walt Disney World. The Grand Canyon Concourse, with monorails silently gliding by the massive art installation by Mary Blair, remains both nostalgic and forward-looking.

You should also know: Guests can enjoy water sports such as boat rentals, waterskiing and parasailing, and other recreation options: volleyball, a playground and two swimming pools. There are gift shops, a game room, laundry service, child-care and a health club for those who think they just haven't walked quite enough on their vacation. For the lanyard-wearing types, the resort features 90,000 square feet of meeting space, including a 44,300-square-foot grand ballroom.

Getting to the parks: Buses to all the resorts and attractions except for the Magic Kingdom; Walk to Magic Kingdom; Monorail to Magic Kingdom; boats to the Magic Kingdom. Guests can also take the monorail to the Ticket and Transportation Center and catch another monorail to Epcot.

Mousejunkie U *President Richard Nixon delivered his "I am not a crook" speech during a gathering of Associated Press editors at the Contemporary Resort in November of 1973.*

Bay Lake Tower at Disney's Contemporary Resort
Theming: Ultramodern
Facts: Connected to the Contemporary Resort by a sky-bridge, this Disney Vacation Club resort has 295 units, including studio, one- and two-bedroom villas, and Magic Kingdom-view three-bedroom Grand Villas. The décor is modern, with striking artwork, flat-screen TVs, full kitchens complete with granite countertops and modern appliances and laundry facilities.

Feed me: The sixteenth floor Top of the World Lounge provides guests with some of the most dramatic views available anywhere at Walt Disney World Resort. Light appetizers and drinks are served.

Feels like: Minimalist, futuristic, quiet. Disney after the robot revolution.

You should also know: This resort is a Disney Vacation Club resort, but rooms can be reserved for paying customers if any are available. Access to the Top of the World Lounge is available only to DVC members staying at the resort using points.

Getting to the parks: Bay Lake Tower offers the same transportation options as the Contemporary Resort: Buses to all the resorts and attractions except the Magic Kingdom; Walk to Magic Kingdom; Monorail to Magic Kingdom; boats to the Magic Kingdom. Guests can also take the monorail to the Ticket and Transportation Center and catch another monorail to Epcot.

Grand Floridian Resort and Spa
Theming: Turn-of-the-century Victorian
Facts: Disney's jewel on the monorail line has 867 rooms and suites, including 181 concierge accommodations. This ultra-swanky resort on the shores of the Seven Seas Lagoon opened in 1988. Inspired by turn-of-the-century east coast Florida resorts, its Victorian look is modeled after the Hotel del Coronado in San Diego—complete with sparkling whites and an eye-catching gabled red roof. The marble in the floor

of the lobby was recently redone and features stylish representations of Disney characters. A cavernous five-story open lobby is dotted with invitingly soft chairs and couches, overlooked by a bird cage elevator. Live music throughout the day and into the night adds atmosphere to the extravagant surroundings.

Feed me: Cítricos (expensive), Victoria & Albert's (really expensive), Gasparilla Grill and Games, Grand Floridian Cafe, 1900 Park Fare (a character buffet), Narcoossee's (expensive) and two lounges.

Feels like: Money.

You should also know: Boat rentals, including the Grand 1 52-foot Sea Ray yacht, are available. Guests can also swim, visit the playground, health club and game room. There is shopping and child-care and laundry facilities. There's also a meeting facility with nearly 40,000 square feet of meeting and convention space.

Getting to the parks: The Grand Floridian is on the Magic Kingdom monorail line. Watercraft transport is also available to the Magic Kingdom. Other parks and attractions are accessible by Disney's bus system. Guests can also take the monorail to the Ticket and Transportation Center and catch a connecting monorail to Epcot.

Polynesian Village Resort

Theming: South Pacific Isles

Facts: Set on the shores of the Seven Seas Lagoon, the Polynesian has 847 rooms, suites and concierge service designed to transport you to the Hawaiian islands. The resort is undergoing a massive refurb, with villas being constructed out over the water and the removal of the once beautiful atrium, which greeted guests in the Great Ceremonial House (Tahitian for "lobby," evidently.) Just outside the Great Ceremonial House is the Nanea Volcano Theme Pool—a zero-entry pool that starts at ground-level and dips gradually like a natural beach.

The entire resort is set on beautiful white sand beaches facing the Magic Kingdom. Grab a lounge chair and you've scored one of the best spots for viewing the Wishes nighttime fireworks display this side of the Main Street Hub.

Feed me: Dining options include 'Ohana—a ton of food served family style—which also has a character dining experience for breakfast. The Kona Café, Captain Cook's, the "Spirit of Aloha" dinner show, The Tambu Lounge, and room service.

Feels like: Hawaii.

You should also know: Recreation and amenities include swimming, boating (rent several kinds of boats at the Mikala Canoe Club Marina), a playground, a game room, shopping, childcare, and laundry facilities.

Getting to the parks: The Poly is on the Magic Kingdom monorail line, but guests can also use watercraft transportation to get across the lagoon. Other parks and attractions are accessible via Disney's bus transportation system. Guests can also take the monorail to the Ticket and Transportation Center to catch a connecting monorail to Epcot.

The Straight Dope *Watch the nightly "Wishes" fireworks display and the Electrical Water Pageant from the beach at the Polynesian. The music accompanying each show is piped-in, and there's plenty of room to spread out and even lie down.*

Wilderness Lodge
Theming: National park lodges of the Pacific Northwest
Facts: Designed to feel like the Old Faithful Inn at Yellowstone National Park, this impeccably themed resort boasts 727 guestrooms. A jaw-dropping six-story lobby, finished with teepee-topped chandeliers, Disney-themed, hand-carved totem poles and an 82-foot-tall stone fireplace, leaves many first-time visitors gazing upward, taking it all in. A hot spring bubbles up from the ground inside the lobby and flows outside and down toward a geothermal geyser that erupts hourly—thanks to Disney magic. Chairs and couches placed strategically throughout allow visitors to take in the overwhelming surroundings in comfort.

Feed me: Dining options include Artist Point (fancy), Whispering Canyon Café (loud), Roaring Fork Snacks (listen

MOUSEJUNKIE BARRY The Wilderness Lodge will always hold a place in my heart. It was our resort of choice on the first Walt Disney World vacation we took with our daughters and it made such an impression on us that it served as home base for the return trip some fourteen months later. I'm a sucker for tall pines, rustic log cabins, mountain air, geysers, honking geese—the works.

The Wilderness Lodge is as close as you'll get to a visit to Yellowstone without actually being there, down to its own Old Faithful. Yeah, it's man-made—Old Fakeful. I still love it. You get the Old Fakeful show every hour on the hour and my girls made sure to attend each and every eruption they could. When they weren't riding Small World of course.

What else did I love? There's the boat launch at the edge of Bay Lake which offers quick trips to either Fort Wilderness or, best of all, the Magic Kingdom. There are two table-services restaurants on-site, including one of my favorites, Whispering Canyon Cafe. The lobby is phenomenal. Six stories of pine and stone edifaces, carvings, Mission-style lighting fixtures. When we visited the first time, we were lucky enough to be there for the Christmas season so we got to enjoy the huge Christmas tree that stands in the dead center of the lobby. There's the bubbling brook running from the elevator area leading outside to a falls and into the main pool. There's the pool itself, in which the resident ducks like to take a dip now and then. Those same ducks will often visit you when you're eating your breakfast out by the pool and aren't averse to sampling your croissant, if you feel like sharing.

for music by Bela Fleck and the Flecktones,) Territory Lounge, a pool bar and room service.

Feels like: The biggest, most opulent log cabin ever.

You should also know: A Disney Vacation Club resort—the Villas at Wilderness Lodge—is located through the lobby, right next door. For business travelers, there is one 750 square-foot boardroom/meeting room. Guests can rent bikes and boats, swim, visit the playground or take advantage of the laundry room, game room or on-site childcare.

Getting to the parks: By boat to the Magic Kingdom and bus to all other parks and attractions.

Fort Wilderness Resort and Campground
Theming: Wilderness camping
Facts: 799 campsites and 409 Wilderness Cabins all set in a relaxed 700-acre wilderness setting. The campsites are level, paved pads with electric, water and sewer hookups, and have charcoal grills and picnic tables. All campsites have close access to air-conditioned comfort stations with private showers, coin laundry facility, vending machines and telephones. There are also sites where guests can pitch a tent.

The Wilderness Cabins are air-conditioned accommodations that sleep up to six guests and feature vaulted ceilings, fully equipped kitchens, full bathrooms, television, VCR, outdoor grills, picnic tables, and a private patio deck. Wilderness Cabins also come equipped with hair dryers, foldaway cribs and ironing equipment, and daily housekeeping is offered.

Feed me: Dining options include Crockett's Tavern, Mickey's Backyard BBQ, Trail's End Restaurant and "Hoop-Dee-Doo Musical Revue" nightly dinner show at Pioneer Hall. Campfire and marshmallow roast with Disney characters and a Disney movie.

Feels like: F-Troop come to life. (Kids, ask your parents.)

You should also know: Amenities include watercraft, beach, fishing, tennis courts, two heated swimming pools, arcade game room, laundry facilities and kennel. Groceries and camping supplies at Meadow and Settlement Trading Posts. Unique to Fort Wilderness is the Wilderness Back Trail Adventure Segway Tour. Guests can explore the campground and Wilderness Lodge area via off-road Segways.

Getting to the parks: Buses link Fort Wilderness with all Walt Disney World parks and attractions. Boats will take guests to the Magic Kingdom.

Fort Wilderness is so unique as a Walt Disney World resort, it deserves a more detailed look. Mousejunkie Jenna is the veteran Fort enthusiast in our group.

MOUSEJUNKIE JENNA I have spent three vacations camping at The Fort with my parents, and have loved every minute of them. Now, when I say "camping," I mean "camping in an RV." While I have nothing against tents, when it comes to camping at Walt Disney World, I'm with my mother on this one—I want air conditioning, a refrigerator, and something more than nylon between me and the alligators (or armadillos, turkeys and lizards).

The Fort is ideally suited to whatever kind of camping you choose. I've seen families with tents, pop-up campers, and the kind of luxury motorhomes the most spoiled rock star would crave. Campsites range from small sites suitable for a tiny teardrop trailer to large pull-through sites for the big diesel pusher coaches. All sites feature a concrete pad for parking or a rig, and a picnic table, charcoal grill, water and electricity, and all sites except for Premium sites feature a sand pad suitable for a tent. Preferred and Premium sites also offer sewer and cable hook-ups. The Premium sites are designed for the longer rigs and don't have a sand pad for tents. The one thing missing is campfire pits. Fires at individual sites are absolutely forbidden.

There's even "camping" for people who don't want to camp, at all. The "resort" part of Fort Wilderness Resort and Campground comes into play with more than 400 Wilderness Cabins. The cabins sleep 6 people, with 2 bedrooms (one with a double bed and one with a bunk bed), and a Murphy bed in the living room. They have full kitchens and dining areas, bathroom with tub/shower, TV in the living room, and your own deck and charcoal grill. The cabins also feature daily "Mousekeeping," so while you're in accommodations that feel like a snug little cabin in the woods, you also get the benefits of staying in a hotel. The only things

(Continued on next page)

you really need to bring are food, bug spray, and a flashlight. Every camper worth his salt needs a good flashlight.

Fort Wilderness is made up of a series of loops that branch off the three main roads. The loops have conveniently located comfort stations, which are very clean and spacious (but you still may want to shower early to avoid a line). Bus stops for Fort Wilderness's internal bus system are also convenient to loops. Campers are discouraged from driving their own vehicles around the campground when not checking in or out of their site. This contributes to the sense of peace and quiet around the campground. The bus system consists of three bus lines—orange, yellow and purple—which run through different areas of the campground. All busses visit both the Outpost Depot (check-in, bus transportation to theme parks, kennel and trail rides) and the Settlement Depot (Pioneer Hall, the Marina/Boat Launch, Tri-Circle-D Ranch), only the orange and yellow buses go to the Meadow area. The Settlement is where you will find the Hoop-Dee-Doo Musical Revue, Mickey's Backyard BBQ, Trail's End restaurant, carriage rides and anything to do with a boat (fishing, boat rentals, transportation to the Magic Kingdom).

At the Meadow, you can find the newly refurbished Meadow Swimmin' Pool, featuring slides and a great kiddie pool, and Chip n' Dale's Campfire Sing-A-Long. The Campfire Sing-A-Long is one of those hidden treasures of Walt Disney World. It's a free program featuring songs, jokes, and a visit from Chip n' Dale. As you might guess, there are two campfires (attended by cast members). Bring your own s'mores, or buy supplies from the chuck wagon. Afterward, stick around for classic or current Disney movies shown on the big screen. The Meadow is also the home of one of two arcades at The Fort, bike rentals, the Meadow Trading Post grocery store, a Segway tour, and an archery program. Another arcade and grocery store may be found at the Settlement.

One feature that makes Fort Wilderness unique among all Walt Disney World resorts is that campers staying in their own air conditioned trailer or RV can keep their pets with them. Pets are welcome on designated pet loops for an extra $5/day. On our last trip, we stayed on a pet loop even though we didn't have any pets with us. It was great seeing all of the different dogs out for walks. At the front of each pet loop, there is a post with a container of baggies and a waste bin to encourage owners to clean up after their dogs. Last year, The Fort opened the Waggin' Trails Dog Park for dogs staying at The Fort to enjoy a little time off-leash. For safety's sake, dogs are not permitted in tents or in vehicles without air conditioning.

The one "problem" I have with Fort Wilderness Resort and Campground is that there's almost too much to do there. I have to confess, I haven't done most of the activities offered at The Fort. When I visit WDW, I am all about the four theme parks, so I miss out on a lot at The Fort. I do know that some devoted Fort Fiends can

(Continued on next page)

spend a week or more at Fort Wilderness and not visit a single park. That may not be the Mousejunkie way, but I think I'm actually a little jealous. There's something to be said for kicking back and enjoying the more rustic side of Walt Disney World"

The Wilderness Lodge is as close as you'll get to a visit to Yellowstone without actually being there, down to its own Old Faithful. Yeah, it's man-made—Old Fakeful. I still love it. You get the Old Fakeful show every hour on the hour and my girls made sure to attend each and every eruption they could. When they weren't riding Small World of course.

What else did I love? There's the boat launch at the edge of Bay Lake which offers quick trips to either Fort Wilderness or, best of all, the Magic Kingdom. There are two table-services restaurants on-site, including one of my favorites, Whispering Canyon Cafe. The lobby is phenomenal. Six stories of pine and stone edifaces, carvings, Mission-style lighting fixtures. When we visited the first time, we were lucky enough to be there for the Christmas season so we got to enjoy the huge Christmas tree that stands in the dead center of the lobby. There's the bubbling brook running from the elevator area leading outside to a falls and into the main pool. There's the pool itself, in which the resident ducks like to take a dip now and then. Those same ducks will often visit you when you're eating your breakfast out by the pool and aren't averse to sampling your croissant, if you feel like sharing.

Shades of Green

Facts: Shades of Green is also unique among Disney resorts, as it is operated as an Armed Forces Recreation Center for the exclusive use of active and retired military personnel and their families. Shades of Green has 586 rooms in a relaxed, country atmosphere overlooking golf courses, gardens and pools.

Feed me: Full-service dining is available, as are snack bars, a lounge and room service.

You should also know: Guests can take advantage of tennis facilities, swimming, and a fitness center and game room. Walt Disney World maintains golf operations on the two PGA championship 18-hole golf courses and nine-hole walking course adjacent to Shades of Green.

Getting to the parks: Buses link to all Walt Disney World parks and attractions.

Epcot Area Resorts

Pop Century Resort

Theming: Twentieth-century pop culture

Facts: A value-level resort, Pop Century features 2,880 rooms with décor inspired by the 1950s, '60s, '70s, '80s and '90s. Outsized icons from each decade are plopped throughout the resort, including a four-story Rubik's Cube, a giant Big Wheel and 65-foot high bowling pins.

MOUSEJUNKIE AMY I really like Pop Century. It's bright and interesting and welcoming. The food court has a good variety. It's one of the newer resorts and it feels that way. If you're choosing among the value resorts, it would be my first choice.

Feed me: Snacks are available at the Petals Pool Bar, but Pop Century has, hands-down, the best quick-service food court in Disney's resorts.

Feels like: Your weird uncle's attic. (Only a lot cleaner.)

You should also know: Swim in three pools, enjoy a kiddie pool, and visit the Pop Jet Playground and Fast Forward arcade. This resort is convenient to the ESPN Wide World of Sports Complex.

Getting to the parks: Buses whisk guests to the parks and attractions from the front of the resort. Only Disney buses can whisk.

Caribbean Beach Resort
Theming: The Caribbean isles
Facts: This sprawling resort is divided into 6 Caribbean-themed resort villages featuring 2,112 rooms located on 200 acres surrounding a 42-acre lake. The 6 themed villages are

Aruba, Barbados, Jamaica, Martinique, Trinidad North, and Trinidad South. There are no elevators in any of the two-story buildings. If you are unable to use the stairs, request a first-floor room. The main building, Old Port Royale, can be quite far from some of the buildings. The Martinique and Trinidad North buildings are closest to Old Port Royale.

Feed me: Dining is available at Shutter's restaurant for table service and the Market Street food court.

Feels like: Pirates of the Caribbean.

You should also know: Pirate-Themed Rooms (in Trinidad South—the furthest village from the main building) immerses guests in the adventure-filled world of buccaneers. Pirate ship beds and wooden "ship's deck" flooring are among the details added to 384 rooms near a zero-gravity pool themed to appear like an old Spanish fort with cannons guarding the walls. All guestrooms include mini bars and coffee makers. Also available: boat rentals, swimming, a playground, a game room, bicycling, nature walks, jogging track, laundry facilities and shopping. Each village has its own pool, white sand beach with hammocks and playground, laundry facilities, bus stop (so distance from the main building may not be an issue,) and parking area.

Getting to the parks: Buses are available at several locations throughout the resort. You're never too far from a bus stop, and therefore your park or attraction of choice.

Yacht Club Resort

Theming: Upscale Cape Cod

Facts: The oyster-gray clapboard buildings on the shores of Crescent Lake feature 621 rooms and suites. Brass fittings, nautical hardwood floors and rich millwork welcome guests into the warm lobby. All rooms feature French doors that open onto porches or balconies.

Feed me: The Captain's Grille, Yachtsman Steakhouse and two lounges. Heads-up here: There are no counter service offerings at this waterfront resort, but if you feel like going for a walk you're not far from the BoardWalk Bakery.

Feels like: Kennedy country with Mouse ears. If they could stage the Barnstable vs. Falmouth football game on the croquet lawn, it'd be perfect.

You should also know: Let's talk location: Stay at the Yacht Club and you're within simple walking distance of Epcot's International Gateway (the back door to Epcot) or Disney's Hollywood Studios. Bunking down at the Yacht Club also gives guests easy access to all the amenities of the BoardWalk, just across the lake. A marina lighthouse that stands out on Crescent Lake adds an almost tangible ambience to this elegant but comfortable resort. Centrally located to the Yacht Club and its kissing cousin, the Beach Club, is a 73,000-square-foot convention center that includes a 36,000-square-foot ballroom that can seat as many as 2,800 for dinner.

Getting to the parks: Walk to Epcot or Disney's Hollywood Studios; Boat to Epcot or Disney's Hollywood Studios; Buses to the other parks and attractions.

Beach Club Resort
Theming: New England beach cottages
Facts: Designed to resemble New England beach cottages of the 1860s, the Beach Club has 576 rooms and suites in sun-washed structures of white stick-style architecture. The welcoming lobby features plenty of white wicker furniture in which to kick back and take in the airy atmosphere, and 24-foot-high ceilings.

Feed me: Beaches and Cream, an old-fashioned ice cream parlor. (Though as the home of the Kitchen Sink, "ice cream parlor" seems a bit modest. Maybe "Citadel of Cream: Where Dessert Warriors Go to do Battle" would be more appropriate. More on that in "Mousejunkies Eat.") Guests can also dine in the Cape May Café (a character dining experience for both breakfast and dinner) and two lounges.

Feels like: Saltwater taffy. Fancy, but a little less stiff than it's neighbor, the Yacht Club. (And I'm still lobbying for a Dunkin' Donuts at the guard shack.)

You should also know: Location, location, location. Guests are so close to Epcot, it often feels as if IllumiNations: Reflections of Earth is going off in the bathroom. (Eat at 'Ohana and it might sound like that anyway.) The Yacht and

Beach Club resorts share Stormalong Bay—the best theme pool in all of Walt Disney World. Stormalong Bay features three lagoon areas and a water slide created to look like a shipwreck. Guests can also take advantage of a health club, a marina, childcare, a barber shop and laundry facilities. The Beach Club Resort also includes the Beach Club Villas—a Disney Vacation Club resort.

Getting to the parks: Walk to Epcot or Disney's Hollywood Studios; Boat to Epcot or Disney's Hollywood Studios; Buses to the other parks and attractions.

The BoardWalk Inn

Theming: Turn-of-the-century Atlantic seaboard

Facts: Dripping with charm, the 372-room BoardWalk Inn is more than a hotel—it's an entertainment and dining district that offers guests a seemingly endless array of merrymaking options. (I did, in fact, say "merrymaking.") Located on Crescent Lake and across from the Yacht and Beach Club Resorts, the BoardWalk features shopping, a children's activity center, a health club, tennis courts, a themed pool and a 20,000-square-foot conference center. See? Plenty of places to make merry.

Feed me: Disney's BoardWalk restaurants include Flying Fish Café, Kouzzina by Cat Cora, Big River Grille and Brewing Works, ESPN Club, Atlantic Dance nightclub, Jellyrolls dueling piano bar, and Seashore Sweets Bakery. Like its counterpart, the Yacht Club, there is no counter service.

MOUSEJUNKIE WALT My favorite hotel is the BoardWalk, and the location is a big reason why. It's between my two favorite theme parks—Epcot and Disney's Hollywood Studios. And then there's the atmosphere. During the day it's a beautiful place to relax. At night there's entertainment from one end of the boardwalk to the other. There are jugglers, games of chance, musicians—all of which draw a crowd. I also like the fact that it's its own little resort. There are restaurants, a piano bar and a microbrewery there. Think of it this way: If you went on a vacation there and didn't want to ride any of the attractions, you could just hang out at the BoardWalk Resort, maybe it the pool and relax during the day. At night you can choose from any of the restaurants nearby, or walk right next door to Epcot and enjoy a different country every night. One night you could be drinking wine in Italy. The next you can be enjoying great French cuisine. If you want a trip where you just relax, it's the perfect place to do it. Or you can go to the Magic Kingdom and be with all the screaming kids. Whatever floats your boat.

Feels like: The Great Gatsby. Only with less disillusionment and unfortunate pedestrian accidents.

You should also know: Live entertainment keeps the BoardWalk jumping well into the night, as do the restaurants and lounges. It's proximity to the ESPN Club, and that establishment's chicken wing and football-fueled Sundays, is yet another reason this place will forever feel like my home away from home.

The resort's themed pool, Luna Park, features a fantastic water slide—the Keister Coaster—and there are two quiet pools.

The BoardWalk also shares space with the Disney Vacation Club's BoardWalk Villas. The Villas offer studio, one and two-bedroom suites, and three-bedroom Grand Villas.

Getting to the parks: Walk to Epcot or Disney's Hollywood Studios; Boat to Epcot or Disney's Hollywood Studios; Buses to the other parks and attractions.

Walt Disney World Swan and Walt Disney World Dolphin

Theming: Think pink coral and turquoise waves

Facts: While these striking resorts are on Disney property, they are run by Westin Resorts. This doesn't mean the Swan and Dolphin are any less enjoyable, they just look and feel quite different from what you might find elsewhere on Disney property. The resorts, designed by Michael Graves, offer 2,265 rooms and 254,000 square feet of meeting and exhibition space. The massive statues topping each resort—the Swans are 46 feet high and the fish 56 feet high—can be seen from all over the Walt Disney World resort.

Feed me: There is a long list of restaurants and lounges between these two resorts. Notably: Todd English's Blue Zoo, Il Mulino New York Trattoria, Kimonos, and Shula's Steak House.

Feels like: Floribbean.

You should also know: There are four swimming pools, two health clubs and a wide array of recreational activities. The location is ideal to Epcot, Disney's Hollywood Studios and the BoardWalk via water and walkway. There is a parking charge for guests at this resort. If you park it yourself, you'll pay $9 per day. Valet parking is $12 per day (and the state of Florida takes its piece, as well.)

Getting to the parks: Guests can either walk or take Friendships to Epcot and Disney's Hollywood Studios. Buses are available to all other parks and attractions.

Downtown Disney Area
Disney's Saratoga Springs Resort and Spa
Theming: An 1800s upstate N.Y. resort
Facts: The spirit of Saratoga Springs, N.Y., with its horse racing history and placid up-state feel, is recreated accurately in the 924-unit fifth Disney Vacation Club resort.

Victorian architecture and gurgling springs evoke a gentler age. Comfortable, overstuffed chairs make the lobby a comfortable place to fall into after a hard day of walking, and its spa offers a relaxing way to get away from the theme parks.

Constructed on the site of the old Disney Institute (and before that the Disney Village, and before that some alligator's house...probably), guests can walk to Downtown Disney, or take a quick ferry across the lake. Rooms facing Downtown Disney have a fantastic view of the nearly 24-hour restaurant, shopping and nightclub district.

MOUSEJUNKIE WALT   My only criticism of Saratoga Springs, which is my Disney Vacation Club home resort, is that it's so big. You can walk forever just to get to the main building depending on where you stay.

MOUSEJUNKIE RYAN   My favorite resort is actually a tie between Saratoga Springs and All-Star Music. I know, I know, those are complete opposites. Let me explain. Saratoga Springs is our home resort, so I've stayed there a lot. And having visited Saratoga Springs, N.Y. twice a year for roughly half of my life, I have a bit of a connection there. Throw in the fact that my dad used to be a jockey, and you can see why I love the fancy racetrack themed resort.

This is a Disney Vacation Club resort, but rooms can be booked when available.

Feed me: The Artist's Palette—a counter-service restaurant and market—serves breakfast, lunch and dinner. The Turf Club is a table-service restaurant where you can get ya meat on (prime rib, angus chuck cheeseburger, grilled New York strip.)

Feels like: Upstate New York. With palm trees.

You should also know: The resort is located across the lake from Downtown Disney and adjacent to Disney's Lake Buena Vista golf course. Also, this place is big.

Getting to the parks: Bus transportation is provided to all the theme parks, water parks and Downtown Disney.

The Straight Dope *For a room closest to the check-in desk, request The Springs. For a room closest to Downtown Disney, request a room in Congress Park.*

Port Orleans—French Quarter
Theming: New Orleans' French Quarter
Facts: Storm shutters, spicy Cajun food, garishly colored décor, ornate wrought iron fixtures and a feeling of perpetual Mardi Gras recreates New Orleans' French Quarter in this moderate-level, 1,008-room resort. The shuttered windows and doors along the main thoroughfare recreate perfectly the feel of Bourbon Street, as do the street signs, which are identical to those found in New Orleans.

Feed me: Sassagoula Floatworks food court and pizza delivery.

Feels like: Mardi Gras without the risqué bead-tempting antics.

You should also know: The French Quarter boasts one of the more eye-popping pools, Doubloon Lagoon, which is themed like a Mardi Gras celebration. A large dragon twisting around one end also serves as a water slide, while an all-alligator

Dixieland band stands guard nearby. But, as it usually does, it all comes down to the food. Beignets and café au lait, ribs and cornbread make this a food court you will not want to overlook. And that, in itself, might be reason enough to stay at this resort.

Getting to the parks: Bus transportation is provided to all the theme parks, water parks and Downtown Disney. Boats can take guests to the neighboring Port Orleans Riverside, and to Downtown Disney.

Port Orleans Resort—Riverside
Theming: The old South
Facts: Accordion and washboard music lilts teasingly from behind bushes throughout this 2,048-room resort. The Sassagoula River winds through both the Magnolia Bend (Southern-style mansions) and Alligator Bayou (rustic lodges) sections.

Feed me: Dining includes Riverside Mill food court and Boatwright's Dining Hall.

Feels like: *Song of the South.* But don't tell anyone. Disney pretty much ignores that film.

You should also know: Recreation includes Ol' Man Island, a 3½-acre old-fashioned swimming hole with slides, rope swings and playgrounds; quiet pools; boat rentals; game room; lounges and a gift shop. If it wasn't for the ribs at the French Quarter's food court, Riverside would top my list of moderate resorts. Never underestimate the power of barbecue.

Getting to the parks: Bus transportation is provided to all the theme parks, water parks and Downtown Disney. Guests can also take a Riverboat to Downtown Disney and to this resorts neighbor, Port Orleans French Quarter.

Old Key West Resort

Theming: The most relaxing aspects of the Conch Republic

Facts: The first Disney Vacation Club resort built, this resort offers the laid-back charms of Key West with the service and amenities Disney resorts are known for. There are 549 units in this Disney Vacation Club resort, with studios, one and two-bedroom suites and three-bedroom, absolutely gargantuan 2,375 square-foot Grand Villas that can sleep the entire defense of the Miami Dolphins. (Up to 12, actually.)

Feed me: Dining includes Olivia's Café, poolside fare at the Gurgling Suitcase, and Good's Food to-Go quick-service restaurant.

Feels like: A take-home version of Key West.

You should also know: Rooms include wet bar, microwave and small refrigerator, or a full kitchen. There is a health club (for those who think exercising on vacation is a good idea), tennis, swimming pool, sauna and planned recreation. Guests can use DVC points or book through central reservations. After dark the resort comes alive with festive yet muted lighting, rather successfully recreating the feel of the original location several hundred miles to the south.

MOUSEJUNKIE AMY If I was going to Walt Disney World and not go to the parks, this is one of the resorts I'd pick to just relax. It's quiet and out of the way. The theming isn't overpowering. The Wilderness Lodge hits you over the head with its log cabin and wooden feel. At Old Key West it doesn't scream "I'm at Disney!" You can just go and hang out next to the water and enjoy a drink.

Getting to the parks: Bus transportation is provided to all the theme parks, water parks and Downtown Disney. Guests can also travel to Downtown Disney by boat, which is a much more enjoyable option than the typical bus trip.

Disney's Animal Kingdom Area Resorts

Animal Kingdom Lodge
Theme: African savanna

Facts: This 972-room deluxe level resort is themed to convey the feeling of being transported to an African wildlife reserve. The architecture, plant life and variety of animals that freely roam the 33-acre savanna just outside the Jambo House lobby contribute to a vivid and convincing atmosphere.

Feed me: The Animal Kingdom Lodge, and the Disney Vacation Club's Kidani Village located just next door, features two full-service restaurants—Boma: Flavors of Africa and Jiko: The Cooking Place. There's also a counter-service restaurant and two bars—Uzima Springs and Victoria Falls. Kidani Village has its own table-service restaurant, Sanaa.

Feels like: All the beauty of Africa.

You should also know: The resort features hand-carved furnishings, African art and a giant fireplace in a soaring lobby. Guests can stroll along a rock outcropping, Arusha Rock, and enjoy nearly panoramic views of roaming animals and flowing streams. Guests with savanna-view rooms—on the inside of the horseshoe-shaped resort—can view the animals from the comfort of their beautifully themed accommodations. Animal Kingdom Lodge has Disney Vacation Club rooms, and is located next to the 449-unit DVC Kidani Village Resort.

Kilimanjaro Club-level guests are offered a safari experience unique to resort guests: The Sunrise safari. It takes guests on an early-morning trek through the Kilimanjaro Safari land. The safari includes a break for a breakfast buffet, featuring African-inspired fare, in a private room at Pizzafari. The Sunrise Safari is $75 for adults and $40 for children, and admission to Disney's Animal Kingdom is required.

Here's the real lowdown: The Disney public relations would like you to imagine sitting out on a hotel room balcony in the morning, sipping coffee as a giraffe slowly moves by, grazing on leaves just a few feet away.

In reality, that is *exactly* what it's like to stay at the Animal Kingdom Lodge (assuming you score a savanna-view room.) There's no marketing sleight of hand at work here. It is as beautiful and unique an experience as you'll find without actually traveling to Africa.

MOUSEJUNKIE KATIE One time we were staying on the third floor of the Animal Kingdom Lodge. I was keeping a journal during that trip, and we were hanging around the hotel room. I decided to go out on the balcony to write. I was sitting around in the chair, watching the animals and I was swinging my legs back and forth out of habit. Suddenly, my foot got stuck between the bars on the railing of the balcony. I panicked and tried to pull it free. It came out, but without the shoe. My flip-flop flew off and plummeted to the grass below—where the animals were! Luckily it wasn't where they could reach it, but I didn't know that at the time. I immediately assumed one of the animals would eat it and die. I ran back into the hotel room. My mom asked me why I had one shoe. "Well, I was swinging my legs, and my foot got stuck, and my shoe fell off, and now one of the animals is going to eat it and choke and die!" I explained. My mom was really concerned because the shoes were expensive. My dad was laughing. I told him this was a serious matter. He joked and said he thought he saw a flip-flop shaped thing inside a giraffe's neck. We went down to the front desk to tell them what happened. About two weeks after we got home a box arrived in the mail—and there it was. My flip-flop was found and sent home by Disney's great cast members.

More than three hundred animals and birds populate the grounds, which surround the resort on three sides. The animals can be seen from private balconies as well as several public-viewing areas.

There's nothing like sharing a caffeine buzz with a zebra first thing in the morning.

Getting to the parks: Bus transportation is provided to all the theme parks, water parks and Downtown Disney.

Coronado Springs Resort
Theming: American Southwest
Facts: Inspired by the American Southwest and regions of Mexico, this 1,917 room resort encircles a 15-acre lagoon called Lago Dorado. There are three quiet pools and a five-story Mayan pyramid that serves as the splashy centerpiece for a family-fun pool with a water slide.

Feed me: Dining includes the Maya Grill full-service restaurant, the Pepper Market food court, Rix Lounge, Laguna Bar lounge, Siestas Cantina poolside bar and limited room service.

Feels like: A breezy siesta.

You should also know: Special services include in-room coffeemakers and ironing equipment, La Vida Health Club, hair-styling salon, bike rentals, watercraft rentals, arcade, sand volleyball court, kiddie pool and playground. A 220,000-square-foot convention center includes the 60,214-square-foot Coronado Ballroom. This place is huge, but a new internal shuttle system helps guests get to and fro. (I'm not sure which is preferred, to or fro.)

Getting to the parks: Bus transportation is provided to all the theme parks, water parks and Downtown Disney.

Art of Animation Resort
Theming: Disney and Disney/Pixar animation
Facts: From the first step into this resort, guests are thrust into the vivid world of feature film animation. All 1,120 family suites and 864 standard guest rooms are designed to evoke one of several of Disney and Disney/Pixar's well-known films. From the big blue world of *Finding Nemo*, and the colorful under the sea haunts of Ariel's Grotto to the pride lands of *The Lion King* and the high-octane Radiator Springs of *Cars*, this resort captures it all.

Feed me: The Landscape of Flavors counter service is located in the lobby, along with a poolside snack bar and pizza delivery.

Feels like: Living on the big screen.

You should also know: The 308,527 gallon, zero-entry Big Blue Pool—straight out from the lobby and adjacent to the Nemo wing—is massive and surprising. Underwater speakers play audio from the film. Just remember to surface occasionally. The Cozy Cone Pool, themed around *Cars*, and the Flippin' Fins Pool are also nearby.

Getting to the parks: Bus transportation is provided to all the theme parks, water parks and Downtown Disney.

All-Star Sports Resort
Theming: Sports

Facts: Colorful, clean, fun, and affordable. This 1,920-room value resort is dotted with buildings surrounded by larger-than-life sports icons representing surfing, basketball, tennis, baseball and football. My only knock: Needs more hockey.

Feed me: Food court, a pool bar, pizza delivery.

Feels like: Tom Brady would stay here.

Wait, who am I kidding? Tom Brady is married to Giselle Bundchen and jets around the world in his own crime-fighting plane. He'd build his own resort with a special wing for his Super Bowl rings and there would be a supermodel stable. But other than that I bet it would look like this.

You should also know: This value-level resort features a commercial center with check-in and guest service facilities, laundry facilities, a gift shop and game room. There are two swimming pools and a kiddie pool. The design, feel, layout and style of this resort is virtually identical to the All-Star Movies and All-Star Music resorts, save for the décor.

Getting to the parks: Bus transportation is provided to all the theme parks, water parks and Downtown Disney.

All-Star Movies Resort
Theming: Movies

Facts: This 1,920-room value resort has facilities and amenities that mirror Disney's All-Star Sports Resort. Towering icons from favorite Disney movies adorn the resort, from *101 Dalmatians, Toy Story, Fantasia, The Mighty Ducks* and *The Love Bug.*

Feels like: An animation fan's dream.

Getting to the parks: Bus transportation is provided to all the theme parks, water parks and Downtown Disney.

How much? Rooms range from $82 to $174 depending on season and whether it's a standard room or a preferred room (closer to the lobby).

All-Star Music Resort

Theming: Fine art. No, I kid, I kid. Music.

Facts: This is the resort that saved my vacation and turned me into a Mousejunkie. Like the other All-Star resorts, it is colorful, clean and fun. There really is not a lot that feels "budget" about this value-level resort. It features 1,489 rooms and 215 family suites in buildings with larger-than-life icons representing jazz, rock, Broadway, calypso and country music. Facilities and amenities are the same as the All-Star Sports and All-Star Movies resorts. The family suites sleep up to six and offer two bedrooms, two full baths, a kitchenette and two 27-inch flat screen TVs.

Feels like: Disney's rich musical history

Getting to the parks: Bus transportation is provided to all the theme parks, water parks and Downtown Disney.

MOUSEJUNKIE RYAN I can't help but love the piano pool, the brightly decorated rooms, and the ridiculously '80s-styled pop stars painted throughout the café. It's just a fun environment, and being a music lover who has stayed there many times, it just seems like home for me.

To reserve a room at a Walt Disney World resort, call 407-WDISNEY (934-7639).

Resorts by the Numbers

According to Walt Disney World figures:

➤ Total number of resorts at Walt Disney World—36
➤ Number of Disney owned/operated resorts—26
➤ Number of Disney owned/operated resorts that J and Deb have stayed at—24*
➤ Total number of guestrooms at Walt Disney World Resort—more than 30,000
➤ Total number of guestrooms where Bill took too much cold medicine and stared at the wallpaper for hours—1*
➤ Number of Disney owned/operated guestrooms—more than 24,000
➤ Number of Disney Vacation Club units—3,293 (2-bedroom equivalents)

➤ Number of campsites at Disney's Fort Wilderness Resort and Campground—799
➤ Number of resorts where Mousejunkie Katie almost choked a giraffe with a flip-flop—1**

* These figures provided by Mousejunkies researchers.
** Not really.

Nearby Options

There are a number of non-Disney-owned hotels located near Downtown Disney. Many of these offer conference and convention space. Here's a quick rundown of these resorts:

Buena Vista Palace: 1,013 rooms and suites and 90,000 square feet of meeting space in a 27-story, lakeside setting.

Regal Sun Resort: 626-room lakeside resort. Features more than 17,000 square feet of meeting space.

Doubletree Guest Suites Resort: 229-room resort consisting entirely of suites with living room and separate bedroom, refrigerator, microwave and coffee maker. Dining at Streamers Restaurant.

Holiday Inn: 323-room high-rise hotel featuring in-room coffee makers, four restaurants and lounges, two swimming pools, a fitness center and a game room.

The Hilton: 814-room resort with seven restaurants and lounges, three swimming pools and a tropical outdoor spa. Offers more than 61,000 square feet of meeting space.

Hotel Royal Plaza: Features 394 rooms, conference facilities, on-site dining and entertainment.

Best Western Lake Buena Vista Resort: 325-room Caribbean-style resort featuring a game room, fitness center, swimming pool, playground and shopping.

Another benefit of staying on-site is that there's always the option of a midday nap. Midday naps can be valuable. That is, if your kid will nap. Ours usually won't, but a little down time can help. It certainly helps her mother, I'll tell you that. Plus, it gives me time to watch Stacey on the in-room resort TV channel.

No matter where guests stay on-property, from the most exclusive suite at the Grand Floridian Resort to the most affordable studio at Pop Century, there is one element that unites them all, and that is Stacey J. Aswad.

Stacey is the super-friendly, ultra-perky host that guides viewers through the Disney parks on its in-room resort information channels. Love her or hate her, there's no escaping her high-energy welcome. Turn on the TV in any Disney resort, and there she is—colorful, cute, enthusiastic, and ultimately helpful.

There are two guarantees on every Walt Disney World trip: I will start and end each day by watching Stacey for a while, and Amy will roll her eyes every time I do it.

Interview:
The Human Exclamation Point
(Walt Disney World's In-Room
Resort Channel Host, Stacey Aswad)

To anyone who has stayed on Walt Disney World property in the past few years, she is the face of the vacation kingdom.

Walk into a hotel room at Walt Disney World—any hotel room in any resort—turn on the TV, and there she is. She's perky, enthusiastic and perhaps most importantly, omnipresent. Guests can't help but feel like they've got a cute, dark-haired woman traveling along with them.

But just who is that girl?

Stacey J. Aswad is the host of Walt Disney World's in-room resort channel. She'll tell you about the "Top Seven" attractions, she'll outline the "Must-Do" activities and provide a few insiders' tips along the way. And if you're staying on Disney property, there's no avoiding the infectiously happy tour guide.

"It's starting to hit me, after five years, that I'm seen as this kind of real-life Minnie Mouse," Stacey said from her home in Los Angeles. "I know in Disney culture, I'm 'that' girl and the face of Disney World, but I don't take myself so seriously. I have been called the human exclamation point."

Stacey got the part after auditioning in Atlanta, going through callbacks, meeting the director and then receiving the original twenty-five-page script.

"I had four days to learn the script," Stacey said. "I had to have everything memorized. There were no Teleprompters, no ear prompters. I had to learn it word for word. I remember having this moment of, 'Oh my gosh, what have I done?' That was my first real acting/hosting gig. I had been a dancer my whole life, but I hadn't really done any on camera. It was a great baptism."

Stacey hosts two shows that are on a constant loop in the resorts: the 30-minute "Top Seven Must Sees," and the newer "Must Do Disney."

"When we shot the first time, no one knew who I was," she said of the relative ease with which she moved around the theme parks. "People would look at us and not care. Now people have gone back time after time, and they end up watching me and not getting away from me. People think I live in the park. I get these great emails—'We were at Disney World and didn't see you.' People think I live in the Cinderella castle."

Over the course of the two shows, Stacey has taken viewers on a virtual tour through Walt Disney World. She interacts with characters, walks through the parks and experiences the resort firsthand—including a few of the more hair-raising attractions.

"Some of attractions I had to do multiple times while shooting," she said. "Like Summit Plummet (at the Blizzard Beach water park.) I had to do that three times in a row."

Her blindingly fast plunge down Summit Plummet—the second tallest and fastest free-fall water slide in the

(Continued on next page)

world at the time—is the perfect example of how the Julliard-trained dancer throws caution to the wind and gives in to her boundless energy.

"I went down, fixed my bathing suit and went right back up," she said. "It was very bizarre. I remember saying to ride operator, 'All I have to do is cross my feet, cross my arms and lean back? Seriously? There's no restraint?' I think I may have said a small prayer, leaned back and off I went. I screamed like crazy."

Which prompts the Binghamton, N.Y. native to explain: "I don't really scream that much in real life."

Stacey flies to Florida to update the shows now and then, and also provides new voice-overs when needed. During the time she's been the inescapable emcee of every Disney resort guest's off-hours TV viewing, she's learned a thing or two about the place. Her number one, top-secret tip?

"Wear comfortable shoes," she laughed.

Surprisingly, someone who is so closely identified with Walt Disney World had very little time in the resort prior to landing the hosting job.

"I had heard about it, but I had a large family so it was like we had our own Disney World at home," she said. "I'd had friends that had gone, but it was this whole mysterious place. So when I first got there I had some expectation of it, but it blew me away—the sheer volume of it. Everything about it is very magical.

"I love challenges, but I had to kind of stop and look around to see exactly what was going on. I was so focused on doing a good job, but I couldn't believe the logistics of it."

The shoot itself is always somewhat of a delicate dance. The timing of each segment is deliberate and mapped out. If a monorail comes by a certain location, they have one chance to get everything right. She often has to board a certain ride car at a certain time, and if they don't get the shot everyone has to wait around for the next timed opportunity.

And as for that famous Stacey energy?

"When I got the first job and we were first shooting it, there was a moment where they said, 'Let's pick it up a little more.' I was like, 'gosh, really?' I thought I was being over the top.

"I do tend to be free and energetic, but I do have moments of being calm and chilled out."

The segments are updated from time to time, and a few times a year Stacey will find herself back in the parks, raving about one thing or another and enjoying the atmosphere.

"What I find interesting—and the attractions are amazing—is that every time I go back I'm more in tune with the landscaping and architecture," she said. "Don't overlook those things. It's incredible. It's all obviously part of the whole palate of fantasy. Nothing is random, and everything has a meaning or purpose."

Mousejunkies Sleep Checklist

❑ Decide if you'd like to stay on Disney property or have a terrible vacation.

❑ Check your budget/needs to see if you'd like to stay at a value, moderate, deluxe, or home-away-from-home/ DVC resort.

❑ Call 1-407-WDISNEY to make your reservation.

❑ If you are an Annual Passholder, see if there are any AP room rates.

❑ If you belong to AAA, see if there are any AAA room rates.

❑ Ask the cast member taking your reservations if they are running any specials (free dining promotion, etc.)

❑ **Disney's Value Resorts**
All-Star Movies
All-Star Music
All-Star Sports
Pop Century
Art of Animation

❑ **Disney's Moderate Resorts**
Caribbean Beach Resort
Coronado Springs
Fort Wilderness
Port Orleans: French Quarter
Port Orleans: Riverside

❑ **Disney's Deluxe Resorts**
Animal Kingdom Lodge
The Beach Club
The BoardWalk Inn
The Contemporary Resort
The Dolphin
The Grand Floridian
The Polynesian Resort
The Swan
The Wilderness Lodge
The Yacht Club

❑ **Disney Vacation Club Resorts/**
Home Away From Home Resorts
Animal Kingdom Villas
Bay Lake Tower
Beach Club Villas
BoardWalk Villas
Kidani Village
Old Key West
Saratoga Springs
Treehouse Villas
Villas at Wilderness Lodge
Villas at the Grand Floridian Resort and Spa

Mousejunkies Eat

PITY THE POOR PEOPLE AT CHEF MICKEY'S, for they could not know of the perfection within their grasp.

I speak, of course, of the Marinated Beef Flatbread at the Contempo Cafe at the Contemporary Resort.

The Contempo Cafe is a counter service restaurant located in the Grand Concourse of the resort. It sits just adjacent to Chef Mickey's—a much more well-known restaurant where it's infinitely more difficult to get a seat. Blame the presence of the Big Cheese. It's a character buffet featuring the most popular Disney characters.

If only these people, blinded by the Big Five, knew what they were missing.

First, a quick aside: To my many Disney friends—Bad. You are very, very bad. Very, very, very bad. Why didn't you force me to know of this wondrous creation before now? It is your job to force me to know something this wondrous. It's for my own good, and this is what friends do.

But hey I can forgive, for I have been awash in the haze of the beefy, garlicky afterglow brought on by heretofore undisclosed foodstuff of joy: the Marinated Beef Flatbread.

It's separate elements sound enticing: marinated beef, oven roasted tomatoes, garlic, caramelized onions, arugula and goat cheese. Combine them together into a magical slab of ultimate goodness designed to transport you to the land of wow, and it becomes transcendent. And here's the best part: The arugula is easily removed.

Let's face it, greens of any kind are there just to obscure the beef or food of a greater caste of deliciousness, so let's just move that to the side and dive in.

The discovery began earlier in the evening as we sat in our room at Bay Lake Towers without any dinner plans. I know, that's crazy. But we had tossed our itinerary out the window and decided to freelance. We wandered up to the Top of the World Lounge but it was packed. Defeated, we headed to the Contempo Cafe right next door at the Contemporary.

I sidled up to the self-service kiosks, saw the word "beef" and tapped that. I paid the nice lady, waited for our buzzer to go off and had a seat. Mousejunkie Amy, who wasn't feeling well, struggled to toss down a banana, and Mousejunkie Katie dug into her rather unappetizing looking chicken nuggets.

Meanwhile, I poked through the arugula while trying to get a look at what I had ordered. Luckily, I have the expertise and wits enough to know that the arugula had to go. As I raked through the offending greens, the true treasure beneath began to reveal itself. I was hungry, and therefore I was intrigued.

I broke off one of the eight squares the flatbread had been sliced into and took a bite.

As the flavors jackhammered into my psyche, I uttered this phrase: "Oh my God I'm losing my mind."

Ask Amy. I'm not exaggerating.

Fighting with the half-eaten banana, she rolled her eyes. I took a second bite.

"Amy, I'm not joking. I am absolutely losing my mind."

They were the only words that raced to mind as I began to lose touch with reality amid the overwhelming fugue enveloping my senses. (Just a reminder: I'm still basically talking about a fancy pizza here. Sometimes I get a little excited.)

They certainly did not skimp on the beef, and there was a full bed of caramelized onions and goat cheese below—certainly a winning combination.

The flatbread in question had been sitting there for some time, waiting for me to discover it. Well, not that flatbread, in particular, but the menu item. And that's the beauty of dining on Disney property: There are changes and undiscovered items that even regular visitors will eventually stumble across.

Keep drilling down through the levels of Disney's many culinary offerings. It will happen.

You've been traipsing around theme parks all day and you're hungry. But you can't decide between escargot with champagne, schnitzel and a beer, or a burger and a coke.

Don't sweat it—Walt Disney World's got you covered.

What's New with Walt Disney World Dining

For years, getting a good cup of coffee on Disney property was a bit of a challenge. Now, however, it's as easy as walking up Main Street.

The Main Street Bakery, a long-time favorite of Mousejunkies for its early-morning offerings and gigantic ice cream cookie sandwiches, has been transformed into a Starbucks. There was much gnashing of teeth when the changeover was first announced, but the protests have quieted somewhat. It might be the effects of a potent caffeine buzz, or it could be that Disney's Imagineers have kept the overall Main Street USA feel of the place intact, rather than staffing it with insufferable, trendy baristas. Fear not—it fits right in. Muffins, scones, breads, cake pops, cookies and rolls will satisfy any sweet tooth, and breakfast sandwiches of many stripe will take care of any early morning needs. The wide range of Starbucks drinks are all available, bringing in a welcome alternative to the old Nescafe fallback.

Despite early misgivings, it seems as if guests have gotten on-board the Starbucks train to jitterville. An early trend had guests providing Disney-themed names for their order and posting them to Twitter with a #CoffeeWithCharacter hashtag.

There are also Starbucks locations at Epcot, where the Fountain View Cafe was, and at Downtown Disney by the World of Disney and on the West Side near the Characters in Flight balloon.

Cat Cora's first foray into Disney dining, outside the Epcot International Food and Wine Festival, has come to a close. Kouzzina, the celebrity chef's restaurant at Disney's BoardWalk Resort, was shuttered after a three-year run. In its place, guests will find **Trattoria al Forno**—an Italian eatery offering Neopolitan pizza, pastas, meats, seafood and desserts. The wine selection will be 100 percent Italian, with offerings hailing from Tuscany, Veneto and Piedmont. The restaurant will be located in the same space Kouzzina occupied.

Trying to take the pulse of Disney dining has been a bit difficult. With new additions going up all over the property, there's always something different to try. New menu items are being added on a pretty regular basis, and even the counter-service spots are benefitting. **Columbia Harbour House**—the quick-service restaurant in Liberty Square near the Haunted Mansion—has recently added seafood mac-and-cheese and chicken pot pie.

The ESPN Club on the boardwalk may be just pub fare, but the chefs behind all those TVs always seem to take it to the next level. Take, for example, the PB&J burger. No, I am not joking: Peanut butter, jelly, bacon and sliced jalapenos piled high atop a burger. It's sweet, salty and spicy all at once, and it's a winner. If burgers are your thing, don't stop there. The Picnic Burger at the **Sci-Fi Dine-In Theater** slaps two all-American favorites together—a hamburger topped with a hot dog. What could be more perfect while eyeballing some of those Tex Avery cartoons up on the screen?

Don't go anywhere, burger freak. First you'll need to head to **Cookes of Dublin** in Downtown Disney for the Battered Burger. The cooks at Cookes drop the burger into its fantastic batter and then they deep fry it. Throw a little chunky tomato chutney and garlic mayo on it, and you're miles from the meat-puck-with-ketchup.

The new thing, around Walt Disney World lately, seems to be adding fried eggs to burgers. It's about time. Whatever breakfast cook accidentally dropped someone's over-medium on another customer's no. 3 special deserves a medal. Grab a lunchtime Advanced Dining Reservation for the **Whispering Canyon Cafe** and order the Chuck Wagon Angus Bacon-and-Egg Burger with Tillamook cheddar and chipotle ketchup to investigate, or head to the Rose & Crown Pub in the UK pavilion in Epcot for an English Breakfast Burger. It's what you think it would be, but with applewood smoked bacon and house-made HP sauce (think of it as a British version of A1 steak sauce.)

Drop a little brie cheese onto anything and it automatically gets fancified. That's canon—I checked. So the Surf-and-Turf Burger at the **Kona Cafe** gets a head start before they even add spicy shrimp to the stack.

Steer away from the burgers, just slightly, for the bacon cheeseburger mac-and-cheese at the **Friar's Nook** in the Magic Kingdom, where you can also find blue cheese mac-and-cheese with balsamic dressing.

Finally, be prepared to leave a credit card number to hold your Advanced Dining Reservation. For years, indecisive guests would make several reservations and just show up for the most convenient. That took up valuable ADR space and left others out in the cold. Now, if you don't show, you get charged. Skipping a reservation will result in a $10 charge, per person. Of course, in reality things are slightly less draconian. If you make an effort and run a little late, you'll be fine. The policy is just a way of keeping people from hoarding all the best reservation times at the most popular restaurants.

The great thing for a foodie is that these changes are happening all over the place. There are upgrades, new items and unusual tastes across the property.

Dig In

Interested in stuffing yourself at a buffet? Be sure to hit Boma at the Animal Kingdom Lodge. How about a character meal? Chef Mickey's at the Contemporary is your answer. Have you pawned the kids off with your in-laws for a romantic evening out? Narcoossee's at the Grand Floridian should do the trick.

There's something for every taste at Walt Disney World, it just might cost you a bit. (And by "a bit," I mean "a lot." And by "a lot," I mean that there may be a bit of hyperbole ahead. Try to eat healthy and smart. Unless you don't want to—in which case, go nuts.)

Dining at Walt Disney World is expensive. I never fail to experience sticker shock when I see what my meal cost. Yet I don't opt to skip this part of the trip. The service, theming and quality of Disney's eateries make them just as much a part of the vacation as any theme park attraction.

MOUSEJUNKIE RANDY Some people find the high-end restaurants at Disney World pricey. But I think they are well worth the value for the money you pay. I have gone to "expensive" places in Boston and paid twice as much as the high-end places at Disney. You can't beat the quality, the service, or the variety of food choices at Walt Disney World. These places to me are a much better value for your Disney dollars than an $8 cheeseburger at Peco Bill's at the Magic Kingdom. (But how I love that cheeseburger.) I would rather spend $18 for a perfectly cooked steak served with fresh, hot macadamia nut bread and Yukon Gold mashed potatoes at the Kona Café. It's all what value you think you're getting for your dollar. It's vacation, live it up a little.

Of course, there are ways to save a little money, it just takes a little creativity. Just not "Corn People" creative.

Several years back an early Internet legend tore through the DISBoards—one of the biggest Walt Disney World fan forums online. A family visiting the World thought they'd save a little money by bringing along their own food. Specifically, canned corn.

Said family used a can opener to crack open the golden treats, sat down on a sidewalk on Main Street USA and shoveled those sweet niblets down their gullets with plastic spoons as other guests wandered by.

I'm not one to pass judgment on anyone trying to save a little money at Walt Disney World, but this family, whoever they were, became unknowing celebrities among the Disney fanatic community. These "Corn People," as they came to be known, were the topic of conversation for the better part of a year. Every once in a while they'll still be referred to by an old-timer on the boards as an example of slightly odd behavior at Walt Disney World.

The truth is, there are countless restaurants (actually, they are quite countable, but they keep opening new ones and closing older ones and I'm easily confused while under the influence of bread pudding) ranging from affordable to shamelessly expensive. And everyone has a favorite. But there are a few generally accepted rules: Le Cellier is always good, and Tonga Toast is one of the best, if most over-indulgent, breakfast you can get on-property.

A Disney Breakfast Coup

Recently there has been a seismic shift in the Disney breakfast hierarchy, however. The mighty Tonga Toast—long the stuff of breakfast legend amongst Walt Disney World guests—may have been knocked from its lofty perch by an unassuming and yet irresistible alternative.

Will there be those who scoff at this subjective proclamation? Surely. But there were those who said man could not reach the moon; that the Red Sox would never win the World Series; that I should probably wear pants in public more often.

And yet I must make this claim: Tonga Toast is dead. Long live the Samoan.

Anyone who has ever eaten breakfast at the Kona Café at Disney's Polynesian Resort has no doubt crossed paths with its signature breakfast dish, Tonga Toast. It's a deep-fried banana-stuffed French toast reportedly brought to the resort by cultural advisor Auntie Kaui. It's bigger than your head and probably has more calories than a footlocker full of Big Macs. But it tastes amazingly good and probably precludes any need for lunch reservations.

And yet it now sits firmly in second place. On the Mount Rushmore of Awesome Disney Breakfast Options, Tonga Toast would be Teddy Roosevelt. Sure, it's up there, but it's kind of looking the other way and you can't really see that he's wearing glasses unless you pay the seventy-five cents to look through the binoculars and you left all your change back in the car.

Tonga Toast will always remain near and dear to my heart, primarily because that's where my stomach is and it's probably still digesting from the last time I had it in December of 2006. Now, however, I have eyes for another.

It happened rather innocently. I perused the menu and my eyes accidentally tripped down the page past Tonga Toast. It was inadvertent, but the repercussions have become very real. A single word jumped out at me and seared itself into my eyes. Hollandaise. This egg yolk and butter-based sauce has magical properties that turn even the most mundane meal fantastic. So imagine my shock when I saw that

"Hollandaise" was paired with two other words that render me weak and defenseless: "pulled pork."

The Samoan, in its entirety, is poached eggs with Hollandaise sauce served over smoked pulled pork hash.

The Samoan is made up of three elements that are good individually, but collectively reach perfection. Topped with a pile of greens that look like clover but serve to only temporarily obscure the golden glow of the Hollandaise, it captured my imagination the minute I saw it.

I tore through the greens, tossing them to the side of my plate as I drilled down to the gooey, aromatic treasure below. I pierced one of the poached eggs and it seeped down onto the pulled pork hash. It was like adding together the vital elements of a potion. Once intermingled, the magic could not be undone. I was enraptured by the visual presentation. But this was nothing compared to when I actually tasted it. It was salty with a hint of sweetness. The pulled pork gave it a tangy bite that tied it all together in a way that I heretofore had not experienced. I temporarily lost the power of speech. My vision grew dim. I swam in a lake of Hollandaise buoyed by a raft of pulled pork while egg whites sang a siren song drawing me closer to an island of toast. After a few moments of this inward trip, I heard—distantly—someone calling my name.

I snapped to.

"Daddy, I have to pee," my daughter said.

"Take the kid to the bathroom," I droned to my wife.

I was focused on continuing my journey. I took another bite and jumped back into my eggy rapture. I saw an order of Tonga Toast delivered to the table next to me, and for the slightest moment felt a tinge of sadness. Because I knew that the Samoan had forever chased it from my palate. I would not attack that mountain of deep fried goodness only to feel full to the point of puking ever again.

But it was O.K., because the Samoan had stolen my heart.

There may have been Hawaiian Kona coffee served in a French press pot, but I'm not sure. I marched through the Samoan until it was gone, and then I emerged—sated in every possible way and ready for another.

But this was Kona, not 'Ohana. That over-indulgence would have to wait for another day.

The Straight Dope *Make your reservations as early as possible, or plan on standing in line at counter service during your stay. Advanced Dining Reservations (ADRs) can be made 180 days out from your trip on the My Disney Experience app or by calling (407) WDW-DINE (939-3463). You can also make all your ADRs online at disneyworld.disney.go.com/reservations/dining. The interface is incredibly easy to use, and it gives you options if your time or restaurant isn't available.*

Considering the sheer number of dining choices and options, figuring out where to eat has become as important as any other part of our trips to Walt Disney World. Whenever a friend comes home from a visit, the questions invariably go like this: How was the weather, how were the crowds, where did you eat?

We literally plan entire vacations around where we want to eat. Not because we're unusually bacchanalian, but because it can be a hassle to get a reservation.

Here's the key: When you've booked your trip, count 180 days out from your arrival date, and either hit your My Disney Experience app or call (407) WDW-DINE (939-3463) or visit disneyworld.disney.go.com/reservations/dining to make your advanced dining reservations that day. Delay, and you may never know the cool, candle-lit, beefy goodness of Le Cellier or what Fantasyland looks like from inside Cinderella Castle.

Can't-Miss Restaurants

Everyone has a favorite Disney eatery, and judging by how difficult it is to get an Advanced Dining Reservation, it must be Le Cellier. The buzz surrounding this restaurant is deafening, however it has dimmed a bit since it became a signature dining experience. That means this once expensive restaurant has gotten even more pricey, and it takes two dining credits if you're on the Disney Dining Plan.

For me, however, if I have a pint of Guinness in my hand and some kind of meat on my plate, I'm pretty happy. Add some great traditional Irish music and I'm in heaven. At Raglan Road you get all this. The food revolves around Irish themes, but is much better than anything I've sampled while actually in that section of the world. The Simple Salmon appetizer—smoked salmon served with capers, shallots and creme fraiche—is still a favorite, along with Ger's Bread and

Butter Pudding. The music is fantastic, and the Irish step dancers, who perform nightly, are the best you'll find outside of the Emerald Isle.

Then there's the statue.

Mousejunkie U *Outside the restaurant, which is tucked between a main entryway near the massive parking lot and the waterfront at Downtown Disney (soon to be Disney Springs), is a statue of Irish poet and novelist Patrick Kavanagh (identical to the one located along the Grand Canal in Dublin). Kavanagh wrote the poem—later set to music—"On Raglan Road."*

One night, Kavanagh met Irish singer Luke Kelly—leader of the traditional Irish group The Dubliners—in a Dublin pub called The Bailey. The two talked for a while, and the conversation eventually turned to Kavanagh's poem. By the end of the night, the two had struck an agreement. The result was the wild-haired Kelly recording what many believe to be the definitive version of the song, "On Raglan Road."

To sum up: The statue of the thin, long-legged man sitting on a bench and thinking quietly to himself is not, despite much confusion, Walt Disney.

The next time you pass by, pause and say hello to the man who penned "On Raglan Road," and remember him as the haunting tune calls out from inside the restaurant named for one of his finest works.

On a quiet street where old ghosts meet
I see her walking now
Away from me so hurriedly my reason must allow
That I had loved not as I should
A creature made of clay
When the angel woos the clay
He'll lose his wings at the dawn of day

The Straight Dope *Schedule your dinner for after
8 P.M.—which is when the live entertainment begins at
Raglan Road.*

While Raglan Road snares me every time, everyone's got
their favorites.

MOUSEJUNKIE J I've said it before, and I'll
say it again: It's all about the food. So here are
a few of my favorites:

The Kona Café, located in the Polynesian Resort
I have eaten all three meals there and they were all
excellent. It is laid back but the food is great. It's not
cheap, but it's reasonable by Disney standards. The
fresh bread with the honey-macadamia nut butter is
to die for. And let us not forget the best breakfast item
in Walt Disney World—Tonga Toast. How can you
go wrong deep frying anything and then rolling it in

cinnamon sugar? I had a pulled pork sandwich there for lunch and it was very good.

'50s Primetime Café at Disney's Hollywood Studios

The place has a fantastic atmosphere and the fare is comfort food at its best—plus there's not much over $20 on the menu. Just be prepared to "play the game" with the servers. The pot roast with mashed potatoes is excellent. Just remember to ask for no green beans if you are not going to eat the green beans. Standing in the corner because you did not finish them is a drag. (Yes, seriously.) To top it off, the dessert menu is presented to diners on a ViewMaster. It's the perfect ending to a meal that takes guests back to their youth.

You'll very likely find the place to be crowded and loud—just the way it is intended to be. The Tune-In lounge before the meal is really neat as well. Just like you were transported back in time. Most importantly, they serve Yuengling Lager.

Les Chefs De France in the World Showcase at Epcot

For a real nice meal that makes you feel like you are dining five-star but on a budget eat at Les Chefs De France—*for lunch*. It is a beautiful dining room, the service is very good and the lunch prices are a bargain by Disney standards. They serve fresh French rolls with butter that are mouth watering. The wine by the glass is reasonable as well. I always get the Bier Kronenbourg

(Continued on next page)

1664. Despite the setting—white linen tablecloths and servers in white dress shirts with black ties—I still felt fine in a polo shirt and shorts. The flatbreads are excellent as well as the stuffed crepes. You can go more expensive and get a dinner-type meal at lunchtime.

Le Cellier in the World Showcase at Epcot

Normally I would put Le Cellier on any list but it can be pricey if you get a drink and a filet mignon. The menu normally is really a steak menu with a single pasta and seafood choice. Don't get me wrong, I love the place. If I knew the people going had lots of disposable income, I would tell them to go there in an instant.

The Best Places to Pig Out

I have a love/hate relationship with 'Ohana—the family style, Polynesian island themed restaurant in the Polynesian Resort across from the Magic Kingdom. For the normal person, there's nothing to hate about 'Ohana at all. It's a wonderful restaurant where the atmosphere is fun, the entertainment fantastic and the food delicious and plentiful.

And this is where our problem occurs. I'll say it again: The food is plentiful. Normal people know when to stop eating. When a Cast Member walks by with a skewer of meat and asks, "More steak cousin?" most people would know to say, "No thank you." Especially if they feel nauseous. And especially if the bread pudding has yet to arrive.

MOUSEJUNKIE RANDY Lets talk about that banana bread pudding for a second. If you're a big fan of 'Ohana's signature dessert, like I am, but find yourself sitting in the Kona Café because you couldn't get a reservation for 'Ohana, remain calm. When they bring the dessert menu, ask for it, Kona and 'Ohana use the same kitchen, and they will be more than happy to get it for you.

In the time honored contest of me vs. food, there are few restaurants that consistently beat me to an absolutely stuffed pulp and then throw me out on the sidewalk, drunk on an assortment of meats and ready to heave it all into one of the conveniently-located trash barrels.

The Straight Dope *If your reservations at 'Ohana are earlier than the nightly "Wishes" fireworks display, finish up your meal and trudge uncomfortably down to the beach. Stake out a spot in the sand—or if you're extremely lucky, sack out in a hammock—and enjoy the show from there. After "Wishes" you'll have a front-row seat for the Electrical Water Pageant. The water borne parade floats across the Seven Seas Lagoon and Bay Lake nightly, weather permitting.*

It's so good, I can. Not. Stop.

It's a cry for help I tend to elicit on every trip when we visit 'Ohana. Which is usually every trip. Luckily Mousejunkie Amy will remind me of my history of 'Ohana-induced nausea

MOUSEJUNKIE AMY He does it every time. He can't resist the phrase "More (insert type of skewered meat here) cousin?" Someone walks by with a pile of food and his brain goes out the window. We certainly get our money's worth.

and throw me a life preserver—which in my peel-and-eat-shrimp-induced haze appears to be made of turkey tips floating in a peanut dipping sauce.

It's to the point where you can predict the entire evening:

1. We arrive at the Polynesian Resort, check-in at the 'Ohana podium.
2. Order a couple drinks at the Tambu Lounge while we wait to be called.
3. As we are led to our table, the hostess asks, "Have you dined with us before at 'Ohana?" We laugh and laugh. Oh, how we laugh.
4. Before my butt hits the seat I'm shoveling something into my face.
5. As I emerge from the feeding frenzy, I begin complaining loudly about how sick I feel.
6. Stuffed beyond capacity, I waddle down to the lakefront to watch the "Wishes" fireworks display over the Magic Kingdom.
7. I fervently wish there was such a thing as a Star Trek-type transporter that could just get me to my resort room without all that awful, you know, walking.

8. I swear I will be smarter about dining at 'Ohana next time. (I won't.)

Here's something the Mousejunkies have come up with to ensure your safety in a post-'Ohana splurge-coma. Simply cut out the tag, pin it to your shirt before the meal begins and make sure you fall face-up at the end of your rapacious feast.

My name is _____.

I am staying at the _____ resort.

I have just eaten at 'Ohana. I am dangerously engorged and cannot speak. Please roll me onto the nearest bus heading for the _____ resort.

There is a FastPass+ for Toy Story Midway Mania in my top pocket. Please take it as a token of my thanks.

It's become more and more difficult to get an Advanced Dining Reservation at 'Ohana, and Mousejunkie J, who savors Disney Dining almost more than anyone I know, details why.

MOUSEJUNKIE J 'Ohana means family. But what 'Ohana means to *me* is a homerun. A great meal every time I show up. The food is served family-style, coming to your table in large plates, bowls and skewers. The server will continue to bring said food until you say stop. This is a dangerous proposition for people like myself who just don't know when to stop.

There are four food courses at 'Ohana. The first course is the salad course. A mixed field green salad is served tossed with Lilikoi dressing. The server also brings three dipping sauces to the table: a sweet peanut sauce, chimichurri sauce, and harissa sauce. For you folks who like to avoid fiber or anything green, the 'Ohana pineapple-coconut welcome bread is good and will hold you over until the appetizer course is delivered.

The appetizer course delivers with a bang. Honey-coriander chicken wings arrive next. I could be happy if I just ate these addictive wings for the meal. I made this fatal mistake once and regretted my decision once dessert arrived. The wings are messy but well worth the effort. Small, hot towels can be brought to help clean your sticky fingers. In addition, pork dumplings are brought as an appetizer. These are standard dumplings you would get a Chinese restaurant.

The third and main course arrives next. Lo Mein noodles and stir-fry vegetables hit the table which is the prelude to skewers of hot, juicy, and tasty meat that will be arriving shortly. Three skewers consisting of sweet and sour pork loin, Szechuan sirloin steak, and spicy grilled peel-n-eat shrimp arrive hot off the grill. Because there are choices here try one piece of each and then decide which one you want seconds on.

Dessert is in no way to be an afterthought or overlooked. If you have paced yourself properly, there should be enough room to partake of the decadent 'Ohana bread pudding served with vanilla ice cream and a rich bananas foster sauce. I was never a bread pudding fan until I visited 'Ohana for the first time. Let's face it, anything served hot and a la mode is going to be very good. A little known secret: If you prefer, ask for the pineapple chunks served with a hot caramel dipping sauce. Mousejunkie Deb always asks for, and gets the pineapple and caramel.

'Ohana is one of my favorite dining establishments at Walt Disney World. The food is fantastic, but the atmosphere puts it over the top. The meat is grilled in a huge open fire pit in the middle of the dining room. There is also a lovely Hawaiian woman who walks around playing the ukulele and coaxing children into limbo and coconut rolling contests. 'Ohana means family and this is a top notch, family dining restaurant.

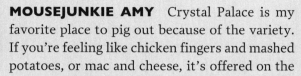

MOUSEJUNKIE AMY Crystal Palace is my favorite place to pig out because of the variety. If you're feeling like chicken fingers and mashed potatoes, or mac and cheese, it's offered on the buffet. But if you want to put in the work of peeling shrimp, you can load up your plate and get your hands dirty. There's a nice array of different salads as well. I'm not a big fan of fish, but there are some great fish choices. My favorites are the prime rib and turkey at the carving station. The turkey is my go to entree, because it's moist, tasty and never disappoints.

MOUSEJUNKIE BARRY When you're on vacation it's incredibly easy to allow yourself to go completely nuts with salty, fatty, sugary and otherwise bad-for-you food. For a Mousejunkie in the throes of a hedonistic Disney World vacation, the diet goes straight out the window. Case in point Whispering Canyon Cafe, the table service restaurant found adjacent to the lobby in the Wilderness Lodge Resort. I always get the skillet—and endless supply of ribs, chicken, mashed potatoes, cornbread and a bottomless ice cream milkshake. It's insane, really. It's ridiculous, painful, shameful, awesome eating. And what do you have to show for it at the end of the meal? A slack-jawed dopey gaze looming over a pile of gnawed-upon rib bones and stained napkins.

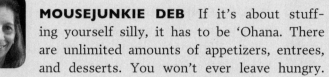

MOUSEJUNKIE DEB If it's about stuffing yourself silly, it has to be 'Ohana. There are unlimited amounts of appetizers, entrees, and desserts. You won't ever leave hungry. Nor will you leave with your shorts buttoned. Fashion tip Elastic waistbands or loose-fitting muumuus are recommended.

MOUSEJUNKIE WALT My favorite place to stuff myself has got to be Le Cellier in Epcot. Again, being French Canadian, I love everything about it. I love the breadsticks, I love the cheddar cheese soup, I love the steak, I love the maple crème brulee. There isn't anything about that place I don't love. I love the cold beer, I love the atmosphere— I could go on all day. And when I do eat there, I order appetizers, entrée, dessert, and plenty of those amazing bread sticks.

MOUSEJUNKIE RANDY I have to say my favorite place for pigging out is Boma in the Animal Kingdom Lodge. It doesn't matter if its breakfast or dinner—that is the place. I can't seem to control myself. I love the variety of foods. my favorite is the authentic African dish, Bobatie. This is a baked pork and goodness dish, which is served at both breakfast and dinner, with a slightly different recipe for each. I think Bobatie is African for "comfort food." If you go to Boma, don't be afraid to take a little taste of everything. Have a food safari. But don't go too crazy, because they have the best dessert buffet on the planet.

MOUSEJUNKIE JENNA I'll always love the old favorites of 'Ohana, Raglan Road and the Brown Derby. But it's nice to venture out to new—and new to me—restaurants, too. On my most recent trip, I found two new favorite restaurants: Jiko and Tutto Italia.

Jiko is a wonderfully elegant choice for dinner. I love Boma for all its African flavors and new discoveries, but sometimes, I just want to eat in a quiet restaurant and have a really great server bring me my food. I got to blend both of those wants at Jiko. The service there is excellent, and the menu is varied and well designed. With a mix of exotic and familiar flavors, you can be as adventurous as you want to be. For instance, I had the seared ostrich filet as an appetizer, the oak fired filet mignon with macaroni and cheese for my entree, and a lemon white chocolate mousse for dessert. The ostrich was new to me and very tasty, the filet mignon was a lovely rendition of my favorite cut, and the macaroni and cheese was sublime. The lemon mousse was just the right size and richness to cap that dinner. Jiko has an extensive wine list and I got to try a varietal created in South Africa, pinotage. I had the Eros tea with dessert, which I had previously seen only at the Grand Floridian's Garden View tearoom.

Tutto Italia was quite different from Jiko in a lot of respects, but shared the same attention to detail and excellent service. I was seated in the main dining room and honestly, I never wanted to leave. The decor is a great blending of opulent formality and welcoming coziness. I was served a basket of assorted breads, dipping oil, and giardiniera (olives, peppers, artichoke, etc.). My appetizer was the bufala mozzarella and tomato. The mozzarella is so fresh and soft, with an outstanding flavor. My entree was the farfalle with peas, prosciutto and cream sauce. It was a great combination and I loved it, but people who don't like their pasta chewy should be advised that Tutto's view of "al dente" might be a little firmer than expected. For dessert, I had one of the most ridiculously extravagant dishes I've eaten at Walt Disney World, copetta sotto bosco. It arrived in a goblet and was made up of zabaglione cream, fresh berries, crunchy

(Continued on next page)

little amaretti cookies, and a drizzle of delicious chocolate sauce. It's delicious, but it's also the most expensive dessert on the menu. To accompany my dessert, I had a cup of espresso—with a gorgeous crema—and a glass of limoncello. The limoncello had to grow on me, because the scent was unmistakably Lemon Pledge. I left Tutto Italia with a box full of leftovers and a belly so full of delicious Italian food that I decided to skip Illuminations and head back to my room to sleep it off.

Meals with Character

Getting your picture taken with a Disney character at breakfast or dinner is pretty much a rite of passage for guests at the Walt Disney World resort.

As guests are seated, Disney characters, ranging from the most popular to a few fringe personalities depending on the restaurant, tour the room. Guests do not need to chase after the character or stand in a lengthy line. They stop at each table to interact with diners and pose for pictures, so a little patience goes a long way.

Awesome/Stupid Disney Idea *Install seatbelts in the chairs at character meal restaurants. There's nothing like having a clinging kid from the next table over in all your family's photos.*

Have a seat and wait, they will come.

Character meals are either buffets, family-style or pre-plated affairs. The food ranges from quite good to merely passable. Cinderella's Royal Table, for example—a princess fan's dream—serves one of the best breakfasts I've had on-property. It's also one of the most difficult reservations to get, and it is the most expensive character meal.

Chef Mickey's, on the other hand, has decent food, but a great character experience. Mickey and Minnie have a celebrity aura about them that can't be denied.

The Straight Dope *Combine a character meal with the correct timing and you'll have Main Street USA and Cinderella Castle to yourself for an incredible photo opportunity. The park itself may open at 9 A.M., but if you book an Advanced Dining Reservation for 8 A.M., Cast Members allow you to pass. Inside you'll find very few people and an amazing view up the street toward the Castle. Fire up the camera and strike a pose for a rare opportunity.*

When we brought our three-year-old daughter, we went to a few character meals. It was fun the first time, fun the second time, but then it got to be "how many of these character meals do we really need?" They're fun, but two seems to be enough. It all starts to feel repetitive by the seventeenth photo-op. Of course, your mileage may vary, so book as many as you think might feed your need.

Here's a list of character meals throughout Walt Disney World's theme parks, and which characters you'll encounter during your meal:

Park	Restaurant	Meal	Characters
Magic Kingdom	Cinderella's Royal Table	Breakfast, Lunch, Dinner	Cinderella, Fairy Godmother, assorted princesses
Magic Kingdom	Crystal Palace	Breakfast, Lunch, Dinner	Winnie the Pooh characters
Disney's Hollywood Studios	Hollywood and Vine	Breakfast, Lunch	Little Einstein and Jo Jo's Circus characters, Jake the Neverland Pirate, Handy Manny, Special Agent Oso
Animal Kingdom	Tusker House	Breakfast	Donald, Goofy, Mickey, Pluto

Park	Restaurant	Meal	Characters
Epcot	Akershus Royal Banquet Hall	Breakfast, Lunch, Dinner	Belle, Jasmine, Aurora, Snow White, Mary Poppins, Pocahontas, Ariel, Mulan
Epcot	Garden Grill	Dinner	Chip and Dale, Mickey Mouse

Here's a list of character meals in various resorts around Walt Disney World, and what characters you'll meet at the character dining experience.

Resort	Restaurant	Meal	Characters
Grand Floridian	1900 Park Fare	Breakfast, Dinner	Mary Poppins, Alice, Pooh, Eeyore, Mad Hatter
Beach Club	Cape May Café	Breakfast	Goofy, Pluto, Donald
Contemporary	Chef Mickey's	Breakfast, Lunch, Dinner	Mickey, Minnie, Chip and Dale, Goofy, Donald, Pluto

(Continued on next page)

Resort	Restaurant	Meal	Characters
Polynesian	'Ohana	Breakfast	Mickey, Minnie, Pluto, Lilo and Stitch

Dealing with Food Allergies

You're sitting in a restaurant far from home, eyeing a decadent Pate a Choux Puff, its crème Chantilly center bursting outward as it glides by on a server's tray.

Your taste buds begin their seductive assault, attempting to convince that lobe of your brain that controls dessert choices that this would be a fine way to end the evening.

A separate, far less fun lobe—probably way in the back in the responsible sector—sends a message:

"Would it be worth a bit of anaphylaxis shock?"

For many people, it's just a fact of living and traveling with food allergies. And traveling to Walt Disney World is no different. One of the more impressive things we've come across is the resort's attentiveness to food allergies and their potential affect on guests' health.

Walt Disney World's restaurants, servers and chefs treat dietary restrictions very seriously. Our daughter, Mousejunkie Katie, is allergic to eggs, fish, and tree nuts of all kinds. When we make our Advanced Dining Reservations months in advance, we're asked about any food allergies in our party. When we arrive at the podium to check in, we're asked. When our server comes to take our order, she asks. And when it's been triple-checked, the head chef comes out, sits down with us at our table, and makes specific notes about Katie's allergies. He talks to us about what she can have, what she can't have, and on more than one occasion she's had a special dish created just for her. It helps us feel more comfortable, it keeps her safe, and it makes her feel special.

One of our first experiences after finding out about Katie's allergies was at 'Ohana, where the head chef came out to talk to us.

As he leaned over to ask Amy a question, my eyes were drawn to his name tag. I'm always interested in seeing where cast members are from, so I always make sure to steal a glance.

My eyes grew wide, I pointed at him and let loose with an involuntary torrent of geeky excitement.

"I know him!" I shouted in barely controlled excitement.

Everyone stopped what they were doing and turned to look at the sputtering weirdo. (That'd be me, having a Disney freakout moment.)

"I know him! Boma!"

The chef stood up straight and laughed as I stuttered incoherent phrases at him.

I slowed down and managed to give a complete explanation to the other people at the table. Chef Tjet Jep, "TJ" for short, had been the chef at Boma in the Animal Kingdom Lodge. We would make it a point to talk to him on each of our visits. He's very friendly and talkative, but more importantly, he's a very skilled chef. On more than one occasion he gifted us with a special deep fried Oreo desert not available on the menu or by request. And if there's one way to this Mousejunkie's heart, it's through his stomach. A deep fried sneaker would make me your friend for life. You can imagine the influence a gooey Oreo tucked into golden-brown, crunchy batter might have on my affections. Chef TJ is as big a Disney star as Pluto in my eyes.

Only now TJ was miles away from where we were used to seeing him, standing at our table talking about my daughter's food allergies as I started spitting crunchy wontons and praise at him.

"Yes, I work here now," he said as we started snapping pictures and explaining our excitement. He was now creating savory coriander wings and tangy turkey tips nightly instead of Pap or Fufu (which, again, I mention any time I get the chance since it's so fun to say).

"Where do you prefer?" he asked. "Boma or 'Ohana?"

I thought for a minute as my pulse began to return to a normal rate.

"Wherever you are!" I answered as he laughed and rolled his eyes.

TJ finished up taking notes on Katie's food allergies and headed back to the kitchen with a big wave. It felt like we had run into an old friend—despite the fact he had no idea who we were.

A few minutes later we were reminded why we were so happy to see our old friend. Our server approached with a long white serving tray packed with food not normally associated with 'Ohana. She put it down and a sweet, slightly spicy aroma wafted across the table. TJ was working his magic

MOUSEJUNKIE KATIE When the chef made a special dessert for me, I felt really good about it. It was nice of them to go out of their way to make something special for me since I couldn't have what everyone else was having. It made it so I didn't feel left out.

again. In front of us was a platter of scallops and chicken stir fried in a spicy, creamy sauce and resting on a bed of banana peppers and greens.

He came out of the kitchen a few minutes later to see if we liked his creation (we did). He visited us a third time to build a special dessert for Katie, and to bring us the 'Ohana version of his after-dinner surprise: deep-fried banana chunks with a chocolate and strawberry sauce on top. It tasted like a warm, soft, deep-fried banana split.

Meanwhile, as we *ooh*-ed and *ahh*-ed over the crispy, brown creations, Chef TJ focused all his attention on my daughter. With great aplomb, he unveiled an ice cream dessert that took some degree of skill to construct. With a flash of showmanship, he assembled it in front of her—chasing away any feelings of being left out of the evening's fun because of her allergies. On the contrary, his special treatment made her feel like the star of the show.

Things like this seem to happen at Walt Disney World. Its part of what keeps us coming back.

MOUSEJUNKIE AMY   Disney goes out of its way to accommodate people with food allergies. They'll come out and ask what Katie wants, and if it's chicken fingers they'll cook them on a hot plate away from where the other food has been cooked to avoid any cross-contamination. A cautious parent doesn't have to worry. The cast members go out of their way for you. If they don't know what's in the food, they'll go back into the kitchen and read the ingredients. They don't leave the onus strictly on the parent. The last thing you want on your vacation is to end up in the emergency room with anaphylactic shock.

You get spoiled because then you come home and you get some teenager waitress or waiter, and you ask them about food allergies you just get a blank stare.

Snack Time

Eventually you're going to get a hankering for something sweet. It might be a case of the midday munchies, or flat-out sloth. You're on vacation—it's O.K.

Just know there are scores of options for guests to choose from. Disney doesn't just serve belly-busting meals. There are small treats all over the place that become part of the returning guests' tradition. Whether it's a special drink or a sweet reward, it's the unexpected little tastes that help make the experience special.

I'm a fan of spicy food. So every time I visit Walt Disney World, I'm drawn to the ESPN Club on the BoardWalk. Because it's there you'll find the spiciest, most face-melting bloody Mary on the planet.

I ordered the drink and asked the server if the bartender could make it "extra spicy." He laughed and said sure.

He came back with a pint glass full of deep red liquid topped with a pepperoncini. I took a sip and immediately started hiccuping. I shook my head, unable to speak. The heat given off by this drink immediately rocketed my endorphins through the top of my head. After a minute or so the hiccups stopped and I dared a second sip. Same result. I mouthed the words "wow" over and over again as my father-in-law had a good laugh at my obviously pained reaction. Sure, tears may have been streaming down my face and my expression may have read "agony," but inside my brain was screaming: "More!"

Earlier I had purchased a pack of antacid at the Screen Door shop down the boardwalk. I used this opportunity to eat half the pack.

I had discovered the holy grail of spicy Bloody Marys on Disney property. I couldn't tell anyone about it though, since the ability to speak had been melted away by this fiery concoction.

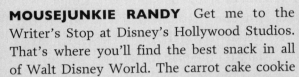

MOUSEJUNKIE RANDY Get me to the Writer's Stop at Disney's Hollywood Studios. That's where you'll find the best snack in all of Walt Disney World. The carrot cake cookie is the sweetest, most amazing confection this side of heaven. It's the perfect combination of a moist carrot cake and thick cream cheese frosting. It's very rich, and I firmly believe it equals two table-service meals in terms of caloric intake.

MOUSEJUNKIE AMY I do love popcorn. But those roasted nuts in Epcot are still my favorite. And on hot days the Mickey Premium Bars are so good. Oooh, the baked potato in the Magic Kingdom by the Hall of Presidents—I love those. No, wait.... The Figaro Fries. Yes, the Figaro Fries—final answer.

(Editor's note: Amy is notified that the Figaro Fries—a one-time offering at Pinocchio's Village Haus in Fantasyland at the Magic Kingdom—are no longer available.)

Curse you, menu changes! (Shakes fist.) O.K. then, the baked potato. It's cheap and filling and yummy.

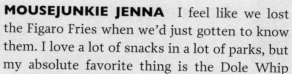 **MOUSEJUNKIE JENNA** I feel like we lost the Figaro Fries when we'd just gotten to know them. I love a lot of snacks in a lot of parks, but my absolute favorite thing is the Dole Whip float. I love the mix of the tangy pineapple juice with the creamy-tart Dole Whip. I like to sit on a bench with my float and take a minute to rest and watch kids play with the tiki mask water sprayers.

 MOUSEJUNKIE DEB When I get hungry I like to grab an apple from the fruit cart in Liberty Square...NOT! I love the chocolate chip ice cream sandwiches at Main Street Bakery.

MOUSEJUNKIE RYAN I like the Mickey Premium Bars. I like them because I can get them anywhere I go. It's basically a Klondike bar on a stick with ears, so I know I like it. It's a refreshing snack on a hot day. Of course having it shaped like Mickey's head makes it taste that much better.

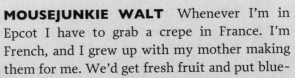 **MOUSEJUNKIE WALT** Whenever I'm in Epcot I have to grab a crepe in France. I'm French, and I grew up with my mother making them for me. We'd get fresh fruit and put blueberries and strawberries on them. I have fond memories of mom making them for me, and having one at Epcot brings back those feelings. If I had to pick a close second, I'd stay put right in France. The raspberry turnovers from Boulangerie Patisserie are to die for. On the last day of my trip I always go over to the bakery and buy a dozen to take home.

MOUSEJUNKIE AMY Yes, it's me again. I need to butt in here. For the budget-minded parent that doesn't want to feed their child chocolate croissants for breakfast every day, the containers of fresh grapes are a go-to for me. If you don't finish them in one sitting, they travel well and make for the perfect snack to stave off a hunger attack.

MOUSEJUNKIE KATIE I love the baked potato in the Magic Kingdom. You can get it at the snack area next to the Hall of Presidents. I love how they have different toppings—I always pile on plenty. I always eat the whole thing, even when it's really hot out.

Picking Up the Check

You've eaten to your heart's content, stuffed yourself beyond bursting, and joined the fraternity of Walt Disney World guests who now know the joys of on-site dining. Don't let that euphoric entrée-based haze cloud your judgment, however: If you want to be the hero and reach for the check, that's your choice. Prepare yourself—Disney dining does not come cheap. Try to keep that considerate smile on your face as you stare into the bill and your hair turns gray while your wallet becomes considerably lighter.

That's not to say there aren't ways to save money. There are options, and perhaps the biggest initial decision is figuring out if the Disney Dining Plan is right for you.

The Disney Dining Plan is a way to pre-pay for your meals using a voucher system. It's available as part of your Disney resort package, or for guests who book using Disney Vacation Club points. There are varying levels of the plan, with varying costs associated. Depending on which level plan you go with, a certain number of snacks, counter service meals and/or table service meal allotments are added. Each time you use the plan, a meal is subtracted from your total.

Here is a look at each level of the Disney Dining Plan, and the cost associated with it:

Magic Your Way Plus Quick Service

What you get: Two quick-service meals per day, one snack per day, one refillable mug.

How much? $41.99 per person, per night of your stay. Children 3-9 are $16.03 per person, per night.

You should also know: This will get you two counter service meals a day (egg sandwiches, breakfast platters, burgers, chicken, tacos, fish, hot dogs), and one snack a day (a Mickey ice cream bar, a bottle of water, chips, popcorn, soda, fruit).

The Plan in Action: An example of how the Quick Service Dining Plan might work—breakfast would be in your room or out of pocket, lunch at the Electric Umbrella at Epcot, a snack of a juice bar or a soda by mid-afternoon, and then dinner at your resort food court.

Magic Your Way Plus Dining Plan

What you get: One counter service meal, one snack, one table service meal per day and one refillable mug.

How much? $60.04 per night (it's more expensive during peak seasons), and $19.23 for children per person, per night.

You should also know: A "table service meal" on this plan is one entrée (or buffet), one non-alcoholic drink, and dessert. The children's plan is one appetizer, one entrée, one dessert and one drink—or a full buffet.

The plan in action: Breakfast would be out-of-pocket, lunch at a counter service restaurant like Pinocchio's Village Haus, a snack of popcorn for the 3 P.M. parade at the Magic Kingdom, and then dinner at a table service restaurant like the Kona Café.

Magic Your Way Plus Deluxe Dining

What you get: A whole lot of food. You get three meals a day—counter service or table service, your choice, two snacks, one resort refillable mug.

How much? $109.53 per person per night. Children 3-9 are $29.86 per person, per night.

You should also know: A "table service meal" in this plan includes one appetizer, one entrée, one dessert (or buffet) and one non-alcoholic drink.

The plan in action: Get ready to eat. This level of the Plan is for those who consider dining at Disney one of the true joys of their vacation. You have the option of eating breakfast, lunch and dinner at a table service restaurant, filling in any voids in your stomach with two snacks, and spackling it all in with a refillable mug of whatever non-alcoholic beverage you might be able to fit down your gullet. Remember: doggie bags are not normally part of the Disney dining experience, so if you sit down to a meal, chances are you're either going to finish it or leave a lot on your plate.

MOUSEJUNKIE RANDY The mistake I always see people make on the Dining Plan is that they hoard their snack credits. This sounds like a prudent plan, until they reach the last day of their vacation and are trying to use up 28 snack credits. I tell people to use them up as fast as you can. If you feel like a bottle of water, don't rationalize by trying to get a better value for that snack credit. This way of thinking is what results in 28 snack credits left at the end of the trip. If you're buying a snack and see that little Disney Dining Plan snack symbol next to your choice, use up those snack credits. If you don't heed my warning you will be making a lot of friends that last day, as you buy everyone within ear shot a Mickey Premium Bar as you try to use up all those hoarded credits.

MOUSEJUNKIE JENNA I always wanted to try the Deluxe plan because I wanted to be able to eat whatever I wanted without considering the cost. When I dine out, chances are what I want to eat just happens to be the most expensive non-lobster thing on the menu. I also like eating three-course meals—even more if I can get it. I'm the kind of person prix fixe and degustation menus are made for. I would rather order three courses of spectacular food and leave half of it on my plate than eat a meager portion of cheap food. A value is only a value if you enjoy the result. But

I digress. When it comes to Disney dining, I may be the only person I know who has stashed away a "someday" plan of a week-long trip on the Deluxe dining plan. I know I could easily eat the cost of the Deluxe plan per night, but it still seems pretty indulgent and something I would only want to do with like-minded traveling partners.

On my last trip, I had a situation with an ideal situation for trying out the Deluxe plan without going absolutely nuts with food. I was checking into a studio at the Animal Kingdom Lodge Kidani Villas on Wednesday and moving to Old Key West on Friday. For the first two days, I was completely on my own, then I was meeting Mousejunkie Ryan for a day at the Animal Kingdom on Friday. The way it worked it out, I could use my two nights of dining credits over those two and a half days. That's one of those tricky things about Disney's Dining Plan. It's based on the nights you stay, so if you're there for full days on arrival or departure, you're technically there for up to a full day longer. I ended up having dinner on Wednesday night, a late breakfast and dinner at a signature restaurant on Thursday night, and a character breakfast and dinner on Friday. I used my four snack credits on Thursday's "lunch" of zebra domes and red pepper hummus from the Mara, and a mid-afternoon snack of chocolate-covered frozen bananas for me and Ryan at Animal Kingdom. Both breakfasts were buffet, so the "three-course meal" thing was kind of moot. However, my dinners at Tutto Italia and Jiko were enjoyed to the fullest—in every sense of the word.

(Continued on next page)

On the other side of the Deluxe Dining Plan coin, my sister took a vacation with her in-laws last year. Her mother-in-law doesn't do counter service, so the whole trip was Deluxe Dining Plan for six adults and three children. That ended up being far too much food for their group and they ended up skipping 'Ohana because by that night they were "fooded out."

I think my conclusion would have to be that three table service meals per day is a bit excessive for most people, but two per day might be perfect for foodies!

Is the Disney Dining plan for you? It depends on your budget. The quick service plan is the cheapest, but you miss out on the resort's fantastic table service restaurants. The Dining Plus plan gets you a good balance of quick-service and table-service dining, but the cost previously included tip and appetizer, so there's a little disappointment on my part.

The Deluxe plan is for anyone who wants to splurge. I'd love to give it a whirl sometime, but I get the feeling my arteries would likely object.

Look at it objectively: Plan where and what you want to eat and then try to figure out if it makes financial sense. Do I spend more than $60 a day dining? Most of the time I do, so the Dining Plus plan would fit my style of touring.

MOUSEJUNKIE JENNA I absolutely did not find the standard Disney Dining Plan to be too much food, although it came close to that when the table service meal plan included an appetizer. I never had unused meal credits. For those that did, I chalk that up to poor planning. You need to put some thought into your meals before going to Disney. If you know you're having a huge dinner at 'Ohana, use your counter service credit for breakfast that day and have a snack for lunch. There were occasions that I had a counter service meal credit and a couple of snack credits left on my last day. Those credits purchased a sandwich meal, wrapped to go. So much better than anything MCO has to offer! And I'm so addicted to the dipped pretzel sticks at Goofy's Candy Co. that it got to the point where I made sure I still had snack credits on the last day.

Now, with all that said, I only recommend the Dining Plan to people who do not have an annual pass and therefore can't get the Tables in Wonderland discount card (see below). And I always ask if they're hearty eaters, because someone who is used to eating less than restaurant portions is going to be overwhelmed.

Still others skip the Disney Dining Plan to create their own experience.

MOUSEJUNKIE J I have never used the Disney Dining Plan. I've always said it was not a good idea for most people. If you are getting it for free as part of a "free dining" promotion, then you might as well use it. (Even though these people are the ones clogging up the ADRs at Le Cellier.) But paying for it? I say no. There's often too much food and people didn't get a chance to use every credit. There are many stories of people buying a half a suitcase of snacks to take home because they did not use them during the trip. I also heard of a man buying ten lunches at the Earl of Sandwich for strangers on his last day at Walt Disney World because he didn't use his counter service credits up. After a cinnamon roll at Main Street Bakery and a Mickey ice cream here and there, a lot of people find themselves just looking for another snack instead of a double cheeseburger from Cosmic Ray's. This leaves those counter service credits for the strangers in line on the last day.

If you are a seasoned Walt Disney World traveler or you seek advice from this Mousejunkie, you can save time and consternation by just doing a little planning. Disney does not scrimp on portion size. Deb and I split counter service meals because there's plenty of food. This also leaves you room for a Dole Whip or Plaza sundae after just a few hours. At all counter service establishments anyone can order off the child menu. They do not ask to actually see the child eating the meal. Deb will often get the kids meals. They are smaller and cheaper.

> Table service is a different story. Since most people are on vacation away from home, doggie bags are out. In my case it makes me eat as much as possible so as to not waste food on my plate. When I know I am going to eat at a table service place at night, I take it easy on food during the day. If I ate a full counter service and then a full table service each and every day, I would not be happy or healthy. That's just too much food.
>
> Don't get me wrong—it is still all about the food for me. But I make sure I plan it out so I am sampling what Walt Disney World has to offer while not over doing it. I have overdone it on occasion. For the most part that took place at 'Ohana. All that food and a couple of 'Ohana coladas and I was not hungry again until lunch the following day.

Florida residents and Annual Passholders have an additional option: The **Tables in Wonderland card**. This card entitles the holder to 20 percent off all food and beverage at participating restaurants. The card costs $100 for Annual Passholders, and $125 for Florida residents who aren't Annual Passholders. The card can be purchased at Guest Services. Tables in Wonderland cardholders also enjoy free valet parking. There are blackout dates, including most major holidays.

Tables in Wonderland cardholders are also offered special dining experiences throughout the year for an additional fee. You just can't get in without the card.

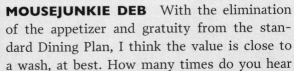

MOUSEJUNKIE DEB With the elimination of the appetizer and gratuity from the standard Dining Plan, I think the value is close to a wash, at best. How many times do you hear about people who didn't use all their counter service meals and/or snacks and either leave with them on their account, pay for other guests' lunches in line behind them, or stuff their suitcases with 19 Mickey Mouse Rice Krispy Treats? Nice for the people behind you, but you clearly overpaid for the DDP.

I would recommend people pay for meals on their own without a plan—likely better for your wallet and your waistline. People tend to over-order and overeat on the DDP. Instead, think about splitting an appetizer or skipping a dessert and having a treat later—where you may not end up tipping on its cost if you get a Dole Whip, funnel cake, Wetzel's Pretzel, caramel apple, chocolate chip cookie ice cream sandwich, popcorn, or one of a hundred other snacks available.

The Tables in Wonderland card is expensive, so you need to think through before purchasing. If you're going to use it over two or more trips, it's probably worth it. And the more people that you dine with, the quicker you'll break even.

Mousejunkies Eat Checklist

❑ Call (407) WDW-DINE (939-3463) or visit disney-world.disney.go.com/reservations/dining to make your advanced dining reservations 180 days from the day of your arrival.

❑ Order the Disney Dining Plan. (Or don't.)

❑ If you are an Annual Passholder, order the Tables in Wonderland card (20-percent off your bill).

❑ Plan character meals.

❑ Note any food allergies with the cast member taking your ADR or on the Disney website form.

The Restaurants of Walt Disney World

Menu descriptions are *samples only*. They are not full menus. Advanced Dining Reservations are recommended for any table-service restaurant. Table service restaurants are rated as relatively inexpensive ($,) not cheap ($$,) quite expensive ($$$,) and stupid ($$$@%&*#.)

Magic Kingdom

Table Service Restaurants

Cinderella's Royal Table (Cinderella Castle): A fixed-price meal—Breakfast: Lobster and crab crepes, steak and eggs, scrambled eggs, cream cheese-stuffed French toast, home fries. Lunch: Pork sandwich, roasted chicken breast, short ribs, pan seared cod. Dinner: Roasted pork loin, grilled sword-fish, roasted beef tenderloin, grilled chicken pasta. Cost: $$$.

Liberty Tree Tavern (Liberty Square): Lunch: Pot roast, fish, traditional roast turkey dinner, burgers. Dinner: Patriot's Platter—roasted turkey, carved beef and sliced pork with mashed potatoes, veggies, stuffing and mac-and-cheese. Cost: $$.

The Plaza Restaurant (Main Street USA): Meatloaf, burgers, steak-and-cheese sandwich, grilled chicken sandwich, grilled reuben. Cost: $$.

Tony's Town Square (Adjacent to City Hall): Lunch: Pizza, meatball sliders, spaghetti, grilled salmon salad. Dinner: Strip steak, chicken parm, shrimp scampi, spaghetti, ravioli. Cost: $$.

The Crystal Palace (Just off Main Street USA): A character buffet—Breakfast: Scrambled eggs and omelet station, pastries, bacon, sausage, cereal. Lunch: Carving station, pasta, fish, veggies, bread, salad. Dinner: Carving station, shrimp, pasta, chicken, salad, potatoes, mac-and-cheese. Cost: $$$.

Be Our Guest (New Fantasyland): Lunch—quick service: Carved turkey sandwich, veggie quiche, roast beef sandwich, grilled ham and cheese, braised pork. Cost $. Dinner: Pan-seared salmon, rack of lamb, strip steak, ratatouille, braised pork. Cost: $$.

Quick Service Options

Aloha Isle (Adventureland): Dole Whip soft serve, Dole Whip float, ice cream floats. Cost: $.

Auntie Gravity's (Tomorrowland): Soft-serve ice cream, drinks. Cost: $.

Casey's Corner (Main Street USA): Breakfast: Sausage breakfast dog, bagels, muffins, pastries. Lunch: Assorted hot dogs, French fries, Polish sausage. Cost: $.

Columbia Harbour House (Liberty Square): Fish and chips, fried shrimp, chicken nuggets, clam chowder, lobster roll. Cost: $.

Cosmic Ray's Starlight Cafe (Tomorrowland): Burgers, rotisserie chicken, pork sandwich, grilled cheese, turkey sandwich. Cost: $.

Diamond Horseshoe (Liberty Square): Turkey sandwich, tuna sandwich, pork brisket, portobello sandwich. Cost: $.

Tortuga Tavern (Adventureland): Tacos, burritos, quesadillas, nachos, Caesar salad. Cost: $.

Cheshire Cafe (Fantasyland): Drinks (Lemonade, slushes, coffee, water,) cereal, muffins. Cost: $.

Gaston's Tavern (New Fantasyland): Lafou's Brew, roasted pork shank, cinnamon rolls. Cost: $.

Golden Oak Outpost (Frontierland): French fries, chicken fingers, chicken sandwich. Cost: $.

The Lunching Pad (Tomorrowland): Chili dogs, hot dogs, cheese-stuffed sweet pretzels, assorted drinks. Cost: $.

Main Street Bakery (Main Street USA): Breakfast sandwiches, smoothies, and now—Starbucks coffees, including espresso, cappuccino, lattes and all that crazy caffeinated goodness. Cost: $.

Main Street Curb: Be one of the Corn People. Open a can of corn and eat it with a plastic spoon.

Main Street Ice Cream (Main Street USA): Haggis. No, I kid. Ice cream sundaes, ice cream cones, ice cream floats. Cost: $.

Storybook Treats (Fantasyland): Soft-serve ice cream, milkshakes, sundaes, assorted drinks. Cost: $.

Pecos Bill Tall Tale Inn and Cafe (Frontierland): Burgers, BBQ pork sandwich, veggie burger, chili cheese fries, Southwest chicken salad. Cost: $.

Pinocchio Village Haus (Fantasyland): Flatbreads, chicken nuggets, meatball sub, salads, mac-and-cheese. Cost: $.

Sleepy Hollow (Liberty Square): Funnel cakes, waffles, sweet and spicy chicken waffle sandwich, ham waffle sandwich, Nutella and fruit waffle sandwich, coffee, floats, cappuccino. Cost: $.

Tomorrowland Terrace (Tomorrowland): Burgers, beef with bleu cheese salad, lobster rolls, pasta primavera, chicken nuggets, mac-and-cheese. Cost: $.

Turkey leg cart (Adventureland): Giant turkey legs.

MOUSEJUNKIE RANDY The Tomorrowland Terrace is also the home of the Wishes Dessert Party. This is a special Advanced Dining Reservation event that runs $25.99 per adult and $13.99 per child. The area is closed off for party guests and the deck is reserved as a special viewing area for the fireworks. The desserts are never ending and are excellent. Carol wasn't that impressed with the exclusive fireworks viewing area, but we both successfully ate our money's worth of desserts. We did overfill ourselves, but here's a tip: Don't come straight from a table-service meal.

Mousejunkie U *Despite rumors to the contrary—and the frighteningly huge size of Disney's giant turkey legs— they are not made of emu.*

Epcot

Table Service Restaurants

Akershus Royal Banquet Hall (Norway): Princess Storybook Breakfast: Scrambled eggs, bacon, sausage, biscuits, potato casserole, fruit. Princess Storybook Lunch/Dinner: Grilled beef sandwich, roasted chicken breast, pan-seared salmon, mushroom-stuffed pasta, kjottkake (Swedish meatballs.) Cost: $$$

Biergarten Restaurant (Germany): Sausages, brats, spaetzle, pork roast, dumplings. This is a buffet experience with common seating areas. Cost: $$

Monsieur Paul (France—upstairs and upscale): Black truffle soup, lobster a l'Americaine, herb-crusted rack of lamb, mussel soup, Grand Marnier souffle. (Note: There is no children's menu at Bistro de Paris restaurant.) Cost: $$$. The prix fixe menu cost: $$$@%&*#.

Chefs de France (France): Sauteed scallops, beef short ribs, flatbread with crème fraiche, onion and bacon, roasted chicken. There is also a prix fixe three-course option: onion soup or lobster bisque, baked macaroni, roasted chicken or short ribs and dessert from that day's menu. Cost: $$.

Coral Reef (The Living Seas): Lunch: Orange glazed salmon, seared chicken breast, sriracha shrimp. Dinner: Lobster orecchiette pasta, seared rainbow trout, strip steak, grilled mahi mahi, braised short ribs. Cost: $$.

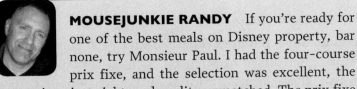

MOUSEJUNKIE RANDY If you're ready for one of the best meals on Disney property, bar none, try Monsieur Paul. I had the four-course prix fixe, and the selection was excellent, the portions just right, and quality unmatched. The prix fixe was a really good value as gourmet meals go. If you have a group of adults who want to check out the finer side, this is the place to go.

The Garden Grill (The Land): Family-style platter: Bread, salad, char-grilled beef filet, roasted turkey breast, fish, veggies, mashed potatoes. Cost: $$.

Le Cellier (Canada): Filet mignon, ribeye, NY strip steak, duck, king salmon, pappardelle pasta, lamb loin, braised short rib, seared scallops, cheddar cheese soup. Cost: $$$, bordering on $$$@%&*#.

Nine Dragons (China): Sweet and sour pork, Kung Pao chicken, hot and sour soup, honey sesame chicken, noodles sampler, fried rice, pot stickers, shrimp and chicken egg rolls. Cost: $$.

Restaurant Marrakesh (Morocco): Chicken kebabs, couscous, shish kebab, roast lamb meshoui, beef brewat rolls, harira soup, lemon chicken tangine, roast lamb meshoui. Cost: $$.

Rose & Crown Pub (UK): Bangers and mash, shepherd's pie, fish and chips, burgers, corned beef sandwich, roasted salmon, Indian-style chicken masala, Scotch egg, potato leek soup. Cost: $$.

La Hacienda de San Angel (Mexico): Carne asada, chile relleno, polla a las rajas, mole poblana. Cost: $$.

Spice Road Table (Morocco): Lamb sausage, fried calamari, lamb slider, harissa chicken roll, mussels tagine, hummus, harissa chicken roll. Cost: $.

MOUSEJUNKIE RYAN The San Angel Inn isn't bad, especially if you like authentic Mexican food. Just don't do what I did. I took a picture of the food with the flash on. I only eat pretty food, and what I had ordered was not pretty food. Now I know why the lights are so dim there.

Teppan Edo (Japan): Sushi, miso soup, and entrees such as filet mignon, swordfish, sirloin, chicken or shrimp with veggies, noodles and beef rice. Cost: $$.

Tokyo Dining (Japan): Assorted sushi and bento box meals, mixed fry with shrimp and chicken, vegetable tempura, edamame. Cost: $$$.

Tutto Italia Ristorante (Italy): Lasagna alla Bolognese, ravioli di ricotta, baked salmon, spaghetti, fettucine vecchia roma, calamari, antipasto, prosciutto di parma. Cost: $$$.

Via Napoli (Italy): Lasagna, pastas, chicken parm, eggplant parm, meat tortellini, minestrone and a wide assortment of wood-fired pizzas. Cost: $$.

Quick Service Options
Boulangerie Pâtisserie les Halles (France): Pumpkin soup, lobster bisque, toasted ham and cheese, cheese plate, ham and cheese on a croissant, crème brulee, eclairs, tarts, cakes, ice cream, pastries. Cost: $.

Cantina de San Angel (Mexico): Tacos, nachos, empanadas, refried beans, churritos. Cost: $.

Electric Umbrella (Future World): Assorted burgers—including a mac-and-cheese burger, meatball sub, veggie flatbread, Caesar salad. Cost: $.

Fountain View Starbucks (Future World): Breakfast sandwiches, smoothies, coffees, tea, latte, espresso, cappuccino. Cost: $.

Fife and Drum (America): Turkey leg, popcorn, pretzels, slushes, soft-serve ice cream, frozen lemonade. Cost: $.

Kringla Bakeri Og Kafe (Norway): Sweet pretzel, Lefse (potato bread with cinnamon sugar), waffles, custard, Danish, Norwegian Club (turkey, ham and bacon), salmon and egg sandwich. Cost: $.

Liberty Inn (America): Burgers, chicken nuggets, strip steak, hot dog, grilled chicken Caesar wrap, BBQ pork sandwich. Cost: $.

Lotus Blossom Cafe (China): Pot stickers, orange chicken with rice, veggie stir-fry with rice, beef noodle soup, sesame chicken salad. Cost: $.

Promenade Refreshments (Future World): Chili dog, hot dog, ice cream, beer. Cost: $.

Refreshment Outpost (World Showcase): Soft-serve ice cream, soda, frozen lemonade, slushes, coffee, ice cream floats.

Refreshment Port (Between Canada and UK): Chicken nuggets, croissant donut (Cronut,) soft serve ice cream, coffee, soda. Cost: $.

Sommerfest (Germany): Hot dog (known at Sommerfest as a Frankfurter), bratwurst, soft pretzel, apple strudel, German beers. Cost: $.

Sunshine Seasons (The Land): Rotisserie chicken, grilled fish, roast pork chop, sweet and sour chicken, Mongolian beef, spicy curry shrimp, roast beets and goat cheese salad, turkey ciabatta, flatbreads, tacos, mac-and-cheese. Cost: $.

Tangierine Cafe (Morocco): Shawarma platters (hummus, tabouleh, couscous salad, bread), lamb wrap, chicken wrap, falafel wrap. Cost: $.

Yorkshire County Fish Shop (UK): Fish and chips, shortbread, Bass ale, Harp lager. Cost: $.

Disney's Hollywood Studios

Table Service Restaurants

'50s Prime Time Café (Echo Lake): Chicken pot pie, pot roast, chicken sandwich, meatloaf, fried chicken, pork chop, poached salmon, peanut butter and jelly shake. Cost: $$.

Hollywood and Vine (Echo Lake): Character buffet—short ribs, pasta, lobster and shrimp mac-and-cheese, orange BBQ chicken, pork loin, maple and mustard salmon. Cost: $$.

Hollywood Brown Derby (Hollywood Boulevard): Cobb salad, glazed pork chop, chicken breast, filet of beef, scotch-glazed salmon, grilled loin of lamb, seafood cioppino, noodle bowl. Cost: $$$, just a shade away from $$$@%&*#.

Mama Melrose's Ristorante Italiano (Streets of America): Chicken parm, strip steak, grilled pork chop, seafood arrabbiata, spaghetti, flatbreads, baked chicken, penne alla vodka. Cost: $$.

Sci-Fi Dine-In Theater (Commissary Lane): Salmon BLT, strip steak, turkey sandwich, shrimp/chicken pasta, burgers, Reuben and the All American Picnic Burger—a burger topped with a hot dog, sauerkraut, onions, pickle and served with french fries. Cost: $$.

Quick Service Options

ABC Commissary (Commissary Lane): Burgers, seafood platter, chicken club, assorted salads, burger/shrimp combo meal. Cost: $.

Backlot Express (Echo Lake): Burgers, hot dog, chili dog, grilled turkey ciabatta, Buffalo chicken nuggets. Cost: $.

Catalina Eddie's (Sunset Boulevard): Pizza, Italian cold cut sandwich, Caesar salad. Cost: $.

Dinosaur Gertie's (Echo Lake): Ice cream shakes, waffle cone, Mickey premium bar, ice cream sandwich, waffle cones. Cost: $.

Fairfax Fare (Sunset Boulevard): Giant turkey leg, chicken and ribs, BBQ pork sandwich, mac-and-cheese and truffle oil hot dog, BBQ pork and coleslaw hot dog. Cost: $.

Pizza Planet (Streets of America): Um, well...Pizza. Cost: $.

Rosie's All-American Café (Sunset Boulevard): Burgers, veggie burgers, chicken nuggets. Cost: $.

Starring Rolls Cafe (Sunset Boulevard): Assorted sushi, ham sandwich, peanut butter and jelly, turkey sandwich, fruit. Cost: $.

Studio Catering Company (Streets of America): Buffalo chicken sandwich, turkey club, Greek salad, chicken Caesar wrap, sloppy joe, Tuscan deli sandwich (ham, turkey, provolone with Caesar dressing on a Tuscan roll.) Cost: $.

Toluca Legs Turkey Co. (Sunset Boulevard): Turkey legs, pork shank. Cost: $.

Writer's Stop (Commissary Lane): Coffee, tea, espresso, latte, cookies, muffins and pastries. Cost: $.

Animal Kingdom

Table Service Restaurants

Rainforest Café (Oasis): An assortment of burgers, fish, pasta, beef, pork and chicken: Portobello mushroom burger, salmon, crab cakes, NY strip steak, fried chicken, ribs, sweet and sour stir-fry, Tuscan chicken. Pretty much what you get at the Rainforest Cafe back home. Cost: $$.

Yak and Yeti (Asia): Crispy mahi-mahi, tempura shrimp, Mandarin chicken salad, seared miso salmon, pot stickers, lo mein, Kobe beef burger, stir fried beef, crispy honey chicken. The Yak and Yeti has a quick service counter in front of the restaurant that has some limited options from the main menu. Cost: $$.

Quick service options

Dino Bite Snacks (DinoLand): Churros, ice cream, cookies, sundaes. Cost: $.

Dino Diner (Chester and Hester's): Glazed nuts, cotton candy, snow cones. Cost: $.

Flame Tree Barbecue (Discovery Island): Ribs, chicken, giant turkey leg, pork sandwich, hot dog. Cost: $.

The Straight Dope   *The Flame Tree Barbecue seating is outside, much of it under cover. There are a few tables under the lush trees that dot the area. Do not sit at a table under a tree. Doing so ensures your already-seasoned barbecue will have a little extra flavor in the form of bird poo.*

Pizzafari (Discovery Island): Scrambled eggs, breakfast pizza, French toast, muffins, pizza, Caesar salad. Cost: $.

Restaurantosaurus (DinoLand): Burgers, mac-and-cheese hot dog, chicken nuggets, turkey wrap. Cost: $.

MOUSEJUNKIE AMY Flame Tree Barbecue offers you choices that aren't fried. It's not a hot dog, not a hamburger, not chicken fingers. There's barbecue chicken breast and some great ribs. I'd rather gnaw on a drumstick than a burger. You can get a burger anywhere.

Tusker House (Africa): Character buffet at lunch only— carving station, fish, veggies, potatoes, salad, desserts. Cost: $$.

Resort Dining

All-Star Movies
World Premiere Food Court.

All-Star Music
Intermission Food Court.

All-Star Sports
End Zone Food Court.

Animal Kingdom Lodge

Table Service Restaurants

Boma—Flavors of Africa (Jambo House): Breakfast buffet— Omelets, bacon, sausage, ham, scrambled eggs, brioche, bobotie, cereal, pastries, West African Frunch. Dinner buffet—carved meats with assorted sauces, peanut rice, pasta salad, Fufu, grilled seafood, chicken tenders, roasted chicken, assorted soups, and couscous. Cost: $$.

Sanaa (Kidani Village): Indian-style bread service with assorted sauces, lamb kefta, burger wrapped in naan bread, tandoori chicken, tandoori shrimp, grilled pork chop. Cost: $$.

Jiko—The Cooking Place (Jambo House): West African jerk scallops, filet mignon, beef short ribs, lamb two ways, pork loin, wild boar tenderloin, flatbreads, fire roasted oysters on the half shell. Cost: $$$.

Quick Service Options
The Mara (Jambo House): Breakfast: Scrambled eggs, potatoes, bacon, sausage, oatmeal, cinnamon roll, bagel, muffin, Danish, and croissants. Lunch/dinner: Burgers, flatbreads, chicken nuggets, turkey ciabatta, half chicken dinner. Cost: $.

BoardWalk and the BoardWalk Inn and Villas
Table Service Restaurants
Big River Grille & Brewing Works: Burgers, pork sandwich, Atlantic salmon, chicken Alfredo, meatloaf, salads, strip steak, ribs, ribeye, assorted beer. Check-in with head brewmaster Kent—he knows his stuff and brews a fantastic beer. Cost: $$.

ESPN Club: Assorted burgers, ahi tuna burger, sirloin steak, lobster bites, wings, Rueben panini, turkey and brie sandwich, Philly cheesesteak, clam chowder, nachos. Cost: $$.

Flying Fish Café: Yellowfin tuna filet, gulf shrimp pasta, Maine sea scallops, lamb chops, strip steak, red snapper, crab cakes, tuna tartare, veggie sushi. Cost: $$$.

Trattoria al Forno: Neopolitan-style pizzas, braised beef Bolognese, chicken parm, whole roasted fish, seasonal risotto, slow-cooked lamb shank. Cost: $$.

Quick Service Options

BoardWalk Bakery: Croissants, muffins, parfait, pastries, cereal, ham and cheese panini, tuna salad, chicken salad wrap, lobster roll, roast beef sandwich, pork loin sandwich. Cost: $.

The Pizza Stop: On the boardwalk in front of Kouzzina, serving pizza by the slice and the pie until midnight. Cost: $.

Caribbean Beach Resort

Table Service Restaurants

Shutters at Old Port Royale: NY strip steak, jerk-crusted tuna, Caribbean pork ribs, roasted chicken, and pasta with shrimp. $$.

Quick Service Options

Old Port Royale Food Court: Breakfast—eggs, bacon, sausage, French toast, oatmeal, grits, Mickey waffle, and omelets; Lunch/dinner—Pizza, burgers, ziti, fettucini Alfredo with chicken, meatball sub, hot dog, chicken nuggets, chili dog, and buffalo chicken sandwich. $.

Contemporary Resort

Table Service Restaurants

The Wave...of American Flavors: Breakfast: Buffet-style with ham and cheese omelet, smoked salmon, eggs Benedict, multigrain pancakes, multigrain or brioche French toast, spinach and feta scrambled eggs, and for the truly different... 'make your own muesli.' Lunch: Burgers, sirloin steak salad, Reuben, Cobb salad, tuna salad, Cuban sandwich. Dinner— Pork tenderloin, grilled fish, penne pasta, beef tenderloin, lamb chops, flat iron steak. Cost: $$.

Chef Mickey's: Character buffet—Breakfast: Scrambled eggs, omelets, Mickey waffles, potatoes, breakfast pizza, pancakes, biscuits and gravy, sausage, bacon, pastries, croissants, muffins, and Danish. Dinner: Carving station, pork ribs, baked salmon, parmesan mashed potatoes, pizza, chicken. Cost: $$.

California Grill: Its borderline criminal to try to summarize the California Grill in anything short of a loving ode composed in rhyming couplet using flowery prose set to a swelling string section. However...assorted flatbreads, sushi, filet mignon, jumbo scallops, bison tenderloin, pork two ways, seafood stew. Cost: $$$@%&*#. That's right, flat-out $$$@%&*#.

⭐ **The Straight Dope** *When the nightly fireworks extravaganza kicks off, the lights in the restaurant are lowered and the accompanying music is piped-in over the sound system. Guests who are not eating at the restaurant can watch the fireworks from an outdoor observation deck adjoining the restaurant.*

Quick Service Options

Contempo Café: Breakfast: Eggs, bacon, French toast, potatoes, breakfast burrito, waffles. Lunch/dinner: Assorted flatbreads (including, yes, the marinated beef flatbread,) sushi, burgers, chicken sandwich, salads, turkey BLT. Cost: $.

Cove Bar: Roasted veggie and quinoa wrap, hot dog, chicken Caesar wrap, turkey BLT. Cost: $.

The Sand Bar: Burgers, hot dogs, turkey sandwich, chicken nuggets, and Caesar salad. Cost: $.

Coronado Springs

Table Service Restaurants

Maya Grill: Duck confit, enchiladas, chimichanga platter, pork shank, fajitas, shrimp tacos, pork ribeye, glazed salmon, strip steak, filet mignon. Cost: $$.

Quick Service Options

Cafe Rix: Cobb salad, chicken Caesar wrap, Greek salad, fruit, quinoa salad. Cost: $.

Pepper Market: Breakfast: Pancakes, biscuits and gravy, eggs, French toast, omelets, waffles, hash. Lunch/dinner: Pizza, carving station, tacos, Philly cheesesteak, empanadas, BBQ ribs, burgers, crab cake sandwich. Cost: $.

Siestas Cantina: Burgers, hot dogs, chicken nuggets, buffalo chicken sandwich, Caesar chicken wrap, and assorted frozen drinks. Cost: $.

Fort Wilderness Resort & Campground

Table Service Restaurants

Trail's End Restaurant: Breakfast buffet: Scrambled eggs, Mickey waffles, biscuits and gravy, sausage, bacon, grits, cereal, oatmeal, and pastries. Lunch buffet: Chicken and waffles, burgers, BBQ pork sandwich, fried catfish, shrimp po' boy. Dinner buffet: Ribs, peel-and-eat shrimp, fried chicken, pasta, chili, pizza, veggies, carving station, fish, and salad bar. Cost: $$.

Hoop-Dee-Doo Musical Revue: Fried chicken, ribs, mashed potatoes, baked beans, salad, corn bread and honey butter, a strawberry shortcake worth singing about, and drinks—including wine and beer. Cost: Consarn it, as they say in the frontier. This is a great show but it is expensive. It's staked out a few acres in the land known as $$$@%&*#.

⭐ **Mousejunkie Choice** *This is a classic that every-one should see. It's a hilariously entertaining show put on by immensely talented cast members. It doesn't matter how much it costs. Pawn a cousin or something. It's worth it. The food is great, the show is amazing and you'll be talking about it for years. Recommended 100 percent.*

Quick Service Options

Meadow Snack Bar (seasonal): Bacon and mac-and-cheese-smothered hot dog, BBQ pulled pork-smothered hot dog, chili-cheese hot dog, roast beef sandwich and assorted desserts and drinks. Cost: $.

Mickey's Backyard BBQ (seasonal): Barbecue chicken, pork ribs, burgers, hot dogs, baked beans, mac-and-cheese, corn on the cob, potato salad, corn bread, and ice cream bars. Cost: $$.

Grand Floridian Resort & Spa

Table Service Restaurants

Grand Floridian Café: Breakfast: Lobster eggs Benedict, smoked salmon, steak and eggs, frittata, omelets, citrus pancakes, maple/vanilla French toast, Mickey waffles. Lunch: The Grand Sandwich (open faced turkey, ham, bacon with Boursin sauce), Cobb salad, NY strip steak, chicken sandwich, Reuben, Caesar salad, fish, and assorted desserts. Dinner: N.Y. strip steak, grilled pork chop, salmon, roasted chicken breast, Grand Floridian Burger (with lobster, asparagus and horseradish hollandaise), and assorted desserts. Cost: $$.

The Straight Dope *The Grand Sandwich at the Grand Floridian Café is a criminally well-kept secret. The Grand Sandwich is an open-faced hot turkey, ham, bacon and tomato concoction—and here's the genius of it all—topped with a rich Boursin cheese sauce and fried onion straws. You can top a sneaker with a rich Boursin cheese sauce and fried onion straws and I'll eat it.*

1900 Park Fare: Character breakfast: Omelets, scrambled eggs, bacon, sausage, Mickey waffles, pancakes, cheese Danish, cheese blintz, bread pudding, yogurt, muffins, pastries, bagels, French toast, biscuits and gravy, and grits. Dinner: Carving station (smoked beef and pork roast), pasta, salmon, Durban chicken, salad bar, and assorted desserts. Cost: $$.

Cítricos: Grilled tuna, filet mignon, seared striped bass, beef short ribs, braised veal shank, sauteed shrimp, lamb albondiga meatball. Cost: $$$.

Narcoossee's: Maine lobster, shrimp fettuccine, seared ahi tuna, filet mignon, lobster tail with filet mignon, grilled halibut, seared scallops. Cost: $$$.

Victoria and Albert's: The most upscale restaurant in all of Walt Disney World, the menu at Victoria and Albert's changes daily. Past menus have included: King salmon, duck breast, elk carpaccio, assorted caviar, pork tenderloin, Niman ranch lamb, Kobe beef tenderloin, and assorted insanely rich desserts. Cost: No debate, it's a solid $$$@%&*#. And if you add a wine pairing, it rises to the extremely rare level of "I got a nosebleed when they brought the check." However, it is an unforgettable experience.

Quick Service Options

Gasparilla Grill: Burgers, hot dogs, chicken nuggets, ham and swiss, pizza and flatbreads, roast beef sandwich. Cost: $.

Old Key West

Table Service Restaurants

Olivia's Café: Breakfast burrito, pancakes, omelets, banana bread French toast, bacon, sausage, biscuits and gravy, cereal, and grits (breakfast); Blackened grouper sandwich, roast beef and blue cheese sandwich, Cuban sandwich, penne pasta with shrimp, Key West salmon salad, turkey club, and burgers (lunch); NY strip steak, roasted chicken breast, prime rib, pork chop, fennel-dusted grouper, and mahi mahi (dinner). Cost: $$.

Quick Service Options

Good's Food to Go: Burgers, hot dogs, chicken nuggets, veggie sandwich, Caesar salad, soup, turkey sandwich, fruit, French fries, and onion rings. Cost: $.

Polynesian Resort

Table Service Restaurants

Kona Café: Breakfast: Tonga Toast, steak and eggs, omelets, pancakes, French toast, Mickey waffles, the Samoan, and Kona pressed-pot coffee. Lunch: BBQ pork taco, ahi tuna sandwich, grilled steak salad, Asian noodle bowl, assorted sushi, Kona turkey sandwich. Dinner: Assorted sushi, curry-crusted lamb chops, seared duck breast, teriyaki strip steak, seared sea scallops, coffee-rubbed pork chop. Cost: $$.

'Ohana: Character breakfast: Scrambled eggs, potatoes, pork sausage, Mickey waffles. Dinner served family-style: Welcome bread, honey-coriander chicken wings, pork dumplings, pork loin, sirloin steak, peel-and-eat shrimp, noodles, veggies, and bread pudding with bananas and caramel sauce. Cost: $$.

Spirit of Aloha Dinner Show: Roast chicken, apple pear slaw, potato salad, pork loin, Polynesian rice, veggies, milk chocolate macadamia nut moose. Cost: $$$@%&*#.

Quick Service Options

Capt. Cook's: Breakfast: Mickey waffle, Tonga Toast, scrambled eggs, bacon, sausage, egg and bacon sandwich, potatoes, biscuit, assorted muffins, bagels, Danish, and pastries. Lunch/dinner: Burgers, pork sandwich, turkey club, chicken Caesar salad, stir-fried noodles, grilled cheese, and pizza. Cost: $.

Pop Century

Quick Service Options

Everything Pop: Breakfast: Waffle platter, French toast platter, Scrambled eggs breakfast platter, omelets, scrambled eggs, cinnamon roll, bacon, sausage, potatoes, assorted pastries. Lunch/dinner: Burgers, chicken nuggets, chili cheese dog, fish sandwich, veggie burger, cheesesteak wrap, assorted flatbreads, assorted soups, lo mein, nachos, and assorted pizza. Cost: $.

Port Orleans

Table Service Restaurants

Boatwright's: Prime rib, Voodoo chicken, vegetarian jambalaya, grilled N.Y. strip steak, BBQ ribs, fried oysters, crawfish bites, chicken and andouille gumbo, shrimp and grits, crawfish etouffee. Cost: $$.

Quick Service Options

Riverside Mill: Breakfast: Omelet station, French toast, scrambled eggs, bacon, sausage, fresh-made waffles, assorted pastries and bagels, and grits. Lunch/dinner: Burgers, grilled chicken sandwich, fish basket, chicken nuggets, assorted pizza, carving station, salads, and baked ziti. Cost: $.

Sassagoula Floatworks and Food Factory: Breakfast: Biscuits and gravy, pancakes, create your own oatmeal, omelet, waffles, pancakes, bacon, sausage, potatoes. Lunch/

dinner: Creole burger, beef po' boy, chicken nuggets, chili-cheese hot dog, bayou chicken sandwich, chicken quesadilla. Cost: $.

Saratoga Springs Resort & Spa

Table Service Restaurants

The Turf Club: Grilled salmon, prime rib, root beer brined pork chop, crispy chicken breast, N.Y. strip steak, lamb chops. Cost: $$.

Quick Service Options

The Artist's Palette: Breakfast: Breakfast flatbread, egg and croissant sandwich, omelets, Mickey waffles, assorted pastries. Lunch: Chili-cheese hot dog, lobster club sandwich, pastrami panini, turkey and brie sandwich, turkey club wrap. Dinner: Buffalo chicken panini, assorted flatbreads, chicken nuggets, chicken parm, BBQ pork loin, Caesar salad, Italian hoagie. Cost: $.

Wilderness Lodge

Table Service Restaurants

Whispering Canyon: Breakfast: All you can eat platter with scrambled eggs, home fries, bacon, sausage, waffles, biscuits and gravy. Also eggs Benedict, omelets banana bread French toast. Dinner: Family platter including choice of three—pork ribs, BBQ pulled pork, roast chicken, beef strip loin, sausage, and sides—mashed potatoes, baked beans, corn on the cob. Also buffalo meatloaf, strip steak, pork loin chop, glazed rainbow trout. Cost: $$.

The Straight Dope *Want to shake up the dining experience? Make sure to ask for Ketchup at the Whispering Canyon Café. Every bottle from surrounding tables will suddenly be transported to your area by boisterous, mischievous servers. If that's not enough, ask for a refill on your soda more than once. A jar the size of a two-liter bottle may be returned to you filled with whatever sugary beverage you prefer.*

Artist Point: Cedar plank wild salmon, seared scallops, smoked Cornish hen, Korean BBQ pork loin, filet mignon, ahi tuna loin and glazed pork belly. Cost: $$$.

The Straight Dope *Artist Point is known, in particular, for its amazing cedar plank roasted wild King salmon.*

Quick Service Options
Roaring Forks: Breakfast: Scrambled eggs, bacon, potatoes, sausage, pancakes, biscuits, oatmeal, and assorted pastries. Lunch/dinner: Ham and cheddar sandwich, salads, turkey and Swiss sandwich, tuna sandwich, peanut butter and jelly, burgers, chicken breast sandwich, chicken nuggets, and assorted flatbreads. Cost: $.

Yacht & Beach Club

Table Service Restaurants

Captain's Grille: Breakfast: Lobster omelet, poached eggs, citrus-scented French toast, waffles, petite sirloin and eggs, dark chocolate waffles, lemon-ricotta hotcakes. Lunch: Burgers, fish and chips, lobster roll, shaved beef sandwich, tomato and mozzarella sandwich, seared scallop salad. Dinner: Lump crab cakes, braised short ribs, snow crab legs, N.Y. strip steak, rosemary-brined pork tenderloin. Cost: $$.

Cape May Café: Character breakfast buffet: Scrambled eggs, omelets, eggs to order, biscuits and gravy, smoked salmon, Mickey waffles, bacon, sausage, potatoes. Dinner: Carving station, BBQ pork ribs, roast chicken, corn on the cob, crab legs, steamers, mussels, baked fish, fried calamari, tortellini with lobster sauce. Cost: $$$.

Yachtsman Steakhouse: Filet mignon, 32-ounce porterhouse for two, oak-fired ribeye, prime rib, corn flake fried chicken, Kansas City strip steak, lamb loin, wild Alaskan halibut. Cost: $$$.

Quick Service Options

Beach Club Marketplace: Breakfast: Scrambled eggs, bacon, potatoes, French toast bread pudding. Lunch/dinner: Flatbreads, roast beef sandwich, ham and Swiss sandwich, quinoa veggie wrap, turkey sandwich. Cost: $.

Hurricane Hanna's Grill: Burgers, hot dogs, lobster roll, shrimp roll, scallop roll, grilled chicken sandwich, veggie quinoa wrap. Cost: $.

Beaches and Cream Soda Shop: Burgers, roast beef, hot dogs, turkey club, grilled cheese, pot roast sandwich. Cost: $.

Fine, but this place is all about the ice cream, and specifically the Kitchen Sink: Eight scoops of ice cream with every topping you can imagine for $28.99. A hefty tub of icy perfection, the Kitchen Sink can be beaten, but it takes a committed warrior to best this monstrosity. A solid base of peanut butter and chocolate sauce coats the bottom of the bowl. Then comes heaping scoops of chocolate, vanilla, mint chocolate chip, coffee, and strawberry ice cream. The whole thing is dressed with a pile of brownies, Oreos, angel food cake, a Milky Way candy bar, and a can of whipped cream. Yes, the whole can. Still not enough? Toss in a few more brownies, a banana and a few more Oreos. Add a few cherries on top and you've got your dessert of doom.

Individual bowls are distributed so the Sink can be divided. This detail is key, since by the end there's a rather large gray puddle of goo at the bottom.

There are those who claim to have single-handedly consumed the Kitchen Sink. I am dubious of these claims. Although I'd watch someone try.

Water Park

Typhoon Lagoon

Quick Service Options

Leaning Palms: Burgers, hot dogs, chicken nuggets, pizza, chicken wrap, turkey pesto sandwich, BBQ pork sandwich. Cost: $.

Typhoon Tilly's: Barbecue pork sandwich, fish basket, chicken wrap, hot dog, chicken nuggets, salad, fruit cup, and French fries. Cost: $.

Blizzard Beach

Quick Service Options

Avalunch: Giant turkey leg, mac-and-cheese hot dog, chili-cheese hot dog, pretzel hot dog, pulled pork hot dog, Caesar salad with chicken. Cost: $.

Lottawatta Lodge: Pizza, burgers, chicken nuggets, hot dog, mushroom veggie burger, Caesar salad with chicken. Cost: $.

The Warming Hut: Jerk chicken sandwich, meatball sub, pulled pork sandwich, Caesar salad with chicken, chicken wrap. Cost: $.

Downtown Disney

Table Service Restaurants

Bongo's Cuban Café: Cuban paella, Cuban-style skirt steak, fried chicken bites, sauteed fish, roast pork, creole minced beef, fried shredded beef, veggie platter, fried rice with pork, shrimp, beef and plantains. Cost: $$.

Fulton's Crab House: Ahi tuna, crab cakes, shrimp and grits, lobster, pork tenderloin, ribeye steak, snow crab legs, ratatouille, lobster ravioli, filet mignon, Alaska king crab, yellowtail snapper. Cost: $$$.

Paradiso 37: Argentinean skirt steak, Chilean salmon, fish tacos, citrus BBQ pork ribs, enchiladas, ribeye steak, filet mignon, burgers, truffle fries, wasabi fries, sweet potato fries, corn dog bites, nachos, quesadillas. Cost: $$.

Planet Hollywood: Assorted burgers, BBQ ribs, pulled pork, garlic shrimp, homemade manicotti, lasagna, N.Y. strip steak, pasta carbonara, teriyaki salmon, turkey club, Philly steak and cheese. Cost: $$.

Rainforest Café: Burgers, shrimp skewers, fried chicken, chicken parm, pot roast, Tuscan chicken, salmon, assorted salads. Cost: $$.

Raglan Road: Filet mignon, risotto with chicken or shrimp, fish and chips, chicken curry, Guinness beef stew, bangers and mash, burgers, lamb shank, shepherds pie, baked cod, roast chicken. Cost: $$.

T-Rex: Assorted burgers (all with kind of hokey dino-themed names like "Gigantosaurus Burger"), fish and chips, rotisserie chicken, lasagna, ribs, N.Y. strip steak, chicken fried steak, seared salmon, tacos, T-bone steak. Cost: $$.

Wolfgang Puck Café: Flat iron steak, mac-and-cheese, ricotta ravioli, pizza, spaghetti, pork loin, seared salmon, pesto chicken, chicken Alfredo, sirloin burger. Cost: $$.

Mousejunkie Choice *Raglan Road is the be-all, end-all when it comes to dining at Downtown Disney. Sure, there are some fine restaurants there, but Raglan Road is the best. Chef Kevin Dundon is a superstar who has crafted a fantastic menu that keeps us coming back on every trip. Despite being a rather large venue with high ceilings, the room is broken up into smaller alcoves, which helps maintain the cozy feel of an Irish pub. Even if Downtown Disney is basically a work zone at this point, it's worth a trip through the construction walls to find Raglan Road. The music, the entertainers, the dancers, the food and the craic are unmatched.*

Quick Service Options
Cookes of Dublin: Fish and chips, battered burger and chips, beef and lamb pie, chicken wings, salmon wrap, mini Irish sausages, and fried candy bars. Yes, you read that correctly. Perfection. Cost: $.

MOUSEJUNKIE RYAN Best BLT with cheese I've ever had in my entire life. It's really reasonable prices for really good food. You can get a sandwich for $6.

Earl of Sandwich: A surprisingly reasonable sub shop serving delicious, hot sandwiches: Chicken, bacon and avocado wrap, holiday turkey, buffalo chicken, spicy tuna, Italian, grilled chicken, roast turkey club, roast beef, meatball, ham and Swiss, Caribbean jerk chicken, BLT. Cost: $.

The Straight Dope *The Earl of Sandwich is one of the best dining values on Disney property. The food is great and the prices are comparatively cheap. Just get there early or be prepared to stalk fellow diners for a seat. It gets crowded quickly, and I have to admit I'm not above laying across a row of chairs while Amy fetches my sandwich.*

FoodQuest: Burgers, hot dogs, chicken nuggets, chili cheese fries, assorted pizza. Cost: $.

Wolfgang Puck Express: Pizza, rotisserie chicken, mac-and-cheese, roasted salmon, spaghetti, bacon-wrapped meatloaf, chicken Alfredo, turkey club, pesto chicken salad. Cost: $$.

If anyone tells you that eating like this is obnoxiously extravagant, just point out the fact that you'll be walking it all off while traipsing through Disney's vast property. Or simply laugh and tell them they're right.

The way we approach it is to map out your week by theme park destination. Then choose a restaurant either in that park, or convenient to it. Once that's done, it's time to get on the phone with Disney Dining.

The Straight Dope *It's been said before, but it's worth repeating: Make your dining reservations early. It is the number one tip most people give. And still many guests don't always heed this advice. Ignoring it can lead to unimaginable heartbreak. Or at the very least grumpy traveling mates and growling stomachs. You can call 180 days out from the day of your arrival to make Advanced Dining Reservations. Call 407-WDW-DINE.*

The Way of the Mousejunkie

THERE ARE A MILLION WAYS to approach Disney's theme parks, all with different philosophies and goals.

The Commando: This person is intent on doing everything. He or she is up at the crack of stupid and is in a sprinter's stance at the rope drop. This person has a plan, and any diversion from it elicits an outburst of swift, punishing Mouse-Fu.

The Parent: Character meals, character autographs, character photographs, and Dumbo the Flying Elephant. These elements dictate The Parent's touring plans. They can fold and unfold a stroller while boarding and disembarking Disney's buses like a Marine can field strip a rifle. And with boot camp-like discipline, they train by carrying a thirty-pound sack of sand on mile-long hikes. Because at the end of a long day, The Parent must possess the stamina to not only get himself to the bus (always the farthest stop away, it seems,) but he must also be able to carry his completely pooped offspring to the finish line.

The Teen: WhatEVER. *eyeroll* The teen loves fast rides, shopping, and independence. They've done the online research, joined several Disney forums and Facebook Groups, have all the apps and have spoken to (or more likely texted) others of their type about the place. It might be a good idea to listen. They'll usually cite Stitch as their favorite Disney character, and will mock you endlessly for being too scared to ride Expedition Everest even though it's not that you're a chicken, it's that you don't want to get thrown around and go a zillion miles-an-hour backwards first thing in the morning so just leave me alone and stop making fun of me! (I think we're getting a little too personal here.)

The Food Guy: This person builds his touring plans around his dinner reservations. He or she knows a thing or two about the finest culinary offerings at Walt Disney World, can tell you where the finest wine can be had, and knows the sous chef at Narcoossee's by name. Sure, he or she will hit the attractions, but the Main Street Electrical Parade is merely a theory to The Food Guy because it steps off at the same time as the second course at the California Grill.

The Lazy Guy: Hi there. My name is Bill. Can you point me to the closest bench?

The Unprepared: These people are overwhelmed. You'll know them by their stressed expressions. And you'll see them eating at quick service for every meal. They'll ride three attractions and go home and tell everyone that Walt Disney World is overrated. The horror of fleeing Fantasmic! at the end of the show will haunt their dreams for years to come. The will be treated for PTDSS (Post Traumatic Disney Stress Syndrome.) We won't see them again.

The Completely Reasonable Person Who Doesn't Have to Wait in a Single Line, Never Gets Tired, Never Argues with His or Her Spouse and Sees All There Is to See: This person is a myth.

The Mousejunkie: This person loves Walt Disney World. He or she is a sucker for the entire show: the music, the theatrics, the attractions, the food, and the unexpected emotions it all elicits. He or she has a few must-do things, and considers the rest a bonus. A Mousejunkie enjoys the ambiance, people-watching and cast member interaction as much as any other part of the vacation.

Of course, a Commando can be a Mousejunkie. A Parent or Teen or Lazy Guy can be a Mousejunkie. Approach it any way you want, just enjoy yourself, be flexible, and be considerate of those around you. I can't stress that enough: Everyone paid a decent amount of money to be there, everyone is (very likely) hot and tired. Take a moment to be kind to others. Trust me, it'll enhance your vacation experience.

Taking that a step further, a Mousejunkie goes out of his or her way to be patient, nice, and complimentary to Disney cast members. They work long hours for low pay to make your vacation memorable. They have to put up with inconsiderate guests on a daily basis by putting on a smile and taking the abuse. Thank them for what they do, and if you see a cast member doing something exemplary, stop at Guest Services and report their professionalism. Note their name, location and time. It'll only take a few minutes, and it might help someone who could use a little boost.

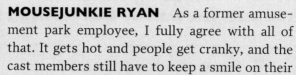

MOUSEJUNKIE RYAN As a former amusement park employee, I fully agree with all of that. It gets hot and people get cranky, and the cast members still have to keep a smile on their faces and deal with it in an amazingly cheery way. It's always nice to feel appreciated by guests.

No matter where you plan to start your vacation, what you want to accomplish or what you *think* you can accomplish, let this advice guide you: You can't do it all in one trip, so don't try. It'll just leave you frustrated and tired. Walt Disney World is, in a word, huge. It's built to accommodate massive amounts of people, and they've all got ADRs at the restaurant you're trying to get into. Disney holds attendance numbers close to the vest, but according to unofficial tallies, Walt Disney World hosted nearly 133 million people in 2013. The Magic Kingdom alone has been averaging around 18 million visitors a year for the past several years. That makes it the most-visited theme park on the planet.

Walking the Walk:
Zen and the Art of Not Melting Down

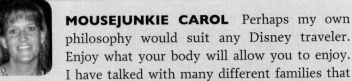

MOUSEJUNKIE JENNA The key to the way I tour is prioritizing attractions. Look over park info, solicit opinions of friends, and then figure out what are your absolute must-sees in each area. Remember that timed shows take longer and are harder to plan around, so try to limit which shows you see. I try to plan no more than two shows per day. Unless you're there on an extended trip or you're there at the absolute least crowded time possible, you can't see everything in one trip. If I'm there on a longer trip and visiting each park multiple times, I like to hit my must-sees on the first day in that park, then revisit my favorites and add in the attractions that were lower priorities on the return day.

MOUSEJUNKIE CAROL Perhaps my own philosophy would suit any Disney traveler. Enjoy what your body will allow you to enjoy. I have talked with many different families that have traveled to Disney. Those that said they had a horrible time felt they had to see everything and tired themselves out. Trying to accomplish that with young children creates a lot of stress. The kids get hot and tired, which in turns creates bad moods and crying. This upsets the parents as they have spent a lot of time in effort in creating the "perfect" vacation and all they remember is how cranky the kids were. Does this sound fun?

I completely understand that the park passes are very expensive and that families will feel they need to get fair value for them. Let me add a little perspective to the price of a pass: The majority of the cost of a pass is in the first three days. Adding on days to the pass subsequent to those first three days is a minimal expense. Over the course of a seven day vacation, if you purchased a seven day pass and got four quality days out of the pass, you've gotten your money's worth.

Other families I talked to like to go in large groups. My very first vacation to Walt Disney World was with my family of fifteen people, ranging in ages from three to sixty. The first day we all tried to stay together and do things as a family. We quickly realized that the older generation did not want to go on Dumbo or see Mickey and that the younger kids did not want the adults to wait an hour to go on Splash Mountain or Big Thunder Mountain Railroad. The answer is simple. Split up! We found that by splitting up the various age groups we all got what we wanted on the vacation. We met every day for breakfast and met every night for dinner. Other than that we were on our own. It was the best vacation I have ever gone on with the family.

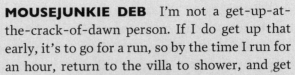

MOUSEJUNKIE DEB I'm not a get-up-at-the-crack-of-dawn person. If I do get up that early, it's to go for a run, so by the time I run for an hour, return to the villa to shower, and get going we're hours behind the opening crowds. We tend to go to the parks that have Extra Magic evening hours so we don't feel rushed. I've heard there are Extra Magic morning hours, but that's just not in my vocabulary, especially on vacation.

I'm married to the Foodjunkie, I mean Food Mousejunkie, so our park touring revolves around where we're eating. If we're having breakfast at the Polynesian, we will probably spend the day at Magic Kingdom. If we're having dinner at an Epcot restaurant, we'll likely be spending our day strolling around the World Showcase.

We don't generally wait in lines longer than twenty minutes. We go during non-peak hours, take advantage of FastPasses, and are willing to pass on something and check later.

We usually split our week up with park days and resort days, meaning hanging out at the pool, maybe shopping at Downtown Disney, doing a watercraft activity, etc. Even when not storming the parks commando-style, it's a lot of walking and a long day, so we break our week into: park 1, park 2, resort day, park 3, shopping day, etc., depending what our plans are. It's vacation!

We always try to see each of the night shows once during our trips. Even after seeing them all many times, they are so moving and provide an exclamation point to the day.

If someone hasn't been to Walt Disney World in a while, I run down the list of all the new things since they were last there so that they can try to see/do those attractions.

Biggest advice: Plan. It's vacation and you want to have fun, but without a plan, dining reservations, etc. you can end up wasting a lot of time trying to get around, being disappointed, and getting frustrated. That's something you can largely avoid with some planning.

I remind them that they won't be able to do everything, so to try to pick out their top choices.

I actually discourage people from park hopping. I do it when I have an annual pass, but when I don't, I avoid it. It's an extra expense that's not necessary if you plan your days and dining and will save you a lot of travel time. Walt Disney World is huge. A bus ride can be twenty-five minutes or longer from one destination to another, so minimizing travel time gets you more park time, more pool time, a more relaxing dining experience, or more sleep!

By the same token, I encourage people to stay on property. It may or may not cost more, but in addition to the total theming immersion and resort perks, you save travel time.

I personally think the night shows are some of the best attractions, so I encourage people to get a later start if that will help them stay up later to see them.

(Continued on next page)

I remind people to try to check out the small things. I love Space Mountain just as much as the next person, but I also love reading the Randy Pausch tribute in front of the Mad Tea Party (see below), looking at all the miniature scenes in the train in Germany, and checking out the celebrity busts in front of what is now the American Idol Experience.

Mousejunkie U *Randy Pausch worked as a Disney Imagineer in virtual reality research. Stricken with pancreatic cancer, Pausch gave a farewell speech at Carnegie-Mellon University known as "The Last Lecture." The speech was a deeply moving, one-hour talk on "really achieving your childhood dreams." Pausch succumbed to complications from pancreatic cancer in July of 2008 at the age of 47. Since "The Last Lecture," he has become known as "the dying man who taught others how to live." His lecture was broadened and published, and the speech is widely available for viewing online.*

In 2009, Disney installed a plaque in Pausch's honor in Fantasyland near the Mad Tea Party. It reads: "Be good at something; It makes you valuable.... Have something to bring to the table, because that will make you more welcome."

Pulling Back the Curtain

There are a number of specialized tours throughout the parks that provide guests with a behind-the-scenes perspective of how this massive machine works. Among them:

Keys to the Kingdom Tour: A five-hour walking tour of the Magic Kingdom divulges some back-stage secrets and tales of Walt Disney's vision and philosophies. This is the much talked about tour that'll give you an up-close look at the tunnels below the Magic Kingdom—the Utilidoors. Lunch is provided at the Columbia Harbour House, but regular park admission is necessary in addition to the $79 fee.

The Magic Behind Our Steam Trains: Walt Disney loved steam trains, something that is clearly evident at the Magic Kingdom park, where this tour takes place. Guests can visit the backstage roundhouse and get an intimate look at one of the trains currently in use, take a spin around the park before it opens and tour the roundhouse nearby. The three-hour tour costs $54.

Wilderness Back Trail Adventure: Glide through the natural beauty in and around the Fort Wilderness Campground on this two-hour trip atop a Segway X2. You'll cruise along paved paths and woodland trails before stopping at the Wilderness Lodge Resort, the stables at the Tri-Circle-D Ranch and along Bay Lake. A half-hour of instruction will help you get the hang of the two-wheeled machine. The tour costs $95, and there is a 250-pound weight limit.

DiveQuest: Certified scuba divers can take a forty-minute exploration among thousands of fish, sea turtles, stingrays and sharks. Your ocean, in this case, is the 5.7 million-gallon saltwater aquarium at Epcot. Family members can look on as you dive with sea turtles, dolphins, rays and sharks. The three-hour experience includes all the necessary dive equipment. Over two hundred feet of visibility comes at a cost of $175. A DVD of your dive can be purchased for an additional $35.

Behind the Seeds at Epcot: An affordable and fascinating (no, seriously) behind-the-scenes look at the Land pavilion's greenhouses and laboratories. A cast member from the Epcot science team leads this interactive experience that provides a close-up look at everything from pest control to hydroponic farming to fish and alligator farming. The tour costs $20 for adults and $16 for children 3-9, and valid park admission is required.

Backstage Safari: Ever want to touch a rhinoceros? The Backstage Safari tour at Disney's Animal Kingdom will give you the chance. This three-hour experience allows guests to observe Disney's animal care facilities, visit the animal housing areas, meet the keepers, and examine the park's veterinary hospital. No photography is permitted, and park admission is not included in this $72 tour.

MOUSEJUNKIE AMY I loved this tour. The rhino experience, in particular, was memorable. It turns out they're very skittish so you need to be rather sensitive to that. On our tour someone moved a little too quickly for the rhino's liking, and it whirled around much faster than I ever would've imagined an animal that size could have. Our tour guide was great, I learned a lot and I'll never forget it.

Backstage Magic: This seven-hour, three theme park tour brings guests to the Magic Kingdom, Epcot, and Disney's Hollywood Studios. All kinds of backstage secrets are revealed, including a look at the intricate American Adventure stage change system, for $249. Lunch is included at the Whispering Canyon Cafe at Disney's Wilderness Lodge Resort.

MOUSEJUNKIE RANDY The Backstage Magic tour is well worth the money. One of my favorite parts was visiting the Magic Kingdom shops—where everything is custom made for the parks. Every animatronic animal for every Disney park in the world is made there. We got to meet a few veteran animatronic builders who had been at Walt Disney World for thirty years. What they told us is that the job is learned through apprenticeship. It's not like you can go to school to become an animatronic

(Continued on next page)

builder. These guys were getting ready to retire and they had found new people who wanted to take the time to apprentice under them.

When we took the tour it was during the pre-production phase of the Pirates of the Caribbean refurb. One of the craftsmen was working on a new parrot that was going to be sitting on the top of the bridge just before the scene with the dog holding the jail cell keys. He showed how this new creation was going to have more moving parts than they had ever put into such a small animatronic.

It really peeled back the skin and showed us all the guts. It was awesome for a Disney freak like me and it also appealed to the engineer in me, as well.

The other great part of the tour is the Christmas warehouse. I've never seen so much Christmas in one place before. This is where every Christmas decoration for every Florida park and resort, and even the DVC resort up in North Carolina, is stored. They have a year-round staff of about fifty people. These people aren't the ones that actually put up the decorations. That department staffs up to about 1,500 people in October to begin getting ready for the holiday seasons. By Thanksgiving they're installing the decorations.

Every five years, every decoration gets some personal treatment or a freshening up. For that staff of fifty full-timers it's just Christmas everyday.

I'd call this tour a bargain for all the history and backstage magic you get to experience.

Contact 1-407-WDW-TOUR (1-407-939-8687) for information about these and other specialized tours.

With a plan in place, park passes in-hand, fanny pack clipped on (and therefore a lack of shame guiding our choices), it's time to unleash these theories on Walt Disney's theme parks.

6 The Magic Kingdom

NOTHING SAYS "WELCOME TO FLORIDA" like the big, wet, hot slap in the face you get upon opening your hotel door first thing in the morning as you head out to the Walt Disney World theme parks.

Inside the room it's nice and cool. Arriving late the previous evening after a long day of travel—and finally making it to the room amid oppressive heat and humidity—always prompts an air-conditioning overreaction. The thermometer dips chillingly through the night as tired travelers are overcome by a fitful sleep. Visions of castles and jungles and pirates prevent a truly restful evening, but eventually the clock works in favor of anticipated adventures and it's time to rise.

Hasty preparations are made—a shower, picking out a favorite touring t-shirt and a double-check to ensure MagicBands and a lanyard heavy with pins are on hand—and it's time to attack the day. Swing the door inward and that blast of early morning air overtakes the artificial arctic environment. Welcome to Florida.

No matter—there are big things ahead. It's early, but stepping into the first light of day reveals that the resort has been awake for hours. Cast members are buzzing about, hosing down the pool area, driving to work stations in oversized golf carts and hustling around the lobby preparing for the day.

There's no time for breakfast. There's a waffle sandwich waiting at Sleepy Hollow, after all. Other early-risers clutching re-fillable mugs of steaming coffee are already lined up in front of the resort, awaiting their transport. There are several bus stops spread out across the front of the resort, but only one says "Magic Kingdom," and against all odds there's a bus pulling up with that designation on its marquee. Chalk it up to Disney magic.

The coach provides another refuge from the surprising early morning humidity, and after everyone grabs a seat it rumbles out of the parking lot and onto Buena Vista Drive. The bus is full of families. Some are seasoned pros, while others are about to experience Walt Disney World for the first time. It's easy to pick them out: A stroller folded and at the ready, a parent going through maps and double-checking FastPasses and a youngster or two firing off questions at a blistering pace. All of them are looking out the windows hoping to catch the first glimpse of the spires of Cinderella Castle rising up over the trees.

Before long, the undeveloped greenery along World Drive begins to give way to signs that the much-anticipated destination is just minutes away. To the left, a massive parking lot. To the right, monorail orange races along its raised beam. And then it comes into view—the royal blue-and-gold peaks of the Castle appear in the distance, along with the conical tip of Space Mountain.

The tease is just that, however. The glimpse of the Castle soon disappears behind the trees as you draw closer. A quick spin around the green, wrought-iron bus stops and your fellow guests deposited—strollers, maps, ear hats and all—into the steamy morning.

A short walk near the Seven Seas Lagoon brings guests up and around to the park entrance itself. There's a reason the buses don't drop everyone off at the front door. This brief trek allows guests to shed the real world and begin to enter the world of the Magic Kingdom. The growling, howling motors of the buses fade into the distance as they unload their cargo, and instead music begins to filter in from behind nearby bushes. It's almost imperceptible at first, but the unmistakable sound of brass, woodwinds and strings begin to serenade visitors as they near the main gates. It's not the music of top-40 radio or the jarring sounds of a distorted guitar. Instead, it's the soundtrack to a fantasy world: Waltzes, rags and jangly melodies that would be more at home in an idealized small town thoroughfare.

A brief security check and we're through. The red brick Walt Disney World Railroad building is the first thing to greet visitors, with its white-faced clock tower and gold lettered sign. The facade blocks everything behind it from view—a deliberate design choice. Everything here is theatrical, and the Railroad acts as a curtain.

Pass by this opening marquee and then take a quick jog to the right, which leads under an archway. Inside, there are posters illustrating the different lands of the Magic Kingdom park—"coming attractions." The smell of popcorn wafts through the air as you emerge into a bright, perfect town square. Cast members stand on the corner and along the street, waving and welcoming guests. The windows looking out from the second story of Main Street USA contain names and professions—actually clever references to the people who helped build the company—and act as "the opening credits."

A few more steps to the corner and the "main attraction" finally comes into full view. Cinderella Castle, the instantly recognizable icon, stands tall over everything. Even more fantastic than in any depiction, the Castle is a fairytale come to life. It's at this point the feature presentation begins.

The Magic Kingdom is the original. It exudes the magic in its purest and most uncut form. It can seduce with tiny details that sneak up and whisper in your ear, and it can shake you to your core with explosive and moving examples of the fantastic. No matter how many times you visit the Magic Kingdom, it reveals new surprises tucked into cleverly hidden corners you may not have noticed previously. It is the shining, unblemished soul of Walt Disney World, and the most direct path to Walt and Roy's vision.

It's never anything less than pure perfection to be standing on the sparkling clean streets of the Magic Kingdom first thing in the morning. Or to be enveloped in ethereal music wafting from hidden speakers and bathed in the early morning Florida sun.

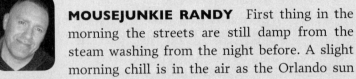

MOUSEJUNKIE RANDY   First thing in the morning the streets are still damp from the steam washing from the night before. A slight morning chill is in the air as the Orlando sun has only been up for about an hour and is still climbing into the sky. Cast members from the Main Street stores beckon early morning guests with waves of their Mickey glove-clad hands. It seems as if it's too perfect and can't be real, but it is. And for me, a fellow Mousejunkie, there isn't a better way to start any day.

Every Walt Disney World vacation has to start at the Magic Kingdom.

There are essentially two ways to approach this park:

1. At a leisurely pace, enjoying the details.
2. Go! Go! Go! Go! Eat! Go! Go! Blister! Spend! Argue! Collapse.

First timers are often tempted to take the latter approach. Don't. Now might be a good time for a reading from the Book of Mousejunkies—Bill, Verse 19:28

"And a good man shall take his family from this place to another place. And that place shall have sustenance and shelter. And roller coasters. And yet the man will remain vexed for his wife wished to complete every task before returning from whence they had come. The children

gnashed their teeth and repeatedly requested items of gifts and corn of the field, which had been popped.

And Mousejunkie Randy spake unto the good man: Slow thine pace. For rushing about causes anguish to all. He bade the man lie down with his wife in his moderately-priced resort for a nap and allow his children to swim in the pool. For it was wicked awesome."

I'll translate: If you try to do it all, you're going to be tired, broke and you're not going to notice all the details that make the place so special.

The Magic Kingdom sits on 142 acres and is divided into several themed lands: Adventureland; Frontierland; Liberty Square; Fantasyland; and Tomorrowland. Unofficial sections include Get Me Out of This Insane Heat Before I Pass Outland, If That Kid Kicks Me Again I'm Going to Screamland, and I'm Not Waiting In One More Lineland.

The Mousejunkies can help with each of these themed lands.

MOUSEJUNKIE RANDY My park touring philosophy is this: Just keep walking. I like to go with the flow and try to pass the crowds. The parks are designed like a wheel with spokes. So I pick either a clockwise or counter-clockwise direction and begin.

(Continued on next page)

If there's a line and it's not a "I have to do this as soon as possible," ride just keep walking. If you continue on with this method, you will eventually get ahead of the crowd. Some might say this approach is touring the park like a newbie. And you might be right in some respects. But where this plan has an advantage over a newbie touring, is that newbies stop at every attraction, wait in the standby line, and then move on to the next one. Since a great number of park visitors are first timers, this plan lets you get ahead of the wave. Just keep walking.

This is also a very relaxed way to tour the park, since you are really not putting any expectations on the next ride or attraction. You should also take advantage of this relaxed, low-pressure pace and just look around as you walk. Most people are attraction-obsessed. If you move away from that approach, you'll begin to notice all the little details that Disney has put in the areas away from rides and attractions. These are the little things that make Disney so much more than just another theme park.

Above all, slow down and just enjoy. Enjoy the park, enjoy the rides, enjoy the time you are spending with your family and friends, enjoy watching all the crazy people driving their families around the park like they're leading a cattle drive. Just have fun.

⭐ **The Straight Dope** *If you or someone you are traveling with is celebrating a birthday, stop at Town Hall and get a birthday button from guest relations. You'll be greeted by dozens of guests and cast members by name throughout the day, and sometimes it will result in some extra magic.*

MOUSEJUNKIE RYAN I was able to finally find out what it's like to sport one of those cool shiny buttons. Actually, I got to find out what it's like to sport *two* of those cool shiny buttons. One said "Happy Birthday Ryan!" and the other said "Just Engaged!" My fiancee, Mike, wore a "Just Engaged" button. We picked up our buttons in the Magic Kingdom and almost immediately started getting the celebrity treatment. Cast members would go out of their way to congratulate us and wish me a happy birthday. Usually they'd notice one button, respond to it, and then see the other button, and raise their eyebrows in approval towards Mike. Throughout the course of our trip, we got several exclamations of congrats from cast members so excited for us, you'd think they were our best friends, we had characters (or their handlers) ask us about the proposal (Tigger slow clapped), I was sung to, got a free cupcake, and in general we felt like celebrities. By the end of the trip, even other guests were wishing us well. If you're celebrating *anything* while you're in Disney, make sure you get a button for it. You won't regret it. I'm a fairly introverted person, but I loved every second of it. I felt like a princess.

What's New at the Magic Kingdom

The largest expansion Walt Disney World's original theme park has ever seen is complete. Fantasyland has doubled in size, offering new attractions, themed dining and immersive experiences.

Awesome/Stupid Disney Idea *A stroller parking deck located near the back of Fantasyland. Think of it—a stroller-free walk past Mickey's Philharmagic? Divine.*

Where there once stood a single castle, there are now three. The towering Cinderella Castle standing at the end of Main Street USA has long been the instantly recognizable icon for Walt Disney World and the Magic Kingdom, in particular. But new attractions, restaurants, meet-and-greets and lands keep the central Florida destination new for even frequent visitors.

New Fantasyland

After a period of planning, announcements, development and making me peek around the construction walls and stare wistfully toward what would become this new land, it's all finished. New Fantasyland—adjacent to regular Fantasyland, home of The Many Adventures of Winnie the Pooh, Peter Pan's Flight, Mickey's Philharmagic, and many, many strollers—has officially been unveiled to guests, bringing new options for when that line at Small World is just too soul crushing.

Walking straight through Cinderella Castle, past the carousel, through newly-constructed castle walls and arches brings you straight into New Fantasyland itself. There, visitors find themselves in the midst of the Enchanted Forest section of the newly-opened land. To the left, Maurice's Cottage—straight from Disney's *Beauty and the Beast*. Inside the quaint, stone and shingle structure is **Enchanted Tales With Belle**, where guests wind through Maurice's workshop and eventually into an ornate library, where Belle and a surprisingly dynamic, lifelike animatronic Lumiere guide everyone through "a tale as old as time."

The Straight Dope *Do not skip this attraction/show. Guests are transported from Maurice's Cottage to the Beast's castle through an enchanted mirror—one of the best illusions in New Fantasyland.*

The cottage is tucked into a wooded grove surrounded by a small river and stands of shady trees and low stone walls. Mountains loom above in the distance (an example of Disney's Imagineers skills with forced perspective), and there atop the tallest is Beast's Castle—the second regal structure in the Magic Kingdom.

Heading toward the mountainous base of that castle along a creatively well-worn path leads to a stone arched bridge guarded by gargoyles. We're in the Beast's domain, and things don't look quite right. But then, visiting that world after Beauty and the Former Beast are married and have kids and spend weekends taking them to soccer games or whatever the

Beasts do would be boring. Here, we enter the same world Belle inhabited. It's visually stunning and slightly dangerous. In other words, perfect.

Across the bridge and inside the base of the mountain is the **Be Our Guest Restaurant**—a large, three dining room creation that takes guests straight into scenes from the animated film. The West Wing recreates the forbidden area of Beast's castle, complete with torn tapestries and slashed paintings. The Rose Gallery is a brighter room open only for lunch, centered by the dancing figures of Belle and Beast. The central Ballroom is taken straight out of one of "Beauty and the Beast's" signature scenes. A high, vaulted ceiling with gold accents and painted with cherubs from which three massive chandeliers hang.

Mousejunkie U *The angelic cherubs flitting about the ceiling of the ballroom are paintings recreating baby pictures of the Imagineers who worked on the restaurant or in some cases, their children.*

Toward the back of the room are tall windows looking out onto an evening mountain scene—complete with falling snow. By day, the restaurant is a quick-service dining option, but by night it is a table-service restaurant where reservations are an absolute necessity.

Right around the corner is **Gaston's Tavern**—identifiable by the fountain/statue of the muscle-bound, blustery character out front—a quick-service eatery offering pork shanks, cinnamon buns and mugs of LeFou's brew: a sweet concoction of frozen apple juice and toasted marshmallow topped with mango foam. Take that, Butterbeer.

Deeper into the new land is **Under the Sea—Journey of the Little Mermaid**: a dark ride that whisks people into the world of Ariel. Guests enter by heading under Prince Eric's castle—the third such palace now in the park, and through a detailed queue line. Sharp-eyed visitors will notice seashells pressed into the walkway and walls, and a clever nod to the location's former tenant, the Nautilus submarine from *20,000 Leagues Under the Sea*. Interactive games help keep any wait times from becoming stale. Boarding a giant clam-shell vehicle takes guests through a musical tour of scenes out of the film.

The other section of the newly opened addition is Storybook Circus—home to **Dumbo the Flying Elephant** (there are now two of these spinning, soaring contraptions,) the **Barnstormer**, a small roller coaster themed around the Great Goofini and the **Casey Jr. Splash 'n' Soak Station**—a circus-themed water play area.

Hot, tired parents are going to love the new Dumbo area. The queue is located inside under a circus bigtop, where they are issued a pager. Kids can then go play in the circus tent, while parents take a load off in an air-conditioned, comfort-able setting with benches and bleachers. When it's time to take flight aboard your own flying elephant, the pager will go off, alerting you to your appointment with the big, blue yon-der. Say goodbye to standing in line for this right-of-passage attraction.

Behind it all is the new Fantasyland railroad station, a handy way to get to other sections of the Magic Kingdom without wearing out those new sneakers.

It's all centered around the **Seven Dwarfs Mine Train**—a family-friendly roller coaster that whisks guests through the world "where a million diamonds shine." And while there's no official word if there was any whistling from the workers who toiled on the massive project for five years, the newest attraction at Walt Disney World is finally open to the public. The final jewel is in place and guests at the vacation Mecca are free to wander into Fantasyland Forest.

Interview with an Imagineer:
Chris Beatty

As with every Disney attraction, this begins with a story. And in this case it revolves around the much-loved and well-known story of Snow White.

"What's great about working at Imagineering is having some of the Walt Disney DNA instilled in us," Chris Beatty, executive director at Walt Disney Imagineering said. "Walt was great with technology and using it in new ways to tell stories, going back and building adventures in brand new ways."

One of the new approaches is featuring the seven sidekicks more prominently than they were in the now-defunct Snow White's Scary Adventures attraction. Where they were cast in a more supporting role there, they are now the stars.

"We had an amazing opportunity to take a story that is fifty years old and re-invent it," Beatty said.

Guests have a chance to board a mine train—the ride vehicle itself—and experience what it's like to go to work with the Seven Dwarfs, sing "Hi-Ho" and mine jewels. Sharp-eyed riders can also keep a look out for Snow White and the Witch as they zip through the carefully constructed world.

For Walt Disney World veterans, the new attraction is roughly located on the spot where 20,000 Leagues Under the Sea once sat, and more recently, Pooh's Playful Spot. In terms of thrills, Beatty said the new coaster drops perfectly between the park's Big Thunder Mountain Railroad and Goofy's Barnstormer.

"I would say it's double the length of Goofy's but not as long as Big Thunder Mountain," Beatty said.

While that may be the case, this isn't just another roller coaster. The one-of-a-kind ride vehicle itself is unique and proprietary to Disney Parks and Resorts. Riders step into the cart and sit side-by-side—an intentional choice so that smaller guests wouldn't be looking out from the middle and missing details.

"We could've widened the train and put more people on it, but we chose to keep it side-by-side because we wanted our youngest guests to be able to see out and experience the adventure," Beatty said.

That's also when things get quite different. The cart is a cradle of sorts that swings back and forth during the ride as twists and turns send it rocking left and right.

(Continued on next page)

The cart takes a corner and you feel the mine train swing out to the side. It's a ride vehicle unlike any other.

The mine cars themselves are works of art. Imagineers working on the ride went back into Disney's archives to pore over drawings and art in order to create the most accurate representation of what fans have seen in the film. There are no traditional metal fittings or modern clues that might give away that this is just a roller coaster train. Meticulous craftsmanship and exhaustive attention to detail help create the illusion that guests are living in the world of the Seven Dwarfs.

"As it pulls into the station, guests' jaws will drop," Beatty said. "It feels like you're riding something hundreds of years old."

With the opening of the Seven Dwarfs Mine Train, the Fantasyland expansion project is complete.

"It will finally complete the vision of Imagineering and Parks and Resorts that was set forward in New Fantasyland," Beatty said. "You leave the Castle Courtyard and step into Fantasyland Forest. For the first time you see Beast's Castle and the rock work of the Be Our Guest restaurant adjacent to the forest of the Mine Train. You see the waterways tying it together and it completes the promise made to guests that we've created an incredibly immersive environment that's lush and beautifully textured, and that there are these incredible adventures that they can go off an enjoy.

"It's the first time we as Imagineers can see five years of this journey and what took place to get to see this overall vision."

Of course, the Seven Dwarfs Mine Train and the Anna and Elsa meet-and-greet are new, which means they will be among the most popular destinations in the park. When these new experiences were first debuted, enthusiastic guests would all-but sprint to them, tearing through the otherwise placid Main Street USA and its shops. Disney didn't exactly smile upon this approach. Now, cast members walk in front of the surge of people upon rope drop to lead a Parade of the Crazed as they do their best to get near the front of the pack.

Festival of Fantasy Parade

Disney does parades on a grand scale, and its newest has stepped off.

The new Festival of Fantasy Parade, a daytime procession at the Magic Kingdom, features more than one hundred performers on stilts, swings and flying rigs, all kinds of floats—some reaching as high as three stories tall—and effects that have yet to be seen in a Disney parade production.

The parade pays tribute to Fantasyland and includes classic Disney scenes as well as some popular Pixar characters. Think of a Broadway show weaving through the streets of the Magic Kingdom and you'll begin to get an idea of what this new parade looks like.

The procession includes floats like The Princess Garden—a fifty-foot long float with Cinderella, Tiana and Belle (and their prince counterparts); Tangled—a long ship on the high seas showcasing Flynn Rider and Rapunzel; Brave—Merida,

Scottish dancers and a giant bagpipe help recreate the Pixar film; and the Finale and Mickey's Airship—a ninety-foot long procession of classic characters, references to New Fantasyland's Storybook Circus and the big cheese himself, Mickey, along with Minnie aboard a hot air balloon. And if there are any fears that Anna, Elsa and Olaf from *Frozen* aren't included, just let it go. Three of Disney's newest and most popular characters are also featured in the new parade.

A highlight: Keep an eye open for the fire-breathing dragon.

★ **The Straight Dope** *The parade starts from one of two places: Right next to the firehouse at the City Hall Hub, or in Frontierland near Splash Mountain. Ask a cast member which end of the park the parade will be stepping off from. If you're at the far end, you won't start to see the parade until 3:20 P.M.*

Additionally, if you can't get a spot right along the rope during the parade, don't fret. The floats are set high up off the ground, making it easy to see—even from behind that guy who showed up two seconds before the parade started and stood right in front of you.

Everyone (who isn't me on our first-ever trip) knows that Disney's nighttime shows are amazing spectacles worth planning for. With Spectromagic, the former after-dark parade, now gone forever, the Main Street Electrical Parade lights up Main Street USA before the Wishes Nighttime Spectacular sets the sky ablaze. Between those two, however, is a can't-miss show that brings Cinderella Castle itself to life.

Celebrate the Magic is a ten-minute show projected right on to the Castle, making it look as if it's moving, changing and evolving. The massive symbol of Disney magic becomes a canvas where Disney's magic-makers paint a story involving some of the most loved film classics. Watch this amazing display unfold and you'll be thinking what everyone else is thinking: "The Imagineers are just showing off now."

The Straight Dope *For the best view of Celebrate the Magic, stand along Main Street USA, the Hub, the Castle forecourt or the Tomorrowland or Liberty Square bridges.*

As Walt Disney World's most popular park, the Magic Kingdom can get crowded at different times during the year. Guests are given an opportunity to make FastPass+ choices to help minimize wait times at certain attractions.

Once that's settled, it's time to set out into the park.

General Touring Tips

Main Street USA

It all starts with Main Street USA. Inspired by Main Street in the town of Marceline, Missouri, where Walt spent part of his boyhood. It's typically buzzing with activity first thing in the morning. The sun is peeking over the rooftops and bathing Cinderella Castle in its very own spotlight, cast members are greeting guests and the park is just coming alive.

Take a moment and look up. Many of the second floor windows along Main Street have names painted on them, which serve as credits for a number of the Imagineers, animators and pioneers who contributed their skills and abilities to the Walt Disney Company.

Mousejunkie U *Walt Disney's window—the only one facing Cinderella Castle—is located above the ice cream parlor at the end of Main Street. (His name also appears above the Main Street train station and on the Casting Agency door.) Roy O. Disney's window is on the southeast corner of Main Street: "If We Can Dream It—We Can Do It!"—Dreamers & Doers—Roy O. Disney, Chairman."*

The names appear as part of fictional businesses and quite often refer to a hobby or interest relating to the job or contribution they made to the Walt Disney Company.

Mousejunkie U *Roy gets another mention on a Main Street window: "Pseudonym Real Estate Development Company—Roy Davis—President, Bob Price—Vice President, Robert Foster—Travelling Representative." Roy Davis was the pseudonym he used while buying property during the initial phases of Walt Disney World's construction.*

Construction throughout the park utilizes forced perspective to create the illusion of height and size, and it's put to good use in particular on Main Street USA. While the ground-level buildings are normal sized, the second-and-third story levels are progressively smaller. The effect helps complete the illusion of an idealized American thoroughfare from the early part of the 1900s.

The Main Street USA Area is lined with gift shops perfect for blowing your budget out before you even hit a single attraction. The Emporium has almost anything you could want, and the Chapeau Hat Shoppe is packed with lids that'll both protect you from the sun and make you look awesomely hysterical.

The Straight Dope *Stop-in at the hat shop on Main Street USA and you'll see an old phone on the wall. Pick up the receiver and you'll be listening-in on someone's conversation.*

The Magic Kingdom was constructed as a two-story structure. When you're standing on Main Street USA, you're actually on the second floor of the park. Nearly a mile and a half of tunnels called "Utilidoors," run below on the real ground floor of the park, allowing cast members to move about without breaking the illusion on-stage, above.

The Straight Dope *For a look at the Utilidoors in action, take the Keys to the Kingdom tour ($79 per person).*

Many guides urge guests not to get sidetracked by the shops and characters on Main Street USA first thing in the morning. I couldn't disagree more. While I don't recommend camping out on a curb for an hour, one of our family traditions is to grab breakfast at the Main Street Bakery. I'll get a chocolate croissant or a muffin, and I have no idea what anyone else gets because I'm pretty much delirious with joy at that point. I'm on Main Street USA with caffeine entering my system, and a light and fluffy croissant dusted with powdered sugar in front of me.

Of course, after the coffee and croissant are gone, my eyes are drawn to the throngs of people moving by the front window of the bakery.

That's when my sense of urgency starts to set in.

Once properly fed and caffeinated, it's time to head for Cinderella Castle.

Mousejunkie U *Don't confuse your superlatives: Disneyland is the "Happiest Place on Earth." The Magic Kingdom at Walt Disney World is "The Most Magical Place on Earth."*

Cinderella Castle—This majestic icon of the Magic Kingdom stands 189 feet high with 18 towers reaching skyward over a moat that holds more than 3 million gallons of water. But Cinderella Castle is more than an eye-catching structure. It captures the hearts of millions of people every year. It is the gateway to the fantastic world that lies behind and around it, silently watching over Walt and Roy Disney's finest work. Cinderella Castle grabs hold of the imagination of anyone who approaches it and creates dreams. It is the beating heart of Walt Disney World made real in a regal, breathtaking structure built of wonder and magic.

Five mosaics located inside the castle breezeway guide guests through the story of Cinderella. Created by Imagineer Dorothea Redmond and artist Hanns-Joachim Scharff, each mosaic is 15 feet high and 10 feet wide.

Mousejunkie U *Hanns Scharff, one of the peo- ple credited with creating the mosaic telling the story of Cinderella, was a German Luftwaffe interrogator during World War II. He was renowned and respected for his tech- niques, which eschewed physical contact, abuse of, or even raising his voice in the presence of captured prisoners. He also helped shape U.S. interrogation techniques following the end of the war. After the war he moved to the U.S., spending the rest of his life working in his medium of choice: mosaic.*

A few steps further and guests find themselves in Fantasyland proper. An idealized world of the playful and fanciful, Fantasyland offers attractions ideally suited for the younger set, but also perfect for adults willing to drop their inhibitions and return to a more innocent time.

It's also boasts the highest concentration of strollers anywhere on the planet. The bottleneck between Mickey's Philharmagic and Pinnochio's Village Haus is nearly impass- able on busy days. What's the best way to avoid this sticky congestion? Get through Fantasyland, especially Peter Pan/ Small World row, as early as possible. I wouldn't skip any of these attractions, but I also wouldn't wait in a long line in Fantasyland if it isn't necessary. And it isn't.

The Straight Dope *Get Fantasyland out of the way early. It gets extremely congested as the day wears on, and lines can become quite long.*

Fantasyland

Mickey's PhilharMagic—Donald is actually the star of this impressive 3-D film, which blends classic Disney music, films, characters and a few unexpected tactile surprises. It all plays out across a 150-foot-wide canvas, one of the largest seamless screens created for such a purpose. FastPass+ is available for this attraction, but normally only becomes necessary on very busy days.

Duration: 12 minutes.

Loads: Quickly. The theater empties out, and the next group of guests steps inside.

Prince Charming's Regal Carrousel—This carrousel features seventy-two meticulously hand-painted, hard maple horses spinning under eighteen Cinderella-themed canopy scenes, all around an antique band organ playing Disney favorites.

Duration: Two minutes.

Loads: It's slow loading, but it's a classic in the shadow of Cinderella Castle. It's certainly worth a few minutes of

---

MOUSEJUNKIE RANDY Every horse on the carousel has a plastic duplicate. These duplicates are used on the carousel when the real wooden ones are being refurbished. One artist's full time job is to repaint every horse, by hand, one at a time throughout the year. Next time you ride the carousel, see if you can find one of the stand-in horses.

your time, but I'd keep walking if the standby is longer than twenty minutes.

Mousejunkie U   *Built in 1917, this Fantasyland staple began its life in Detroit. It spent thirty-nine years at Olympic Park in Maplewood N.J. before Disney bought it in 1967 and had it refurbished in time for the Magic Kingdom's opening.*

Dumbo the Flying Elephant—A pack of sixteen flying pachyderms take guests on a spin around, well, nothing. The staggering popularity of this simple attraction prompted Disney's Imagineers to create two of these as part of the planned Fantasyland expansion.

Duration: 1 minute.

Loads: Very slowly, but now that Disney has relocated to the Storybook Circus section of Fantasyland and doubled down on the attraction, part of the queue is located inside an air conditioned circus tent.

Mousejunkie U   *The Dumbo the Flying Elephant attraction was one of the original attractions available to guests on opening day in October of 1971.*

It's a Small World—The "happiest cruise that ever sailed the seven seas" takes guests on a tour through different lands populated by 472 dolls who drill that familiar song into your subconscious with "the happiest jackhammer that ever cracked a subconscious."

Duration: 11 minutes. (Though for some, seems like 3 hours.)

Loads: Quickly. You rarely stand still while waiting in line for Small World. It might take a few minutes, but you'll be moving.

Go ahead, mock me, but I never miss this attraction. The whimsical feel and the refurbished Mary Blair design combined with the maddeningly repetitive yet classic song by Robert B. and Richard M. Sherman make this an old-school favorite. I love Small World and I don't care who knows it. Except for maybe Jason Statham. I can only guess that he'd neck-kick me if I mentioned it.

Mousejunkie U *The song that launched a million boat rides is sung in five languages through the attraction: English, Spanish, Japanese, Swedish and Italian.*

Mad Tea Party—If Small World launched a million happy cruises, then the Mad Tea Party launched a million lunches. Giant teacups whirl guests around at a breakneck pace. The chaotic trip around a giant teacup is set to appropriately fast-paced music, resulting in a heaping cup of dizzy for anyone dunked in the oversized china.

Duration: Two minutes.

Loads: Medium.

Mousejunkie U *The teacups at the Mad Tea Party can hold 144 gallons of tea.*

MOUSEJUNKIE RYAN   Spin until you puke during your very own un-birthday party at the Mad Tea Party. Actually, speaking as a former ride operator for a New Hampshire amusement park, please don't puke on the ride. It's disgusting, and no one wants to clean that up. But really, whether you're obsessed with Alice, like me, or you just want to spin around for a few minutes, Mad Tea Party is a blast.

The Many Adventures of Winnie the Pooh—Oversized honey pots take guests for a ride through the Hundred Acre Wood in this Fantasyland dark ride. It's amazing how some-thing geared toward youngsters can even affect adults. If Pooh was ever a part of your youth, this attraction will transport you right back to that time.

Duration: Five minutes.

Loads: Medium, but the queue was one of the first to get the interactive treatment from Disney's Imagineers, so there's plenty to do and look at while you wait.

Mousejunkie U   *This attraction, which opened in 1999 on the spot of the old Mr. Toad's Wild Ride, offers a nod to its former landlord. Just as you go through the first set of doors inside the ride, look back and to your left to see a painting of Mr. Toad handing the deed over to Owl.*

When we first took our then-three-year-old to Walt Disney World for the first time, we thought this light-hearted romp through A.A. Milne's world would be perfect for her. No way. Seconds into the attraction she was terrified. From her toddler's point of view, we were heading into a dark tunnel where there was thunder and where Pooh's soul flips up out of his body and floats away. The Heffalumps and Woozles didn't help, either. It took her years to get over what became an irrational fear of the cuddly bear. Now it's one of her favorites. Go figure.

Peter Pan's Flight—Board your pirate ship and take flight out of the Darling's bedroom, over old London, through Captain Hook's grasp, and into Neverland.

Duration: Three minutes.

Loads: Forget it, if you don't have a FastPass+, things could get ugly. The line for this attraction builds very quickly, stretching around the corner and down toward the Columbia Harbour House. It loads deceivingly slowly. However, if you happen to wander by and the standby line is short, jump right in.

New Attractions in Fantasyland

Barnstormer Featuring the Great Goofini—This coaster, perfect for the youngsters in your touring group, is themed to look like an old-time stunt plane show. The track features several nice ups and downs without actually hurtling riders

through any terrifying flips or spins. It's a short, gentle intro-
duction to the world of roller coasters.

Duration: 90 seconds.

Loads: Slowly.

⭐ **The Straight Dope**   *The ride vehicles on this attraction are a bit small, so if you're an adult or quite tall, prepare
to shoehorn yourself in.*

Enchanted Tales With Belle—Join Lumiere, Belle and the
Beast as they lead you through "A Tale As Old As Time."
Guests wander through Maurice's Cottage, into his workshop
and then eventually into the library where the show proper
begins. Guests are encouraged to volunteer for roles in the
story as it is retold.

Duration: 20 minutes.

Loads: Slow. It's theater-type seating, but since it's a newer
attraction, it tends to draw slightly larger crowds.

The Seven Dwarfs Mine Train—Take a spin through the
Seven Dwarfs' mine on this smooth, relatively speedy coaster.
There are no loops or jarring spins, which makes it perfect
for those who have graduated from the Great Goofini, but
have yet to experience Big Thunder Mountain.

Duration: Three minutes.

Loads: Medium. It's new, and therefore very popular, but the queue has several interactive elements that help pass the time.

Under the Sea—Journey of the Little Mermaid—A dark ride that takes guests Under the Sea, this attraction is a slow-moving ride through the world of Ariel, Prince Eric, Ursula and the rest of the denizens of this 1991 film.

Duration: Seven minutes.

Loads: Quickly. The clamshell vehicles that shuttle you through the attraction are constantly in motion, much like the Doom Buggies over at the Haunted Mansion.

By now you've worked your way through Fantasyland and you're staring straight down the barrel of the future: Tomorrowland. Or, more accurately, an idealized, fairly schizophrenic—but still eminently seductive—version of the future.

Schizophrenic, you say? Sure. Buzz Lightyear's Space Ranger Spin fits perfectly. Carousel of Progress? That's a stretch. The Indy Speedway? It doesn't exactly scream "future!" to me. Still, Tomorrowland, which was given a complete makeover in 1994 when Disney's Imagineers opted to avoid trying to keep up with ever-changing visions of the future—is home to some of the best-loved attractions in the Magic Kingdom.

Tomorrowland

Stitch's Great Escape!—You can't see me right now, but I'm crossing my arms and shaking my head. I have a very disapproving look on my face. I'm making that "tsk, tsk" sound that people make when they're disappointed. And now I'm banging my head on my desk.

I'm not going to go any further than that because the head/desk thing kind of hurts and this attraction just isn't worth it.

Set before the events of *Lilo and Stitch*, the show focuses on Experiment 626 (Stitch) and his attempts to slip The Man at the Galactic Federation Prisoner Teleport Center.

If your group is in a hurry, if you're claustrophobic, if you have children in your party that might get uncomfortable in the dark, or if you don't like mediocre attractions, consider dropping Stitch's Great Escape from your touring plans. It's consistently panned by guests and ranks lower than most other attractions in its general vicinity. It's a retrofit of the Extra-TERRORestrial Alien Encounter attraction, and retains much of what made that too frightening for children: It's dark, loud, and you're strapped into a seat and can't move.

Duration: 15 minutes.

Loads: Quickly. This theater-in-the-round show ends, empties out, and a new batch of people who haven't read this book enter.

Buzz Lightyear's Space Ranger Spin—Join Buzz Lightyear's forces to defend the earth against evil Emperor Zurg. The attraction is essentially a dark ride with some really fun extras—primarily a functioning "laser gun" with which guests shoot at targets. Bulls-eyes trigger movement and audio cues, and participants can even keep score. (I'm not going to say trash-talking is one of the finer points of this attraction, I'll just say that Mousejunkie Amy has yet to best her spouse.) But if I keep bringing it up, it's "To the couch! And beyond!"

Duration: Six minutes.

Loads: Medium. The line can get quite long, but since the ride vehicles are constantly loading guests, things tend to move along.

The Straight Dope *To boost your score on Buzz Lightyear's Space Ranger Spin, shoot for smaller, far away targets and anything that moves. Specifically, aim for the back of the robot's left wrist in the first room for a 100,000-point bonus. Target Zurg when you arrive at Planet Z and hit the bottom of his space scooter for another 100,000 points. Also, the volcano at the top of the Zurg room is worth big points.*

Astro Orbiter—Think of this attraction as Dumbo, only higher up. Guests take an elevator up to the boarding area where they pilot their own rockets and spin in circles. That might not sound too gripping, but the Astro Orbiter provides some great views at night and can be visually striking. (Mainly from the ground.)

Duration: Two minutes.

Loads: Slowly.

Ask most Mousejunkies about the Astro Orbiter and the answer will approximate something along the lines of "eh."

Walt Disney's Carousel of Progress—Disney boasts that this musical/comedy stage show "has been seen by more guests than any other theatrical presentation in the history of American Theater since its debut at the 1964 World's Fair."

A showcase for Disney's audio animatronics, the Carousel of Progress follows a family through the years as electricity and technology shape their lives. Guests sit in a dark, cool theater that rotates around the stage, changing scenes and bringing them up-to-date.

Duration: 22 minutes.

Loads: Fast. The theater opens as soon as the previous group has rotated to the next scene in the production.

Call me corny, but I can't miss this attraction. It has Walt Disney's fingerprints all over it. It's classic, and it has that intangible magic that makes the Magic Kingdom so special. It's also relaxing, and who can argue against sitting in a dark, air conditioned theater for a few minutes on a hot day?

⭐ **Mousejunkie U**   *The voice cast of Carousel of Progress is quite notable. Jean Shepherd, author and narrator of A Christmas Story, stars as the father, John; his daughter, Patricia, is portrayed by Debi Derryberry, who is primarily known as the voice of Jimmy Neutron on the Nickelodeon animated series; the family's grandmother— the video game whiz—is voiced by Janet Waldo, who voiced many cartoon characters including Judy Jetson from The Jetsons and Josie in Josie and the Pussycats; finally the great Mel Blanc—Bugs Bunny, Porky Pig and dozens of others—is the grumpy cousin Orville.*

The Monsters Inc. Laugh Floor—An interactive show based on the Pixar film, guests file into a theater where they watch a standup comedy routine hosted by Mike Wazowski. Several screens placed around the theater show audience members as they interact with the characters on stage. During the show, a camera focuses on someone, usually an adult male audience member, who theretofore is known as "that guy." He becomes the butt of the good-natured jokes for the rest of the show. Yes, I have been "that guy."

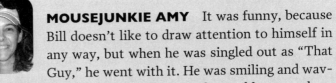

MOUSEJUNKIE AMY   It was funny, because Bill doesn't like to draw attention to himself in any way, but when he was singled out as "That Guy," he went with it. He was smiling and waving, and then later in the day people would approach us and say, "Hey, you were That Guy!"

Duration: 15 minutes.

Loads: Medium. The theater empties out and a new group of guests files in.

During the pre-show, guests are given the opportunity to text jokes for possible use at the end of the show. Shockingly, they've never used my favorite joke. I text it in every time and must deal with crushing rejection on every occasion so far. Experience the genius for yourself:

Q: "How many surrealists does it take to change a lightbulb?"
A: "A fish!"

I'm telling you, they're missing out on comedy gold.

Space Mountain—When this classic coaster debuted in 1975, twenty-eight miles-per-hour may have seemed blindingly fast. Decades later, it still does. Space Mountain still delivers one of the best thrills in all of Walt Disney World. Sure, it's not as smooth as the Rock 'n' Roller Coaster, or as visceral as Expedition Everest, but since it takes place completely in the dark it's got the "unknown" factor going for it. Dips, turns, and drops fling you around with little-to-no warning. FastPass+ is available for this attraction.

Duration: Three minutes.

Loads: Slowly. The standby lines tend to build up rather quickly.

Tomorrowland Speedway—Strap yourself into one of these machines and feel the thunder under the hood rattle your teeth. Or, more precisely, feel the lawn mower-sized engine buzz contently at about 7.5 miles-per-hour as you leisurely tour this 4/10-mile track.

Duration: Five minutes.

Loads: Slowly, and in the open. Bring sunscreen. I got fairly singed one late morning as we slowly shuffled up the ramp, across the track and back down to the loading area.

Tomorrowland Transit Authority PeopleMover—A train of five cars using linear induction motors carts guests on a smooth ride through the upper levels of Tomorrowland.

Duration: 10 minutes.

Loads: Quickly.

As the designated "lazy traveler" in our group, I love the PeopleMover. It gets you off your feet a bit, it lets you cool down, it provides some great people watching from above, and you get a great view of Cinderella Castle as you pass by the outer edges of Tomorrowland.

Cut back across the Castle Hub and across the wooden bridge to find yourself in **Liberty Square**.

The cobblestone streets and colonial architecture bring guests back 200 years. But don't get too comfortable, there are a few minor frights ready to take you by surprise.

Liberty Square

The Haunted Mansion—More giggle than scream, guests tip-toe their way through the stretching room where they "drag their bodies to the dead-center of the room" and then move on to their Doom Buggies for a tour through the home to 999 Happy Haunts.

Mousejunkie U *The voice of Paul Frees (Boris Badenov from the Bullwinkle show) is the "Ghost Host" of the Haunted Mansion. The names of the hitchhiking ghosts at the end of the attraction are Phineas, Ezra and Gus.*

Duration: 9 minutes.

Loads: Medium. Even when the line twists back and forth in front of the Mansion façade, it normally keeps moving. The queue is also covered, and once you get close enough to see the front doors you can spend time checking out the cemetery and the new interactive elements.

Mousejunkie U *There are five singing busts in the graveyard scene. Despite popular urban legend, Walt Disney is not among them. The farthest one to the left, however, is Thurl Ravenscroft, the soloist on "Grim Grinning Ghosts." (He's was also the voice of Tony the Tiger.)*

Hall of Presidents—Every U.S. president who has ever served is represented in audio animatronic form in this classic Magic Kingdom attraction. A combination film, narrative and truly impressive audio animatronic presentation, it's hard to leave without feeling just a little more patriotic. A refurb has made the show more moving, more informative, and better on every level.

What's new?

> Since the 2009 re-launch of the attraction, Abraham Lincoln now recites the Gettysburg address with the original Royal Dano recording directed by Walt for President Lincoln's World's Fair debut.

> Barack Obama is one of three presidents programmed to speak in the updated show. The first contemporary president to speak in the show was Bill Clinton. George W. Bush recorded a segment eight years later.

> In the new update, George Washington speaks for the first time. He explains the importance of the presidential oath of office and uses portions of a speech he actually gave during his second inauguration.

Duration: 25 minutes.

Loads: Quickly. The theater holds 700 people, and empties out every twenty-five minutes. Don't rush to get near the doors—the view is good from anywhere in the theater. Just get inside ten minutes before show time and you'll be all set.

Liberty Square Riverboat—Get on board this steam-powered sternwheeler for a relaxing tour of the Rivers of America. The *Liberty Belle* takes guests on a half-mile trip around Tom Sawyer Island. Grab a spot along the second-level rail and watch Walt Disney World go by from aboard a steamboat.

Duration: 15 minutes.

Loads: Quickly.

Continue down past the Liberty Tree Tavern and the food stand where we must eat outlandishly huge turkey legs, and you'll find yourself in Frontierland.

Frontierland

Country Bear Jamboree—Eighteen audio animatronic bears—and a few other musically-inclined animals—serenade you with an odd collection of funny tunes in Grizzly Hall. Corny? Yes. But it's fun if you've got kids in tow. Big Al is reason enough for me to visit again.

Here's a list of the Bears' greatest hits:

➤ "My Woman Ain't Pretty, but She Don't Swear"
➤ "Mama, Don't Whip Little Buford"
➤ "Tears Will Be the Chaser for My Wine"
➤ "All the Guys That Turn Me on Turn Me Down"
➤ "Blood on the Saddle"
➤ "The Ballad of Davy Crockett"

Duration: 15 minutes.

Loads: Quickly. This is a typical theater-type load-in. As soon as the show is over, the theater is empty and ready for the next group.

The Straight Dope *If you attempt to shoehorn yourself into Grizzly Hall just after the 3 P.M. parade, you might find it quite crowded. The parade ends, leaving thousands of guests standing in front of the Country Bear Jamboree* *looking for the closest attraction. Just wait it out until later in the day for a much more relaxed experience.*

Frontierland Shootin' Arcade—Take a few potshots at harmless targets with these light-activated firearms. At $1 per play, it's inexpensive and mildly entertaining, but I played this exact shooting range at Hampton Beach, N.H. as a teen. It feels like a cheap, pre-packaged attraction you can find anywhere.

Splash Mountain—Now we're talking. Splash Mountain is one of the biggies at the Magic Kingdom—quite literally. The eighty-seven-foot structure stands towering over Frontierland, daring guests to take a trip into the bayou. Based on *Song of the South*, the Disney film no one talks about, Splash Mountain is a tour through the forests and swamps of Brer Rabbit and friends. It ends with a five-story log flume drop that delivers thrills every time.

Duration: 10 minutes.

Loads: Moderately fast. The queue is capable of handling a massive amount of guests, but standby times aren't normally unbearable, except during the busiest times.

Mousejunkie U *A Florida State University graduate who worked on Splash Mountain left his mark on the attraction. Just before your log starts the long climb up Chickapin Hill, a small rodent pokes his head out from the ceiling and exclaims, "FSU!"*

Tom Sawyer Island—Run through caves, trails, hills and explore Fort Langhorn on this island in the middle of the Rivers of America. A playground accessible by raft, there are endless opportunities to relive the days of Tom Sawyer.

Walt Disney World Railroad—Walt Disney loved steam trains, and his infatuation carried over into his theme parks. Board one of the Magic Kingdom's authentic steam trains and take a loop around the park. The trains stop at Main Street USA, Fantasyland and Frontierland.

Taking a few loops around the Magic Kingdom is a great way to get a quick rest, and if you find yourself near Splash Mountain with a burning need to be at the front of the park, Disney's steam trains are an alternate to hoofing it. It takes about fifteen minutes to travel the entire route.

Mousejunkie U   *There are four locomotives in the Magic Kingdom—the Roger E. Broggie (an Imagineer and fellow train enthusiast), the Lilly Belle (named for Walt's wife,) the Roy O. Disney, and of course, the Walter E. Disney.*

MOUSEJUNKIE RANDY Head to the last train car. If you or your child is lucky, you will get to call the "All Aboard" and get a card as an honorary conductor.

Big Thunder Mountain Railroad—One of three "mountains" in the Magic Kingdom range, the Big Thunder Mountain Railroad is a roller coaster that takes guests on an out-of-control train ride through the Old West. Falling rocks, dry riverbeds and an assortment of audio animatronic figures color the red rock caverns that whip by.

Mousejunkie U *According to the legend of Big Thunder Mountain Railroad, a "Rainmaker" was brought to the town of Tumbleweed to break a devastating drought. The audio animatronic snake-oil salesman has a name: Professor Cumulus Isobar. Look for him bailing water out of the back of his wagon as you speed by.*

Duration: Three minutes.

Loads: Medium. This popular attraction can get bogged down in long lines early in the day.

As coasters go, this one is mild. I'm a big chicken when it comes to thrill rides, and this one is just fast enough to give me a slight bump in blood pressure. It's more hairpin turns and jumping over hills than heights or inversions.

The Straight Dope *For a faster feel and a little more tossing and shaking, sit in the caboose.*

There is one final, unexplored land that awaits guests. It is perhaps the most exotically themed, and holds some of the most classic and best-loved attractions.

Adventureland

Walt Disney's Enchanted Tiki Room—This attraction has been returned to a shorter version of its original state. What you get is a ten-minute musical show put on by audio-animatronic birds. Your hosts, Jose, Fritz, Michael and Pierre lead more than 300 fellow fowl as they warble through that insanely catchy tune, "In the Tiki Room."

Duration: 10 minutes.

Loads: Quickly.

★ **The Straight Dope** *A few of the theatrical lights are pointed into the audience from above, and are absolutely blinding if you're sitting in the wrong spot. Keep one eye on the ceiling as you choose your seat.*

Jungle Cruise—A stand-up comedy routine disguised as a cruise down the Nile, the Amazon, the Congo and the Mekong Rivers is led by some of the best cast members at Walt Disney World. As guests cast off into the jungle, a world of animatronic beasts await around every corner. The skipper keeps things lively, showering adventurers with some incredibly bad (great) jokes and puns throughout the attraction. If it wasn't for these quick-witted, pith-helmeted cast members, the dated look of the animatronics might detract from this now classic attraction.

Duration: 10 minutes

Loads: Slowly

Magic Carpets of Aladdin—The third iteration of the Dumbo ride in the park, the Magic Carpets of Aladdin lets guests board their own flying carpet and soar over Adventureland—which is great as long as you don't mind going in a circle. This hub-and-spoke ride works essentially the same as Dumbo and the Astro Orbiters. The ride vehicles can be controlled by the rider, tipping it forward or back, and making it rise and dip.

Duration: 90 seconds.

Loads: Moderate to slow.

Pirates of the Caribbean—Johnny Depp's Captain Jack Sparrow has infused new life into this well-loved attraction. Guests board small boats and are plunged into the midst of a chaotic scene where a coastal town is being pillaged by a motley crew of scurvy swashbucklers. An update added Captain Jack, a creepy Davy Jones, and Jack's nemesis Barbossa to the proceedings.

Duration: Nine minutes.

Loads: Medium to slow, but don't let that dissuade you from getting in line. This queue is among the best in all of Walt Disney World. Walk through the caves, look through prison bars, examine cannon and rifles and soak up the exquisite theming. Believe it or not, this line is half the fun.

Mousejunkie U *125 audio animatronics figures harass and entertain guests—65 pirates and townspeople and 60 animals and birds.*

MOUSEJUNKIE RYAN You can't miss Pirates of the Caribbean. There's just something incredibly exciting about sitting in a boat, listening to pirates sing, and trying to be the first to spot Captain Jack Sparrow. (Editor's note: "Swoon.")

MOUSEJUNKIE RANDY One December 30th evening Carol and I were about to board Pirates of the Caribbean, only to notice some strange looking plain-clothes security people appear. It's not uncommon during the Holiday for celebrities to be about the parks, so I thought "which Hollywood type would need all this security?"

We boarded our boat and survived our trip to the Caribbean. When we were unloading there was additional plain clothes security, so whoever it was must be somewhere on the ride.

We headed up to the gift shop and Carol and I put on a couple of those new Jack Sparrow hats that have the dreadlocks hanging down. We look up and standing right in front of us is President Jimmy Carter and his wife. In my pirates hat I gave him a hearty "Hello President Carter." He gave me an odd look and said, "Well hello." You never know who you will run into at Walt Disney World.

⭐ **Mousejunkie U** *According to cast members who work at Pirates of the Caribbean, there's an oft-repeated legend centering on a ghost named George. The George in this tale worked on the attraction and somehow died inside. Each night cast members must say "Goodnight George" before leaving. If this routine is forgotten or ignored, the ride experiences shutdowns and emergency stops the next morning.*

Swiss Family Treehouse—Climb through the treetop home of the Swiss Family Robinson. You remember them, don't you? The movie is only fifty years old. Get your butt up into the tree. The home of the aforementioned shipwrecked family is recreated faithfully. Explore at your own pace. Full disclosure: My pace is usually set by the bench outside the attraction's entrance.

⭐ **Mousejunkie U** *The Magic Kingdom opened on October 1, 1971. The opening day attractions were Mr. Toad's Wild Ride, the Mickey Mouse Review, the Skyway, Snow White's Scary Adventures, Dumbo the Flying Elephant, Cinderella's Golden Carousel, the Mad Tea Party, It's a Small World, the Grand Prix Raceway, the Country Bear Jamboree, the Hall of Presidents, the Frontierland Shootin' Arcade, the Haunted Mansion, the Jungle Cruise, the Enchanted Tiki Room, the Swiss Family Treehouse and the Walt Disney World Railroad. Guests could also enjoy the Main Street Vehicles.*

Napping in the Kingdom

I tend to whine about the heat and humidity in central Florida any chance I get. ("Bill is hot at 60°. Deb is cold at 90°."— Mousejunkie Walt, copyright © 2010) When things get particularly oppressive, there are places to duck into that will provide some much-needed rest, cooler temps and an inconspicuous place to maybe catch a quick nap.

Disclaimer: I don't nod off on purpose. Sometimes it just happens. Heck, I've seen Mousejunkie Randy with his head back on the Carousel of Progress (his eyes snapped open when I took a photo of him. Either that or his lumbago was acting up), *and* stretched out on Ellen's Energy Adventure at Epcot. And this is a man who will out-tour almost anyone.

If things get too heated, consider these sleep-inducing, comfortable, gloriously air-conditioned oases in the Magic Kingdom:

➤ **The Carousel of Progress**—I've stated earlier that I love this attraction, and that affection is unequivocal. But I have to admit that I've nodded off when John blew the fuse and came to when he was burning the turkey.

➤ **The Hall of Presidents**—While the new refurb has improved this attraction immensely, sometimes days of constant park touring take their toll. Great story, great attraction, great air conditioning. Just remember: Snoring is not patriotic.

➤ **Liberty Square Riverboat**—Most of the seating on this steamboat is located outside along the rail. But I discovered a very soft, comfortable seat on the second, inside level.

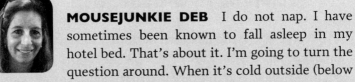

MOUSEJUNKIE DEB I do not nap. I have sometimes been known to fall asleep in my hotel bed. That's about it. I'm going to turn the question around. When it's cold outside (below 80°), my favorite place to warm up is in a rocking chair in front of the fireplace in the Villas at the Wilderness Lodge lobby. The Wilderness Lodge lobby is good, too, but all the rocking chairs are usually taken.

➤ **Mickey's Philharmagic**—You have to be really tired to sleep here, with the noise and audience reaction and tactile surprises, but it is dark and cool and therefore not impossible.

The Straight Dope *If you arrive at the park during the daily 3 P.M. parade, hop on the train at Main Street Station and take it to Frontierland. You'll miss the crowds and be half-way across the park in minutes.*

Above all, approach the Magic Kingdom slowly. It allows for a more relaxed pace, and the opportunity to notice the details Imagineers created through the years.

Epcot

IN A PERFECT WORLD, I'd spend an entire week at Epcot.

The thing is, Epcot *is* a perfect world. A sprawling, wondrous park filled with idealized dreams of technology, exploration and cultural unity.

Every morning Epcot slowly awakens as the Friendships begin crisscrossing the World Showcase Lagoon, their staccato signals providing the soundtrack to a new day. Guests arrive in the shadow of Spaceship Earth—the eighteen-story geodesic sphere that serves as the icon of Epcot—and are greeted by meticulously-groomed grounds, swelling music and the promise of a day-long journey taking them from the very beginnings of written communication to the far-reaches of space, to a showcase of diverse cultures waiting to be discovered.

At the end of every day, guests are sent back to their resorts alternately exhausted by their odyssey and seduced by IllumiNations: Reflections of Earth—a moving display of fireworks, lasers and music that imparts a message of hope and unity.

It's all spelled out on the dedication plaque:

"To all who come to this place of joy, hope and friendship, welcome. Epcot Center is inspired by Walt Disney's creative genius. Here, human achievements are celebrated through imagination, the wonders of enterprise, and concepts of a future that promise new and exciting benefits for all. May Epcot Center entertain, inform and inspire. And, above all, may it instill a new sense of belief and pride in man's ability to shape a world that offers hope to people everywhere."

It's an inspiring mission statement that delivers. Or it could be the frozen margarita stand between Mexico and Norway. (A little pricey at $9.50—or $14.50 if you prefer Patron—but very cooling and quite potent.)

What's New at Epcot

Test Track, the fast-moving, giant slot-car attraction at Epcot has been given a complete re-do by Disney's Imagineers. At one time themed to resemble an auto manufacturer's test facility, it now looks like something out of the film, *Tron.* Neon accents, black light displays and futuristic designs have replaced the factory-like feel of the old attraction. Guests spend the pre-show creating their own car, weighing elements like capability, efficiency, responsiveness and power. **Test Track 2.0** then puts these would-be car designers behind the wheel, whipping them through twists, turns and straightaways—at times reaching sixty-five miles-per-hour. The post-show scores their designs, rating them against fellow designers and recent top scores.

Disney's move to interactivity continues with **Agent P's World Showcase Adventure**. This game drops guests into the world of the smart, funny Disney Channel cartoon, *Phineas and Ferb*. Participants pick up their interactive handheld device (read: really old-style flip-phone) and embark on their adventure. Recruitment centers are located at the Odyssey Bridge, the Norway pavilion, the Italy pavilion or near the International Gateway. Agent P—Perry the Platypus—leads you through one of several World Showcase pavilions, triggering interactive elements and providing narrative and clues along the way. The games are relegated to one pavilion per-mission, which is nice because you're not hoofing it from one side of the World Showcase to the other. Games last about 30 minutes.

The World Showcase's France pavilion was never really an option when looking for a quick lunch. Sure, the bakery was adequate, but we always skipped it in favor of something more. Now, that's all changed. **Les Halles Boulangerie and Patisserie** is a greatly improved dining spot with an expanded menu. Grab a sandwich, some soup or a fantastic dessert at this upgraded eatery. The atmosphere and food are as authentic as anything you'll find in the World Showcase.

Just around the corner, **Monsieur Paul** (formerly Bistro de Paris) provides gourmet dining in a refurbished setting. Don't look for a big, flashy sign. Instead, keep an eye out for an understated awning and a small plaque. It all gives the impression that you need to know the secret handshake to get inside. The word here is "elegant." You might also use "expensive," but a look inside this top-notch restaurant will confirm that.

The noble funnel cake at the American Adventure may now have a worthy opponent across the World Showcase Lagoon. Peckish Epcottians can now head to the Refreshment Port to order up their own **cronut**. Only don't call it a cronut because the term is copyrighted. You can get a croissant-donut, however, which is the same thing.

Epcot doesn't have the number of traditional "ride" type attractions that a park like the Magic Kingdom does. While there are fewer thrillers, they are of the "big bang" type, and everyone heads straight for them. You've heard it before, but it's worth saying again: You'll need to get there early if you want to avoid lengthy queues.

Epcot is separated into two major sections: **Future World** and the **World Showcase**. Future World is located at the front of the park, while the World Showcase is situated around the lagoon at the center of the park.

Future World

Soarin'—Guided through the pre-show by "Patrick Your Flight Attendant" (actor Patrick Warburton), guests are launched on a breathtaking journey over the Golden State. The ride vehicle simulates a hang-glider type flight, navigating over the Golden Gate Bridge, national parks, orange groves and even Disneyland.

Mousejunkie U   *In one scene, guests fly over the PGA West golf course in La Quinta. A golfer drives a ball off the tee, which seems to "fly" right by guests' heads. According to a Walt Disney World exec—who divulged this information to me at great personal risk—the man hitting the golf ball is former Walt Disney Company Chief Executive Michael Eisner.*

The ride provides a bird's-eye view, and a rather convincing experience. The ride vehicle sways gently, and appropriate scents are piped-in during certain scenes. Rumors are circulating that the attraction will be updated with a new film in the not-so-distant future.

Soarin' is where you want to be headed as soon as the ropes drop and the park opens. You, and very likely 90 percent of the other guests, will be heading in the same direction. Walk up past Spaceship Earth, bear right, and walk straight through Innoventions toward The Land pavilion. Soarin' is located inside on the first level. Just follow the crowd.

Mousejunkie Choice   *Soarin' is a perfect example of the ideal attraction according to Walt Disney: It's something parents and grandparents can experience alongside their children and grandchildren. It's a mild ride that provides just enough thrill to keep your blood pumping (which is to say not much, unless you don't like heights.) The bird's eye tour of the Golden State is breathtaking. Feel free to take the youngest member of your party and sit them next to the oldest. It's a top-notch attraction that any visitor can enjoy.*

Head inside the pavilion, go down the stairs, high-five the cast members greeting you with giant, four-fingered Mickey gloves, and prepare to take flight.

⭐ **The Straight Dope** *The Land pavilion is somewhat inconveniently located from the rest of the gate-busters, so once you've hit Soarin' and The Land and maybe had something to eat, you've pretty much exhausted that pavilion.*

Duration: Six minutes.

Loads: Slowly. Either get there early or plan on using a FastPass+.

Living With the Land—The natural follow-up to Soarin' (its load area is right next to Soarin's exit), Living with the Land is part dark ride, part boat ride, part greenhouse tour and part lecture.

Wait, I know you probably don't want to be educated while on vacation, but trust me—there are alligators, so it's

MOUSEJUNKIE WALT Soarin' is one of my all-time favorite rides for a very specific reason—it fulfills Walt Disney's original goal. It's a ride me, my grandfather, and my four-year-old nephew all went on together. It's something families can do together, and it's amazing in that respect.

awesome. It's actually a really interesting look at agriculture all over the world and the work Epcot is doing to revolution-ize farming.

Duration: 15 minutes.

Loads: Quickly.

Spaceship Earth—Yes, "the big golf ball" is a ride. Spaceship Earth takes guests on a journey of discovery, examining how communication and technology have changed the world. Audio animatronic figures populate life-size diorama scenes starting in the Stone Age, going through the renaissance, and into the future. It's a slow-moving ride that underwent a refurb not too long ago, allowing for some interactive elements in the second half.

Duration: 15 minutes.

Loads: Quickly. The attraction's ride vehicles are constantly rotating through and moving people up into the attraction proper.

Since my park touring "type" is The Lazy Guy (which basically means I don't like blisters and I covet bench-time), Spaceship Earth has always been one of my favorites. It's dark, cool, slow moving and it tells an interesting tale. I park my butt in one of the blue, hard plastic seats, and for the next fifteen minutes I'm enthralled. I look for hidden Mickeys and try to pick up subtle details the Imagineers may have hidden among the many scenes.

A ride through communication history is actually very meditative. Everyone usually stops talking, and since it's slow moving it allows for some inner-dialogue time. Without fail, I always fall into a zen-like space and think about our trip, the day ahead, our dining reservations, how lucky I am to be there and how we'll end our day with IllumiNations: Reflections of Earth. It never fails to relax and inspire.

The Straight Dope *Don't feel like you need to rush to Spaceship Earth right away. Lines can form right after the rope-drop, slowing progress. The lines tend to diminish greatly as the day goes on.*

Mission: Space—Experience pre-flight butterflies, the exhilaration of liftoff, all the G-forces of a slingshot around the moon, and a hair-raising finale that'll have you catching your breath. And potentially your lunch.

This simulator puts you and your team on a rocket to Mars. The adventure includes a few close calls, some convincing tactile experiences and a couple of real thrills in the form of visual, audio and tangible sensations.

Guests have, on occasion, complained of motion sickness after experiencing this attraction. The ride compartment sits at the end of a centrifuge, which spins and places a sustained 2.5G on riders. You really don't feel the spinning, but it's absolutely clear that something is going on. The G-forces feel amazing, and there's a weightless sequence that's surprisingly effective.

Mission: Space offers guests two ride options: the original (orange side), and a more mild experience (the green side) that cuts out the centrifuge element. Upon entering the queue, a cast member will ask which side you'd prefer. He or she will hand you an orange card or a green card. Orange indicates you prefer the original, more intense ride, while a green card indicates that you answer to the name "Sally." (Any insult to anyone named "Sally" is purely unintentional. It's just an expression. Sally is actually a wonderful name. My grandmother was named Sally.) (No she wasn't.)

I found the milder side to be only slightly less disorienting, since the visual effects are what made me feel queasy.

Duration: Five minutes.

Loads: Slowly.

Test Track—Design a vehicle and then take it on a test spin through a series of testing grounds to evaluate the car's performance. A futuristic, sleek look gives this attraction an exciting, experimental feel.

The high-speed fan favorite underwent a re-imaging recently, and while the pre-show and storyline has changed, it has retained all of its thrill. Guests hop into vehicles that hold six people and take part in braking, cornering, maneuvering and accelerating. The finale has the car pushed to its limits as it blasts out onto a track that encircles the Test Track building, reaching 65 miles-per-hour.

Duration: 20 minutes.

Loads: Slowly.

MOUSEJUNKIE KATIE If your kid likes fast rides, then go straight to Test Track. It's the fastest ride in the park. You're like a crash test dummy, going through a series of events in the car like low and high temperatures (you don't want the ride to break down in that room,) crashing, going up hills and then finally outside. When the car goes outside is when it gets real fast. It speeds around the track, above a parking lot and if you look on the other side you can see the park. It's one of my favorite rides.

Universe of Energy—Ellen DeGeneres, Jamie Lee Curtis, Alex Trebek and Bill Nye the Science Guy host this journey through time that offers a look at how energy makes the world go around. The attraction starts with a funny pre-show that finds Ellen tanking in a game of *Jeopardy!* against her former college roommate, Jamie Lee Curtis. Bill Nye rescues Ellen and takes her on a trip back to the prehistoric age— that's where things pick up.

A massive, moving theater slowly glides through the rest of the show, giving guests a close-up look at some animatronic dinosaurs.

Duration: 40 minutes.

Loads: Quickly. Head inside and grab a bench along the wall or have a seat on the floor. It's nice and cool, and the preshow keeps things moving.

★**The Straight Dope** *On particularly hot days, be sure to visit The Universe of Energy. It's air conditioned, dark, and lasts about forty minutes. Several of the Mousejunkies have been known to take advantage of these factors to steal a quick nap. Though not all at the same time. That would just be strange.*

Journey Into Imagination with Figment—Figment the purple dragon pops in and out of this dark ride where guests ride through The Imagination Institute. Hosted by Dr. Nigel Channing (Monty Python alum Eric Idle), ride vehicles cart guests through a number of "imagination" experiments where Figment runs rampant, creating both chaos and entertainment. (Author's note: Allegedly.)

Figment and I have a tangled history. I'm not a fan of the attraction, which is now in its third incarnation. There are, of course, those who love it and are confounded by my dislike of the cloying dragon. The cheese-meter needle is pinned throughout this ride.

Duration: Six of the longest minutes ever.

Loads: Quickly.

The Seas with Nemo and Friends—Board your "clamobiles" and take a trip down to The Sea Base. Characters from the Pixar film *Finding Nemo* follow along, somehow swimming alongside fish of the non-animated type inside the main massive aquarium tank.

Essentially, it's a fun way to get guests deeper into the pavilion.

Once you've arrived at The Sea Base, which is essentially an aquarium, there are dozens of aquatic exhibits to check out. The two-story viewing area into the main tank is hypnotic, and provides an amazing view at more than 3,000 types of marine life.

Turtle Talk with Crush—This show where the perpetually spaced-out sea turtle from *Finding Nemo* interacts with guests is a can't-miss. Guests sit in a small theater with a large screen "looking out into the ocean." Crush swims into view, talks a little about ocean life and engages youngsters from behind his "tank." The interactive element is outstanding. Crush speaks to guests, refers to what they're wearing, who they're with and enjoys a little back-and-forth during each performance.

Duration: 15 minutes.

Loads: Moderately. The theater empties and re-fills at the completion of each show.

Club Cool—Essentially a store for Coca Cola, its sponsor, this area is located next to the Fountain of Nations behind Spaceship Earth. Guests are given a chance to sample unusually flavored soda from around the world, and/or buy Coca Cola merchandise.

The fun part comes in the sampling, and attempting to trick your friends into trying an awful concoction from Italy called Beverly. It tastes like a mixture of gin and aspirin, and has garnered a reputation, rightfully so, for its nastiness.

Here's a list of soda flavors available in Club Cool:

➤ Beverly (a bitter concoction from Italy)
➤ Guarana Kuat (berry flavored from Brazil)
➤ Sparletta (a raspberry cream soda from Zimbabwe)
➤ Bibo (kiwi mango flavored from South Africa)
➤ Inca Kola (tastes like bubble gum—from Peru)
➤ VegitaBeta (a Japanese apricot and fruit drink)
➤ Fanta Melon Frosty (melon flavored from Thailand)
➤ Fanta Pineapple (perhaps not shockingly, it's pineapple flavored from Greece)

Innoventions—At the center of Future World, just behind Spaceship Earth, sits Innoventions East and West. Both buildings house interactive exhibits, examples of new technology and a chance to play some Disney-themed video games.

★ **The Straight Dope** *Need to get a few character pictures? The Epcot Character Spot is a fantastic place to do this. There's an entire indoor section adjacent to Innoventions where many the Disney biggies are located: Mickey, Minnie, Donald, Goofy, Pluto and Chip and Dale. Line 'em up and shoot away. You can either use your own camera or take advantage of Disney's Photopass photographers.*

We worked our way through the **Epcot Character Spot** one morning when we got to the end and prepared to head back outside. We turned the corner and who was standing there? Belle. All by herself. There wasn't even a character

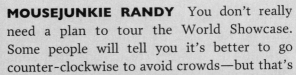

MOUSEJUNKIE RANDY You don't really need a plan to tour the World Showcase. Some people will tell you it's better to go counter-clockwise to avoid crowds—but that's really not the case. Just go in and explore every country. Check out the little corners. That's where you'll find the most rewarding details. And make sure to catch the street performers throughout the day. They're some of the best free shows in all of Disney World. They're not on any map, but they're all fun and interesting.

handler in sight. She kneeled down, opened her arms, and my then-three-year-old ran to her. She had nearly five minutes completely alone, just visiting with Belle and comparing outfits and making small talk. It was one of those moments that can't be duplicated or planned for.

You've now hit the biggies in Future World. If time allows or if you can't think of any reason not to, visit Imagination! on your way to the World Showcase. Or you can skip it and head straight for the World Showcase Lagoon and make your next biggest decision of the day: Clockwise or counter-clockwise?

The World Showcase

The World Showcase boasts eleven pavilions representing various countries from around the world. Clockwise, in order, they are: Mexico, Norway, China, Germany, Italy, the American

Adventure, Japan, Morocco, France, the United Kingdom, and Canada. Each country's pavilion is staffed by cast members who are from that particular country. Spending the day strolling through the World Showcase is a great way to get a taste of different cultures—both figuratively and literally.

Spend a little time in each of the countries. Be friendly. Say hello. It's a great opportunity to speak to someone from another culture and to try out what you learned in some of your high school foreign language classes.

Each country's pavilion has a table service restaurant and at least one quick service option. Several have attractions, all have shopping, and each offers a chance for the adults in your party to grab a beverage. This is just one of the elements that sets it apart from the Magic Kingdom. The Magic Kingdom is a dry park. Epcot, however, is not.

And the benches. Oh, the benches. There are benches everywhere. Glorious, restive, inviting benches designed for camping out and enjoying said adult beverages. The World Showcase promenade runs 1.2 miles—a pittance for Mousejunkies such as Deb, J or Ryan. But for some it can seem to be an uphill marathon.

★ **Awesome/Stupid Disney Idea** *I'm going to throw this one out there to the Walt Disney Company for free—consider it a service. I envision a theme park where roaming teams of cast members carry benches. A tired guest*

pulls over to the side of the walkway, out of the traffic pat-
tern, raises his or her hand. That pair of cast members—let's
call them the "Bench Team"—rushes to that person's aid and
places the mobile bench behind the person's knees. The guest
sits, and all is right with the world. Roaming Bench Teams.
You know, in print, this looks pretty pathetic. How about I
just get skinny and gain some endurance.

If you're traveling with children, take advantage of the
World Showcase Kidcot Fun Stops. Kids are presented with a
mask which they can color on and decorate at craft areas normally located deep within each of the pavilions. This forces
guests to really visit each pavilion, talk to cast members from
that country, and it gives kids something to do in an environment that otherwise has little in the way of traditional theme
park rides.

The World Tour

Mexico: An authentic looking (as far as I know—I've only
been to Tijuana, and it didn't look like this) Mexican marketplace tempts with (what I can only assume are) authentic wares. The Mexico pavilion, constructed to look like a
Mesoamerican pyramid, represents perhaps the finest Inside/
Outside in all of Walt Disney World.

An Inside/Outside is when you enter a building and it's
designed to give the impression you are outside. It's my
preferred way of getting outdoors. It's temperature-con-
trolled, and the chances of me getting a sunburn in an Inside/
Outside are virtually nil. Though I am of Irish ancestry and

my translucent skin can become painfully charred by even thinking about the sun.

Entering the pavilion, the marketplace is spread out in front of you under a starry sky. In the distance a volcano rumbles over a Mayan pyramid as boatloads of guests on the Gran Fiesta Tour Starring the Three Caballeros glide silently past diners.

The Gran Fiesta Tour Starring the Three Caballeros is a seven-minute boat ride that follows the adventures of Donald Duck, Jose Carioca and Panchito. The three are to sing at a soiree, but Donald has gone missing.

The Gran Fiesta Tour comes off as a rather slapdash retrofit of the former El Rio del Tiempo. Kids might find the Donald Duck storyline engaging, but it has stripped the attraction of any dignity and seems to run opposite of the park's theme. It teaches guests nothing about the diverse people and regions of Mexico.

Fairly new to the Mexico pavilion is a tequila bar called **La Cava del Tequila**, which in the literal translation means "I bet I can kick tequila's butt. Pass me some of those chips."

MOUSEJUNKIE RYAN I keep riding the Gran Fiesta Tour starring the Three Caballeros, hoping it will get better. But much like with crème brulee, I continue to be disappointed.

La Cava del Tequila is a somewhat dark, cozy rest stop offering a vast array of tequilas to sample. It's a comfortable location and it becomes incredibly easy to wile away hours without realizing how off-track your touring plan has become.

I ventured into the cavern-like establishment with Mousejunkie Barry during one trip and ordered up a tequila flight. Barry had a margarita.

Our server told us one brand of tequila was "Scorpion." Why? "Because there's a dead scorpion in the bottom of the bottle."

Of course.

I was feeling brave, and maybe just slightly tequilaed (that's a real condition—I checked), so I asked if I could eat the scorpion. I figured if I was ever going to eat a poisonous arachnid, it might as well be now. Our waitress told me she'd be right back with it, and suggested I "don't eat the pincers." She said they were too hard to chew.

I manned up and was totally prepared, only to be disappointed that they didn't have one available. Another guest had beaten me to the questionable tasting.

Barry had a few suggestions:

"Can you just catch a palmetto bug outside, drown it and give it to him?"

"Is there a mouse you can just stick in a shot glass?"

"Can you pour a shot over a dog and let him lick the fur?"

None of these things came to pass. Regardless, we left the Mexico pavilion very happy with our experience.

Norway—Designed to look like a tenth-century Norwegian village, an austere stave church dominates the lagoon-facing portion of the pavilion. A series of shops—where guests can buy staggeringly expensive sweaters, sweets or plastic Viking helmets—lead back into Norway's attraction, which, at this point, is under construction. Old favorite, Maelstrom—a boat/dark-ride—has been excised in favor of a *Frozen*-themed attraction. Though the film, which has taken over the planet, isn't officially set in Norway, it's close enough for Disney.

In addition, Norway has the most statuesque and usually blondest cast members. A friend of the family is from Norway, and taught me the only Norwegian phrase I believe I will ever need: *"Jeg snakker, ikke Norsk."* ("I do not know how to speak Norwegian.")

There are two mandatory tasks that must be accomplished on every visit to the Norway pavilion. I must try on a tiny plastic Viking helmet, and I must try out my single line of Norwegian on a cast member. Some laugh, some stare at me in a confused manner, and Amy usually just stands behind me and shakes her head in embarrassment.

China: The brilliantly reconstructed Temple of Heaven hosts the Circle-Vision 360 film, *Reflections of China*. The film, hosted by ancient Chinese poet Li Bai, showcases sweeping images of the vast country, focusing on seven cities and regions.

Tragically, there are no benches in the theater.

The rest of the pavilion is laid out with ponds, bridges, and a pagoda. Inside, guests can see historic representations of Chinese artifacts such as the famous terra cotta warriors.

Characters from the Disney film *Mulan* appear here, and the Dragon Legend Acrobats perform daily.

The Straight Dope   *The temple in China is acoustically perfect. Stand in the direct center and listen to yourself speak. You'll hear your own voice as others hear you.*

It works amazingly well. If you see a guy looking up at the impossibly ornate ceiling inside the Temple of Heaven and talking to himself, that'd be me.

Germany: Guests are welcomed into an almost impossibly perfect representation of a fairytale German village, complete with a glockenspiel and a statue of St. George slaying a dragon.

A perpetual state of Oktoberfest exists, with brew and German food flowing in equal portions in the Biergarten restaurant, which lies in the back of St. George's Platz.

Next to the pavilion is a miniature train and village, a fantastic place to slow the pace and meditate on the incredible handiwork that went into creating the small scale hamlet.

Italy: A mix of beautiful architecture is punctuated with a recreation of St. Mark's Campanile. This fully functioning bell tower draws guests inward, past replicas of the Doge's palace in Venice and the exterior of the Sistine Chapel.

The landscaping here includes olive trees and grapevines, adding a seductive and evocative feel to the reproduction of St. Mark's Square.

At the rear of the pavilion is the Neptune Fountain, and the new Via Napoli pizzeria.

The American Adventure: A massive, colonial-style building houses the America pavilion's multimedia presentation, "The American Adventure." Narrated by audio animatronic figures of Benjamin Franklin and Mark Twain, guests are taken on an American history lesson from the earliest settlers up through brief glimpses of the terrorist attacks of 9/11.

The show's theme, "Golden Dream," is part of the sweeping, emotional finale that gives a glimpse of the American experience and what it took to build the country. Film, art, animatronics and music combine to present an impressive and at-times, emotional, tribute.

The Straight Dope *Do not miss the Voices of Liberty, an a cappella group, which performs in the rotunda of the American Adventure, an acoustically superior venue. If you visit around Christmas, the Voices of Liberty will perform classic Christmas carols. The group has recently added their own version of Disney's "Let it Go" from the film,* Frozen. *Because* Frozen *has taken over the world. Check your park map for times.*

Mousejunkie U   *Take a close look at the clock on the main building of the American Adventure pavilion. Instead of the Roman numeral, "IV," it instead reads, "IIII." Imagineers say it's to avoid confusion and make it more legible from a distance.*

Japan: The castle in Japan, visible from the waterfront all around the World Showcase, is a replica of the Shirasagi-Jo, a seventeenth-century fortress considered one of the most well-preserved of its like. A torii gate stands out in the water in front of the Japanese pavilion, while venturing further back into the pavilion reveals beautiful gardens and shopping opportunities.

The Straight Dope   *Walk all the way to the back of the pavilion, go into the shop and take a left. There you'll find a counter where you can sample several different types of sake. Sip on it while shopping for a relaxing break.*

The Matsuriza, or traditional Taiko drummers, are part of the natural background soundtrack that saturates the fabric of Epcot. The sound of the drums echoes all the way across the lagoon, mixing with the piercing horns of the Friendships that ferry guests around the World Showcase and to and from the BoardWalk Resort area.

The waterfront along the Japan pavilion is a great place to watch the nightly IllumiNations: Reflections of Earth performance. You get a great view of the floating globe centerpiece, and an easy exit via the International Gateway.

Morocco: One of the most finely detailed of all the World Showcase pavilions, Morocco was designed to evoke the feel of a city from this north African country. A replica of a minaret in Marrakesh stands overlooking the intricately constructed alleyways and back rooms. Nineteen Moroccan artists spent months recreating the intricate, colorful tile masterpieces of their homeland.

The shops tucked into the maze-like pavilion sell everything from musical instruments to clothing to fezzes (because fezzes are cool, now.)

The Treasures of Morocco is a forty-five-minute tour designed to teach guests more about the culture, people and history of this north African land. This type of tour is unique to the Morocco pavilion.

Plus—belly dancers!

France: Wander through a neighborhood in Paris from La Belle Epoque, complete with shops, fountains and a distant view of the Eiffel Tower. The central Florida version of the city of lights truly comes alive after dark. The bubbling fountain outside Chefs de France is lit up, creating one of the most beautiful spots in a park packed with them.

The Straight Dope *If you're entering Epcot through the International Gateway, stop in at the Boulangerie Paitisserie les Halles—the greatly-expanded, much-improved bakery in this truly evocative location. It opens at 9 A.M.—a full two hours before the World Showcase.*

The pavilion's film, Impressions de France, provides a tour of the country set to stirring classical music.

An amazing chair-balancing/juggling/acrobatic act, Serveur Amusant, is a can't-miss. It is staged just outside the entrance of Chefs de France several times daily.

★**Mousejunkie U**   *The replica Eiffel Tower stands 103 feet tall. The real Eiffel Tower in Paris stands 1,063 feet tall.*

The United Kingdom: A tea shop, authentic phone boxes and a neighborhood pub turn this pavilion into a small slice of the United Kingdom.

The Rose & Crown Pub is a cozy watering hole, offering a fantastic place to pull up a pint of Guinness and grab a seat. It also serves as the UK's table service restaurant.

★**The Straight Dope**   *Photo opportunities with Winnie the Pooh characters are often available in the back of the Toy Soldier shop. It's an out-of-the-way location with very little foot traffic, so the lines are often quite short.*

A picturesque garden tucked in the back of the pavilion is another great spot for a breather. This dad enjoyed one of his beloved benches while Mousejunkie Amy and our seven-year-old wound their way through the hedge maze near the back of a picturesque park. But don't get the impression the UK pavilion is all about relaxation. The British Airwaves provide ripping renditions of tunes made famous by British invasion groups and bands from the '60s and '70s. They perform several times daily in a gazebo just off a large garden area.

Canada: But where is Don Cherry? Do they serve Timbits? Where are the hockey rinks? Where is Rush?

Visitors to this World Showcase pavilion will learn it is so much more than those truly Canadian, yet already quite well known cultural exports. Canada's vast wilderness is illustrated by the splashing waterfalls cascading down a mountainside, and its majesty plays out in a towering version of the Chateau Laurier.

Located near the Le Cellier restaurant, the Circle-Vision 360 movie, *O Canada!*, hosted by Martin Short, was updated in 2007 and goes even further to show the many faces of our neighbor to the north. The updated theme from the film revisits the original, which is now sung by Canadian Idol Eva Avila.

Awesome/Stupid Disney Idea *There's been a great wailing and gnashing of teeth since fan-favorite Off Kilter left the pavilion. I have an awesome/stupid idea—Get Rush in there for a few months. I know it sounds crazy. Just consider it.*

Soused with the Mouse: An Epcot Tradition Exposed

For those drinking around the world: You have reached the finish line (assuming you went clockwise). Please gather your things and move quietly to the exit. While it does seem like a fun way to travel the World Showcase, I've seen the results. And it's not pretty. In Mexico, it's an exciting start to the day. By Italy it's riotously funny. By the United Kingdom it's just sloppy.

However, in the interest of better serving the reader, the  researchers down at Mousejunkie Labs conducted a highly controlled experiment in order to lift the veil of secrecy that surrounds Drinking Around the World. That is, starting at one side of the World Showcase at Epcot, and ordering an alcoholic beverage at each country while traversing the entire loop—from Canada to Mexico.

Drinking Around the World is an activity alternately whispered about in hushed tones or blurted out to no one in particular in slurred torrents of indecipherable yammering. Usually somewhere near the Germany pavilion. Convinced that it could be done without causing a scene and with some dignity (read: still wearing pants by the end), the Mousejunkies huddled and came away with a plan. Consider it a service, as it were. For the betterment of all Disney guests, we would conduct our own Epcot pub crawl.

Drinking Around the World, simply, means partaking of 11 drinks throughout the course of the day. It may not sound like much for the experienced imbiber, but in practice the drinks can start to come quickly. Without proper preparation and focus, it can end poorly. If unsuccessful, draftees can find themselves broke, sick, sunburned and lost—and all joking and hyperbole aside, potentially tossed out of the park. It happens. Cast member harassment is a common side effect when drinking around the world, something that no Mousejunkie would take part in.

As we prepared to embark on our journey, we agreed to adhere to three simple ground rules:

1. An alcoholic beverage must be ordered and consumed at each country's pavilion. The circuit must be completed before the 9 P.M. showing of IllumiNations: Reflections of Earth.
2. Hands-off the Cast Members. Cast Members must be treated with the utmost respect at all times.
3. Also, avoid engaging other guests. Especially the bigger ones with neck tattoos. No matter how bulletproof we get.

When the call went out for brave souls to take on this challenge, Mousejunkie Walt stepped into the breach. He put all thoughts of his own well being out of his head. (More room for margaritas that way.) He knew it would be risky. He knew that it could result in a debilitating hangover that could find him with a head the size of Mickey's the next morning. But he also knew that he was working for a something greater than himself. For this reason, Walt signed on and answered the call to act as the stunt liver.

As your humble scribe, my job would be to follow our stunt liver around the World Showcase, taking notes and reporting progress. And if forced, I would join Mousejunkie Walt in sampling the wares, if only to support him in this noble effort. And only under great duress and protest. A journalist must remain completely detached and impartial. Except when he is thirsty. Or when he doesn't feel like it.

Having had some experience in occasional overindul-
gence, we knew that a proper foundation must be built. We
would begin construction at the Kona Café in the Polynesian
Resort. It would be the base upon which the rest of the day
would be built. It would be constructed of alcohol-absorb-
ing elements: Eggs, cheese, potatoes, hash, and the most
important and magical of elements, hollandaise sauce. This
alone would assure a healthy and energetic afternoon. Oh,
and a Wasabi Mary (Absolut pepper vodka, wasabi, spices
and tomato juice. In my case an extra helping of chili sauce
was brought out to kick up the pain.) Yes, I realized this was
not the best idea. But who can pass up something called a
Wasabi Mary? It was on the breakfast menu, along with a
mimosa. Mimosas are what you drink while knitting. Wasabi
Marys are what you drink if your name is Spartacus. Actually,
Boilermakers are. But I'm not that stupid. As far as you know.
Obviously, the testosterone level was high as we prepared for
the day's challenge.

Walt chose to gird his innards with the famous Tonga
Toast—nearly half a loaf of sourdough, fried and stuffed
with bananas. Sitting like a three-pound stone in his stomach (which translates to approximately 4.5 kilometers for
our European friends), the Tonga Toast was ready to absorb
anything unhealthy that may have been tossed its way. Walt
was ready.

We boarded the monorail outside the Polynesian and a
short time later found ourselves deposited at the other end
into Epcot. With Spaceship Earth looming above and the
World Showcase just behind it, our mission was upon us. We

wound through Innoventions Plaza, and just as we crossed over into the World Showcase, Walt stopped. He looked left toward Mexico and considered tequila. He looked right toward Canada and took the first step on the journey. We knew at that point there was no turning back.

Except when we got to the Canada pavilion. Because the beer stand was closed.

We wandered around aimlessly for a while, seeking our starting point but finding no such purchase. Thankfully, the Rose & Crown Pub beckoned in the distance. Assured by Cast Members in Canada that the beer cart would soon be operational, we opted to kick off in the UK pavilion and return to Canada later.

The United Kingdom: Walt ordered a Bass ale. I couldn't necessarily toast our quest with a glass of air, so I had the air replaced with Strongbow Cider. We were on our way.

A quick backtrack to Canada found us standing in front of the beer cart. As Walt ordered his Labatt Blue, we started talking to the Cast Member, who asked what we had planned for the day. We told her our plan to Drink Around the World. She eyed us warily.

"It can get scary," she admitted. "We get these big guys coming through, and if they start in Mexico and end in Canada they can be really drunk. And we have to shut them down if they're visibly intoxicated. I've been physically threatened, yelled at.... We just call security but it's not fun."

I felt it appropriate that we were reminded of the potential consequences of acting like a pinhead. We could face the traditional Canadian punishment: You go to the box, you know, two minutes by yourself. You feel shame—and then you get free.

We doubled our vow to treat cast members exceptionally well, and struck out toward France. We loitered for a brief time as Walt finished his Canadian beer, before winding our way to a shop around back for a glass of merlot.

It seemed as though things were beginning to move rather quickly as we found ourselves standing in the Tangerine Café in Morocco, holding a cold Moroccan beer. Walt had consumed four drinks in a relatively short time. It was time to start thinking about pacing ourselves. We grabbed a seat and sipped slowly as we watched the day go by.

It was at this point that this whole experiment started to seem like such a great idea, that if there were an award ceremony for amazing ideas, this one would win first prize. A cool, breezy day in Epcot with a head full of happiness? It could only be improved if we were being transported around the World Showcase in litters borne by supermodels. Really strong ones.

Truly, whoever came up with the idea for this magical pub crawl would kick Einstein's butt in a smart guy contest.

With Morocco now a distant memory, we turned our attention to the east (figuratively.) The Taiko drummers pounded rhythmically as we marched toward the walls of the Japanese fortress in front of us. Like two warriors striding into battle (hey, the whole fortress thing left us feeling like we were in *The Seven Samurai*), we strode into the shop with Bushido leading us.

That bravado was soon replaced with really strange facial expressions and the pursing of lips in a decidedly unwarriorlike manner, since neither of us were really fans of the cold sake.

Here's what we learned so far: Plum wine is also offered by the glass. It's got to be better.

After five drinks, we found ourselves at home in the American Adventure. Familiarity embraced us, as we each ordered up a Sam Adams. We walked with our brews and struck up a conversation with a woman now known as "the best cast member ever." Friendly, talkative and down to earth, she kept us company as we finished our beer in time to catch a showing of The American Adventure inside.

Full of patriotism (and not to mention beverages), we passed through Italy (Fumaio wine); Germany (Spaten Oktoberfest); and a Tsing Tao in China.

An $8 Carlsberg is all that stood between us and the finish line: Mexico. Normally, this would be a simple matter of which beer to choose. But there was a wild card facing us that we hadn't really thought about: Tequila.

La Cava del Tequila, a new tequila bar in the bowels of the Mexico pavilion, called out to us. We could not ignore its exotic beacon, and bellied up to the bar.

Walt ordered a Clasica margarita for $12.50, and grabbed a bench outside the bar to reflect on our findings.

First, a disclaimer: We approached this challenge like a pair of forty-year-olds, not twenty-five-year-olds. What does this mean? Walt ordered and consumed a drink in every country along the way. But there may have been a

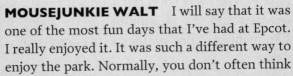

MOUSEJUNKIE WALT   I will say that it was one of the most fun days that I've had at Epcot. I really enjoyed it. It was such a different way to enjoy the park. Normally, you don't often think about going down there to do that. It was such an adult thing to do. I love the countries anyway. I love Epcot, seeing the different cultures and talking to the cast members and wandering through the pavilions. When you think of Germany though, you think of beer. When you think of France you think of wine. When you think of Mexico, it's tequila. I'm not talking about falling down drunk—just about having good time.

We went through the entire World Showcase, taking pictures in every country. We wanted to shoot with something representing the country we were in. So we'd have pictures of us wearing a fez or a sombrero and posting it online. I started getting comments on those pictures immediately. I've had people say they wanted to fly down and take part the next time we plan on drinking around the World. You can go down with a group of people and that's the entire day.

A little advice though: I would always do it the way we did it. I'd always start in Canada and end up in Mexico. Why? I love margaritas. Everywhere else is beer or wine or sake. By time you work your way around to Mexico, you have enough in you to just sit down and relax with a flight of tequilas. Starting with that would've made the day a little rougher.

little left in the glass before we moved on, and I may have lightened his load a bit by sharing at a couple points. Our intent was to complete the spirit of the challenge, not bleurgh all over Epcot.

Second, the final tally for Walt's drinks came in around $150 with tip included. It could easily go much higher if we opted for choices such as the Nuvo sparkling vodka in France or the Campo Azul Extra Anejo tequila in Mexico for $20 a shot.

He had survived the challenge, and emerged a wizened man. (And, to be honest, not exactly soused. We were in it for the fun, not the chaos.)

We finished up just in time for IllumiNations: Reflections of Earth—a fireworks/laser/pyrotechnic show set to music and performed every night over the World Showcase Lagoon. It's viewable from anywhere in the World Showcase, though a few locations are more sought-after than others.

Just before the show is launched, the lights around the park are dimmed, leaving only the lagoon torches burning. A narrator sets the scene:

> "Good evening. On behalf of Walt Disney World, the place where dreams come true, we welcome all of you to Epcot and the World Showcase. We've gathered here tonight, around the fire, as people of all lands have gathered for thousands and thousands of years before us; to share the light and to share a story—an amazing story, as old as time itself but still being written. And though each of us has our own individual stories to tell, a true adventure emerges when we bring them all together as one. We hope you enjoy our story tonight; Reflections of Earth."

MOUSEJUNKIE WALT IllumiNations is one of my favorite things to do, and I always make sure to watch from the Canada pavilion. Most people say you can see IllumiNations from anywhere, and that is true. But to get the best view, head for Canada—and here's why First, there are not a lot of trees in the way. More importantly, you're looking across the lagoon at more countries than anywhere else in the park. Why does this matter? During a certain point in the display the countries are lit up by brilliant white lights. So when the white lights come on, you get a much better view. I've watched IllumiNations from all over the park, and when you're on the other side near Japan or Germany, you look across and see Canada and England. That's it. It's not as good. If you're in Canada you can see the American pavilion and everything to the left of it from there.

Low drums begin to sound as a single rocket hurtles through the night sky. When it explodes it sets off a display of fire, sound, fury, and hope in three acts: Chaos, order, and celebration. The music, reflecting each act, is alternately wild, introspective, and triumphant.

⭐**Mousejunkie Choice** *Illuminations: Reflections of Earth is one of the best things you can experience at Walt Disney World—period. As the sun begins to set, the lights* *around the World Showcase begin to blink on. The torches along the waterline blaze to life, and guests start to line up around the lagoon. When the park is plunged into darkness and a single rocket is launched overhead, it all begins. The whirling music builds to a crescendo as the sky is set alight. The entire production conveys a. sense of belonging and peace told entirely through visuals and a moving soundtrack. It is a majestic ending to a day filled with wonder and hope, every time.*

An Illuminations viewing spot near Mexico or Canada will provide the quickest retreat to the buses at the front of the park. Watching from the UK pavilion will get you to the International Gateway—and boats to the Epcot area resorts—in seconds.

Mousejunkie U *If you're leaving the park at night through the main entrance, look down when you get between the Fountain of Nations and Spaceship Earth. The walkway lights up with hundreds of fiber optic lights that pulse, twinkle and shine beneath your feet.*

Between being tossed around by attractions such as Test Track and Mission: Space, walking endlessly through the World Showcase and ultimately being serenaded by an inspiring performance of hope, I have never left Epcot feeling anything less than completely exhausted and happy.

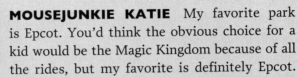 **MOUSEJUNKIE KATIE** My favorite park is Epcot. You'd think the obvious choice for a kid would be the Magic Kingdom because of all the rides, but my favorite is definitely Epcot. There are so many things to do and see while you're traveling around the World Showcase. I like to get the mask and stop at the Kidcot stations to color it and have a cast member stamp it and write something. There are also a few rides or movies that go along with each of the countries in the World Showcase, which are always enjoyable. My favorite is the American Adventure—it's not a movie or a ride, it's kind of both with animatronics like the Hall of Presidents. Plus, it's air conditioned. It's a park you can't skip. Just don't do that.

Disney's Animal Kingdom

THE PROMISE OF PULSE-POUNDING, exotic adventures and heart-racing encounters with a menagerie of beasts might be what lures guests to Disney's Animal Kingdom theme park, but it's the perfectly-realized world that captures their imagination.

The World Walt and Roy Disney first dreamed of, with an army of Imagineers, cast members, and creative types, very likely reached its artistic peak with the opening of Disney's Animal Kingdom. This is not to say that it's the best theme park. The Magic Kingdom has the biggest heart, Epcot's journey is epic and Disney's Hollywood Studios transports guests to another time and place like no other.

There just isn't a theme park on the continent that has perfected its theming, atmosphere, its feel, or its soul—all in one package—as completely as Animal Kingdom.

Joe Rohde, executive designer and vice president, creative, as well as lead designer of the park, has created a convincing world where guests feel as if they have been transported to Africa, Asia and even the prehistoric past.

Hats off to Rohde, because he and his team have set the bar extremely high. This, of course, benefits Mousejunkies everywhere. Because if Disney's Animal Kingdom is now the standard against which new projects are measured, we can look forward to a future of unmatched artistic achievement.

What's New at Disney's Animal Kingdom

Harambe Theater

After six months in exile, the king has returned. The Festival of the Lion King, one of the biggest and best live shows on Walt Disney World property, has fully moved-in to its permanent digs.

The new Harambe Theater, set in the Africa section of the Animal Kingdom theme park, is now host to this colorful, vibrant production. Since it first bowed in April of 1998, the show had been held at a theater in Camp Minnie-Mickey. With expansion plans encroaching on that part of the park, the show was moved to the new theater in Harambe, necessitating a six-month shutdown. The thirty-minute Festival of the Lion King show, a celebration of *The Lion King*-style African culture, remains unchanged since the move—which is a very good thing. The theater isn't markedly different, as guests file in to one of four seating sections. Every seat is a good one, and the glorious, glorious air conditioning makes it a comfortable place to watch this oftentimes emotional production unfold.

One change worth noting is that there is now a FastPass+ queue to deal with. If you haven't selected a FastPass+ for this show, plan on showing up early. FastPass+ holders are allowed in first, filling up a good number of seats. If a seat down close is important, make sure you use one of your FastPass+ selections here.

Wild Africa Trek

A rickety rope bridge spans a chasm over the seemingly treacherous, crocodile-infested waters of the Safi River. As adventurous souls step out onto its aged boards, the bridge creaks and twists just thirty feet above what would appear to be certain death. One misstep will send them hurtling into the nest of toothsome predators.

However, that's not likely to happen.

This particular bridge—and the river it traverses—is located in Walt Disney World, where insurance liability considerations and guest thrills come in equal parts. The crocs and hippos along the path are quite real; it's just that the bridge may not be as rickety as it appears.

It's all part of the Wild Africa Trek. A unique, three-hour tour designed to give guests a one-of-a-kind experience, the Trek takes participants through sections of the park's Pangani Forest and parts of the Harambe Wildlife Reserve not normally open to guests. The environment is incredibly immersive, designed to recreate the natural habitat of its many animals. Just don't call it a zoo.

This VIP, expertly guided expedition is no run-of-the-mill backstage tour. Forget well-worn sidewalks lined with gift shops. The pathways of this trek wind through dense bamboo and fern forests, opening up into surprising and unexpected animal interactions. Every attraction at Animal Kingdom has a story to tell, and the Wild Africa Trek becomes part of that tale.

The Trek starts at the Outfitters' Post. Guests are geared up with vests containing everything they might need, including a safety harness for some of the more "risky" moments. Tour groups are limited to twelve or fewer guests, allowing for a more personal experience.

The section of the route that winds through the Pangani Forest Exploration Trail offers amazing views of massive western lowland gorillas as they move through and loll around a lush waterfall environment. The powerful animals move freely, seemingly just beyond a fingertip's reach. The trucks carting guests through the nearby Kilimanjaro Safaris rumble in the distance as trekkers strap their harnesses onto a safety rack and actually lean out over a cliff that overlooks a hippo enclosure.

Then there's that bridge. A thin, lengthy spit of rope and wood juts out over the Safi River, which is choked with floats of prehistoric-looking crocodiles. Wide, well-traveled bridges with obvious OSHA requirements are for amateurs. Disney's Imagineers have crafted a dilapidated-looking catwalk with missing boards and an aged feel that adds immeasurably to the ambience. A closer look reveals safety netting and a secure safety harness, guaranteeing that adventurers make it safely to the other side.

At the end of the trek, participants are afforded expansive views of the Harambe grasslands, populated by several species of antelope, gazelle, wildebeest, okapi and elephant. The adventure culminates in an open-air meal at a private safari camp, featuring African-inspired cuisine.

For the $189 to $249 per-person Wild Africa Trek fee (varies depending on season), you get the expert-guided three-hour tour, all the photos and the "tastes of Africa" finale. As with most tours, a park-entry pass is necessary.

Pandora: The Land of Avatar

This is a big one. From time to time, Disney will add new features or tweak existing attractions—and that can be exciting. Lord knows I peed a little when I got a look at Talking Mickey in the Town Square Theater.

This time around, however, Disney is creating an entire world. Announced in September of 2011, the untamed, wondrous world of James Cameron's *Avatar* will take root in a back quadrant of Disney's Animal Kingdom theme park. Disney partnered with Cameron and producing partner Jon Landau to created themed lands that will give guests the opportunity to explore the Avatar universe firsthand.

"Why Animal Kingdom?" you may ask. Disney sees it as an opportunity to further the park's theme of conservation. The new land will emphasize living in harmony with nature—a symbiotic fit between the park and Cameron's film series.

According to reports, the new land will feature some of the visually stunning details found in the film: floating mountains, blue denizens and—no surprise here—incredibly immersive theming. Guests can expect several attractions when all is said and done, and given the speed with which Disney is adopting new technologies, expectations for the look of the *Avatar*-themed land are high. For example, Cameron pointed out early in the process that Disney's early animatronics used twelve axis of motion. The new Na'vi are using sixty-four axis of motion just to animate facial features.

At the moment, details about what to expect in the new land are a bit hard to come by. Land is being cleared and Cameron drops in now and then, but with a few years until we get to set foot on Pandora, execs are remaining fairly tight-lipped. What we do know is this: It is happening. When it was first announced, Mousejunkies from sea to shining sea reacted in one of two ways: cautiously optimistic or with stamping of feet and the gnashing of teeth. It seems to be a polarizing project.

Construction finally got underway in 2014—which is why Camp Minnie-Mickey has been shuttered. The budget for this expansion is rumored to be rather Cameronesque—somewhere in the neighborhood of $500 million—and as of right now it looks as if we won't be traveling to the mystical planet until 2017.

Welcome to the Kingdom

Disney's Animal Kingdom is divided into themed areas: The Oasis; Discovery Island; Africa; Rafiki's Planet Watch; Asia, and DinoLand USA

Mousejunkie U   *Zulu craftsmen were hired by Disney to create the thatched roofs located on buildings throughout the Animal Kingdom and at the Animal Kingdom Lodge.*

The Oasis

The Oasis is actually the main entrance area leading deeper into the park. While there aren't any ride-type attractions in the Oasis, don't write it off as a track meet to the more exhilarating attractions like Expedition Everest. Take in all that is around you. It may not spike your adrenalin as much as other theme parks (with a couple notable exceptions,) but Disney's Animal Kingdom is the most completely and perfectly themed park of the four in central Florida. And the Oasis is where it all begins.

As you enter the park, cast members loiter about with cages containing exotic creatures. Don't pass up the opportunity for some early, up-close action.

Cracked and scarred pathways marked with animal tracks and floral imprints lead guests up into lush vegetation. Rock formations loom overhead, as animals begin to present themselves along the route. Assorted birds, wallabies and giant anteaters, roaming in natural-looking environments, line the route as it winds even further upward.

They key to this park is pacing. Go slowly. There are details around every corner. Wherever you find a patch of green, you're likely to find a new animal to observe and learn about. The best approach for Disney's Animal Kingdom is to

MOUSEJUNKIE RYAN Be sure to check out the various trails through each section of the park. Mousejunkie Jenna and I spent almost forty-five minutes watching a father vulture build a nest for the mother vulture, while a baby kangaroo hopped back and forth, back and forth, back and forth.

put any traditional definitions of a theme park out of your head. It's not about rushing from one thing to the next. It's about soaking everything in.

Discovery Island

Crest the hill at the top of the Oasis and the massive, 145-foot tall Tree of Life rises up out of the surrounding verdant plant life that makes up the **Discovery Island** section of the park.

A massive, fourteen-story creation, the tree was engineered from an oil platform and has been the park's icon since opening in 1998. Disney set its Imaginers loose on it, and the result is a rather awe-inspiring piece of art that features more than 325 animals carved into its Kynar surface.

★**Mousejunkie U** *Ten artists worked full-time for eighteen months to carve the 325 animals into the Tree of Life, which is topped by more than 103,000 artificial leaves.*

At the base of the tree, a number of animals are viewable in impressively themed enclosures. Once you're close enough to pick out beasts from the surface of the tree, it's time to start hitting attractions.

Discovery Island is also where the attractions begin:

It's Tough to be a Bug!—Located in a theater tucked inside the base of the Tree of Life, this 3-D, audio animatronic presentation is based on the Pixar film, *A Bug's Life.* The show's host, Flik (voiced by Kids in the Hall's Dave Foley), attempts to teach guests that bugs should be seen as beneficial, and not as pests.

It's a funny, inventive show that, like most of Disney's 3-D films, includes a few tangible smells, sights, sounds and unexpected tactile prods. However, every time I watch this film, there are always a couple youngsters who react by freaking out. The theater is plunged into virtual darkness at one point, and when the lights come back up there are a few new visitors that might send arachnophobes into fits.

In fact, even Foley's kids were a bit bothered at the time.

"I took my two boys to the opening of Animal Kingdom in Orlando," Foley told me during an interview. "We went to watch it—they were four years old and two and one-half at the time—and they were both terrified and had to be taken out of the theater."

The actor laughed at the memory.

"I remember my oldest son kept going, 'Why did they make it like that? Didn't they know children were going to see this?'"

It's not exactly a horrifying experience by any stretch of the imagination, but knowing there is a surprise may prepare the younger kids.

MOUSEJUNKIE KATIE My message to kids is that it's not really scary at all—it's just that it can be startling for a moment if you're extra jumpy. You realize it's not real. It's actually really fun, very funny and I like it a lot.

Duration: 9 minutes.

Loads: Medium. The theater empties and refills after each performance. However, if there is a bit of a line, do not back out. The queue winds around parts of the Tree of Life and offers a fantastic opportunity to view some of the stunning artwork carved into the surface.

The Festival of the Lion King—Puppetry, music, audience participation, dance, dramatic lighting and acrobatics combine to create a sweeping, emotional celebration of African culture and mythology as told through the prism of Disney's film, *The Lion King.*

The performance is not a retelling of the film, but weaves its own tale based around the characters of Kiume, Kibibi, Zawadi and Nakawa. The four playfully poke at one another while involving the audience before launching into the show. Songs from the film make up the soundtrack to this Broadway-quality performance.

A visit to the park would not be complete without catching a performance of this masterful production.

Duration: 30 minutes.

Loads: You know the drill by now—theater loading. When the show ends, the audience files out and the next group heads in. The enclosed, air conditioned theater can hold many guests, and lines tend to form throughout the day.

Africa

Just outside is the completely immersive Africa, where the fictional village of Harambe hosts one of the park's signature attractions, the Kilimanjaro Safaris.

Mousejunkie U *According to Imagineers, Harambe was at one time a Dutch colony, but broke away in 1963 to become self-governing. That's the kind of detail that sets this park off from your average city zoo.*

Kilimanjaro Safaris—Board your safari truck and prepare for a two-week adventure across the Harambe Wildlife Preserve (or so the story goes.) Guests are driven across several African environments, including a forest, wetlands and bush country. Giraffe, crocodiles, hippos, antelopes, lions and elephants are among the animals you'll come across as they roam freely throughout the savanna. Disney's Imagineers have devised some ingenious ways to make sure the wildlife remains fairly visible throughout the day.

Duration: 20 minutes.

Loads: Slowly, but it is worth the wait.

★**Awesome/Stupid Disney Idea** *Make that brief musical interlude that comes into play near the elephant habitat—"Hapa Duniani" by African Dawn—a much longer part of the Kilimanjaro Safaris. Its hypnotic, sets the mood in authentic African arts, and is better than the evolving storyline that's become a bit convoluted through its recent iterations.*

★**Mousejunkie Choice** *All of the theme park's efforts and promise come together during the Kilimanjaro Safaris. These are not audio animatronic creatures thriving just outside your fingertips. When your safari is stalled because of a giraffe in the roadway, that's a real giraffe curiously sticking its head into your truck. When an immense elephant crosses the grasslands just yards away, you can almost feel the ground shake. And when a rickety old bridge shakes and quivers dangerously over a huge float of hungry-looking crocodiles...just hold on.*

Pangani Forest Exploration Trail—This walking tour, which begins outside the Kilimanjaro Safaris exit, runs through a number of animal viewing areas—most notably the hippo pool, the meerkat grasslands and the western lowland gorillas. The gorillas live in and around a rocky area that can be viewed from a glassed-in room, a bridge, and a few spots near some cliffs. Lucky guests can get up-close and nearly personal to these absolutely massive animals if they happen to feel particularly social.

Rafiki's Planet Watch—The Wildlife Express steam train will take guests to Rafiki's Planet Watch—an interactive, backstage examination of the park's operations. There are hands-on displays, a chance to view animal care areas via the Animal Cam, and the Affection Section. (I'll call it a petting zoo, but I'm sure Disney would say its "Nahtapettingzoo," to paraphrase its own marketing efforts.)

Asia

The first expansion to the park was the addition of the **Asia** themed area. Centered around a fictional kingdom named Anandapur, guests tour between two villages: Anandapur itself and Serka Zong, which lies in the shadow of Mount Everest. (Just look up, you can't miss it.)

Expedition Everest—Conquer the sacred mountain as a runaway train plunges guests into the world of the mythical Yeti.

This roller coaster, which climbs, twists and turns through the mountain itself, reaches speeds of up to 50 m.p.h. forwards, and 30 m.p.h. backwards. Yes, backwards. When the Yeti is on the prowl and he shreds the tracks in front of you, there isn't much choice.

Disney Imagineers traveled to the real Himalayas to research this stunningly themed attraction. Actual props brought back from their journey are used as part of the ride queue, adding a sense of reality to the proceedings.

When it opened in 2006, Expedition Everest was awarded "World's Best New Theme Park Attraction" by Theme Park Insider.

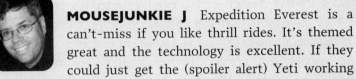

MOUSEJUNKIE J Expedition Everest is a can't-miss if you like thrill rides. It's themed great and the technology is excellent. If they could just get the (spoiler alert) Yeti working correctly. It's supposed to move, but it was breaking all the time. Most people don't notice this as they whiz by at 40 m.p.h. in the dark, but he just stands there now and makes noise. This is the "B" mode. The "A" mode has him moving and swinging his paw at you. "A" mode does not work so well.

This is a true gate-buster. Like Soarin' or Splash Mountain, guests head straight for this towering structure the minute the park opens.

Duration: 4 minutes.

Loads: Moderately slowly. But again, the queue in this attraction is really half the experience.

Flights of Wonder—During my first visit to Disney's Animal Kingdom, I passed by the front of this attraction and said, "I'm not going to a stupid bird show."

I have been paying for that ill-informed remark ever since. Flights of Wonder is a hilarious, impressive production that showcases the surprising talents of some remarkable birds. And unlike the audio animatronic creatures of the Magic Kingdom's Tiki Room, these are real, live birds. Performed at an outdoor amphitheater, macaws and pelicans fly over head

MOUSEJUNKIE J I never miss this interactive bird show. I choke-up every time they bring out the bald eagle. Also, be ready with a dollar bill when they ask. You can be part of the show if when a small bird to flies up to take it from you. (You get it back.)

(and I mean *directly* overhead—just sit very still) and your guide, Guano Joe/Guano Jane learns to overcome his/her fear of feathered friends.

Duration: 25 minutes.

Loads: Typical theater load-in. If you get there and the previous show has just let out, you're in luck.

Kali River Rapids—Get whirled around, tossed up and down, and quite drenched in this rafting expedition along the fictional Chakranadi River.

Twelve-person rafts float guests past a number of staged scenes and ultimately drops them down a twenty-foot rapid. Themes of illegal logging are addressed, although I supposed they had to teach me something before whipping me down the whitewater.

There's a warning telling guests that they might get soaked on the ride. It should be amended to say, "You will get soaked, so just deal with it."

If you're concerned about walking around sopping wet, consider wearing a bathing suit, water shoes (shoes are required in the loading area), and a spare t-shirt. You can rent a locker at the front of the park to store extra or dry clothing.

Duration: Five minutes.

Loads: Fairly quickly. While it is among the more popular attractions, the theming in the queue helps alleviate any line-fatigue.

The Straight Dope *Mobile phones are quite expensive, and losing one on an attraction could put a damper on things. Whipping one out for an ill-advised selfie during the Kali River Rapids could very likely get you mocked and your phone waterlogged. If you're worried about your electronics, bring along a small sandwich bag. Zip your phone up in it during the ride, and it'll help it stay nice and dry.*

Maharajah Jungle Trek—A wildlife trail similar to the Pangani Forest Exploration Trail, guests walk through a rainforest setting to see tigers, gibbons, Komodo dragons, birds and other creatures. Among the "other creatures" are the startlingly large Rodrigues fruit bats.

Nepal, India, Thailand and Indonesia all are represented throughout the Maharajah Jungle Trek.

MOUSEJUNKIE BARRY Someone should get those bats some chinos. How about a little modesty?

Guests who take the walk are treated to jaw-dropping views of Bengal tigers. The massive size of these cats becomes evident when you get to see them up close.

DinoLand USA

The final theme area in the park is DinoLand USA. It's designed to evoke a carnival-like atmosphere, with midway games and a trashy, gaudy feel. Obviously, this is not the official description. Here's the lowdown on DinoLand USA: As much as I am completely enthralled with the rest of the park, this area leaves much to be desired. I get what they're going for, I'm just not a fan of it. I grew up in a somewhat broken-down seaside resort town that had seen better days, and it feels just like parts of DinoLand USA I don't harbor any bad feelings about where I grew up, I just don't want to be plunged back into it when I'm on vacation.

Needless to say, I don't spend a whole lot of time at Chester and Hester's Dino-Rama—an asphalt and particularly out-of-place feeling section of DinoLand USA It's mainly a way to walk from Finding Nemo: The Musical, to the Dinosaur attraction and then out.

Here are the attractions you'll find in DinoLand USA:

Finding Nemo: The Musical—This live-action stage show based on the Pixar film *Finding Nemo* is a colorful, creative triumph. Original music was composed specifically for the show, and Michael Curry, who designed puppets for the stage version of *The Lion King* acted as leading puppet and production designer. The result? A show that looks like nothing else.

Duration: 40 minutes.

Loads: Here it is again: Theater load-in. Only five shows are performed daily, so don't put it off if lines are beginning to form.

Dinosaur—A dark ride with teeth, Dinosaur shoots guests back to prehistoric times aboard a Time Rover to attempt to retrieve an Iguanodon.

The ride is fast, rough and loud. Guests are whipped down unexpected drops, around corners, and away from hungry dinos. Most of the ride is in near dark, and the intensity may frighten younger children.

However, it's a blast. It's funny and exciting and provides enough thrill to get my blood pumping.

Duration: 10 minutes.

Loads: Quickly.

Mousejunkie U *Do the actors in the pre-show look familiar? They should. That's Phylicia Rashad (The Cosby Show) and Wallace Langham (CSI: Crime Scene Investigation) debating your Cretaceous era safety.*

Primeval Whirl—Combine the teacups of The Mad Tea Party in the Magic Kingdom with an off-the-shelf, run-of-the-mill mini-coaster, and you've got Primeval Whirl. The ride car spins in circles while traveling along the tracks.

MOUSEJUNKIE J Primeval Whirl is an evil ride. This ride is a projectile vomiting machine for me. I got off it holding lunch back in my throat and had to sit for a good half hour to regain my dignity. If you like this type of spinning ride, take a shot. I avert my eyes from it when I enter the area.

Duration: 90 seconds.
Loads: Quickly.

Triceratops Spin—It's Dumbo the Flying Elephant, only it's dinosaurs.
Duration: 90 seconds.
Loads: Quickly.

The Straight Dope *Head to the Kilimanjaro Safaris early in the morning, or very late in the day. If you do it in the morning, they've just let animals out of enclosures into the display areas. The animals are wide awake, and they get them out there by using food so they're active. At the end of the day the animals are in transition, being prepared to be led back into the enclosures for the night, and you'll see a lot more activity.*

MOUSEJUNKIE DEB Animal Kingdom has pros and cons for me:

Pros:

➤ Expedition Everest—Awesome coaster.
➤ Legend of the Lion King—Excellent show.
➤ The carvings in the Tree of Life are remarkable.
➤ Dinosaur is a cool ride, although not as cool as the Indiana Jones equivalent in Disneyland.
➤ Divine—a cast member on stilts costumed in remarkably camouflaged vines, leaves, and sticks—is very interesting to watch if you catch a glimpse of her.
➤ Theming is authentic.

Cons:

➤ I don't like seeing the creepy, crawly things in the glass boxes that Cast Members are holding in the morning when you walk in. Sure they're in glass, but if you dropped that thing.... AAAHHHHH!!!!!
➤ I'm a night owl, not a morning person, so any park that's only open until 5 P.M. or 6 P.M. loses points in my book.
➤ It always seems to rain the day we go to Animal Kingdom. Probably not Disney's fault.
➤ Lack of dining options.
➤ Hester's and Chester's Dino-Rama is too tacky for me.
➤ Theming is authentic.

9 Disney's Hollywood Studios

THE SPECIAL BRAND OF TINSELTOWN GLAMOUR on display at Disney's Hollywood Studios never really existed.

Sure, the klieg lights lit up the stars, actresses stepped out in flowing gowns dripping with jewels, and square-jawed actors in tuxedos said things like, "Listen here, doll, we're going to put you in pictures, see?" But it was never really quite like the Walt Disney World version.

Instead, Old Hollywood—more an idealized frame of mind than an actual spot on a map—remains vital and very much alive in the streets and backlots of Disney's glitziest theme park.

Known as "a Hollywood that never was and always will be," the Studios represent all that is enchanting about starry-eyed dreams and movie magic.

What's New at Disney's Hollywood Studios

The biggest thing to hit the Studios in some time is the biggest thing to hit the planet in some time. *Frozen* has taken over the world. It's pretty much accepted that every human has seen the animated movie, and "Let it Go" is likely challenging "Let it Be" for the most-played song of all time. So it's no surprise that Disney is capitalizing on its popularity at the theme parks.

In what is, up to this point, a seasonal move, Disney launched **Frozen Summer Fun Live!** several months ago. A series of events themed around the Oscar-winning film, it includes a daily character procession up Hollywood Boulevard, sing-alongs with Anna and Elsa (you can't escape the song, so don't even try,) *Frozen*-themed fireworks, an area where people can build a snowman (it doesn't have to be a snowman,) and an ice skating rink where you can play "spot the Canadians," or alternately, "spot the native Floridians." (Pro tip: Look for the flailing limbs.)

What's new at the Studios is also about what's gone. Disney has decided to shutter the American Idol Experience permanently. There are whispers about what else could be closing and why (*cough*StarWars*cough*) because closing down rather large attractions leaves plenty of room for something new and Force-related. Apparently.

Walt Disney Co. chief executive Bob Iger revealed during a quarterly earnings conference call that there are plans afoot for "a far greater *Star Wars* presence" in the theme parks. This means much more than the current Star Tours attractions and the Tatooine Traders. What it will translate into is still a bit of a mystery, though there are those attraction closings that may point the way. What is apparent is that Star Wars fans are going to be very happy.

"When we grow the *Star Wars* presence, which we will do significantly, you will see better bets being made that will pay off for us than were made in the past," Iger said.

Hollywood Boulevard

Guests enter the park on Hollywood Boulevard, a glitzed-up version of Main Street USA Lined with shops, it leads to the park icon—the Sorcerer's Hat. Inspired by Mickey Mouse's lid in "The Sorcerer's Apprentice" segment of the 1940 film *Fantasia*, the hat stands 122 feet tall and towers over a replica of the Chinese Theater behind it.

Mousejunkie U *Mickey Mouse would have to stand 350 feet tall if he wanted to wear the massive Sorcerer's Hat. Or, 125 feet tall with a truly glorious afro.*

The Great Movie Ride—Located inside the theater, this is a dark ride capable of seating sixty-eight people in each ride vehicle, it takes guests on a tour through scenes of some of classic Hollywood's most famous movies. The cast member/host/actor leads guests through musicals, gangster films, westerns, sci-fi, action/adventure and fantasy films.

The pilot of the "moving theater" ride vehicle gets involved at one point, taking the audience along for an adventure within the attraction.

Duration: 25 minutes.

Loads: Moderately slowly. The queue area can handle a massive crowd, but once inside guests are treated to trailers from classic Hollywood movies. This is great, although once I've been on the attraction I can't get "Gotta Dance" out of my head for a good hour.

Citizens of Hollywood—Cops, starlets, movie directors, and kitschy newspaper reporters wander up and down Hollywood Boulevard, putting on impromptu shows throughout the day.

Walk part-way up the street and Sunset Boulevard will be on your right. This is the neighborhood where most of the park's heaviest-hitters live.

Sunset Boulevard

The Twilight Zone Tower of Terror—Looming ominously over the entire park, the charred hulk of the Hollywood Tower Hotel dares guests to check-in for a brief stay.

This thrill ride starts in the intricately-dressed lobby, leads down into the dank boiler room basement, and then to the very top of the cursed hotel aboard a rather unreliable elevator. Unexpected shakes, special effects and a random drop sequence will leave your stomach in your throat.

Duration: 10 minutes.

Loads: Slowly.

Rock 'n' Roller Coaster Starring Aerosmith—Zero to 57 m.p.h. in 2.8 seconds, 3 inversions, and Steven Tyler screaming in your ear make this the most adrenaline-jacking attraction in the park.

MOUSEJUNKIE RANDY A fantastically themed attraction, The Tower of Terror starts weaving its story immediately upon entering the queue. One of the little details I really like is that even when there is no wait, the standby wait time never goes below thirteen evil minutes.

Of course, this being Disney, there's more to it than that. The story goes like this: You're in the recording studio watching the Bad Boys from Boston lay down a few tracks. Their manager arrives and tells them they're late for a show.

You, and everyone in your group, score some backstage passes at the Forum. This means you'll have to board a super stretch limo that'll get you to the venue.

Hold on, because your ride is certainly going to be interesting.

Duration: Four minutes (including pre-show with the awesome acting by the boys from Aerosmith).

Loads: Slowly. This is one-half of the Tower of Terror/Rock 'n' Roller Coaster shuffle.

Beauty and the Beast Live on Stage—Currently the longest-running stage show at Walt Disney World, this Broadway-style show uses live performers, puppets, and special effects to present a musical stage version of the Disney film.

The songs performed during the show are:

➤ "Belle"
➤ "Be Our Guest"
➤ "Something There"
➤ "The Mob Song"
➤ "Beauty and the Beast"

Duration: 30 minutes.

Loads: Quickly. The Theater of the Stars can hold 1,500 people.

Fantasmic!—A nighttime spectacular telling the story of Mickey's dreams and a battle of good versus evil, this show uses live performers, fireworks, lasers, music, animation projected onto water, fire, boats and a pile of Disney characters.

Stunts, choreography, running battles, and a giant snake all lead up to a fiery finale with a massive, fire-breathing dragon and the appearance of princes, princesses and almost every Disney character you can think of. Fantasmic! is the only way to finish off a day at Disney's Hollywood Studios.

⭐**Mousejunkie U**   *The character-packed finale features more than fifty performers.*

Duration: 25 minutes.

Loads: The Hollywood Hills amphitheater seats 6,500 people, with space for another 2,500 in standing-room-only.

Echo Lake

To the left of Hollywood Boulevard is Echo Lake. It's identified by its, well, water. Here are the attractions located around the Echo Lake area of Disney's Hollywood Studios:

Star Tours—The Adventures Continue—Blast into the world of George Lucas' *Star Wars* films in this convincing simulator. The attraction was given new life and a much-needed upgrade recently. Guests can now expect to visit one of several intergalactic locations, including Tattooine, Hoth, Naboo, Kashyyk and Coruscant. The new upgrade provides a nearly endless combination of adventures (well, fifty to be precise.) It's all been shot in digital 3D, so the effects are flawless and clear. It's the best 3D experience in any of the Orlando area theme parks.

On one of our many trips on Star Tours, we've encountered R2-D2, C-3PO, Boba Fett, Yoda, Chewbacca, Darth Vader and Princess Leia.

As with many Walt Disney World attractions, the queue is half the fun. This one, in particular, really sets the stage for what's to come. Surprisingly realistic glimpses of alien life provide a thrill, and the hardware on-hand is a Star Wars geek's dream come true.

Duration: Seven minutes.

Loads: Slowly, but this is actually a blessing. Enjoy the world Disney's Imagineers have created.

⭐ **Awesome/Stupid Disney Idea** *Gadgets run out of juice at the most inopportune times. Cameras and phones die just when we need to take that perfect photo. And while charging stations are now more accessible throughout the property, the $4 billion acquisition of Lucasfilm is screaming to be exploited at the Studios. Try this one: Toshi Station Power Converters. Recharge your gadgets in less than twelve parsecs.*

Jedi Training Academy—A live-action show located right next to Star Tours, the Jedi Training Academy allows young guests ("younglings"), to join a Jedi master to learn the ways of the force.

The younglings are brought up on stage and provided with Jedi robes and toy lightsabers. They're put through their paces before facing Darth Vader himself.

The show has become staggeringly popular, so getting your youngling involved can be a challenge. Here's how: Get to the park before opening. When the rope drops, head straight for the Jedi Training Academy with your child in tow. There, you can sign up your 4-12 year-old to take part. There are a finite number of shows daily, and spots fill quickly.

Even if you don't have a youngling of your own, this show is worth making time for. The lead cast member's interaction with the kids is often hilarious.

Duration: 25 minutes.

Loads: N/A. It's an outdoor stage. You walk up and watch and laugh hysterically.

It's worth noting that the viewing area for this show is in the open with no shade. Make sure your sun block is doing its job and be sure to stay hydrated. The Florida sun can sear the unprepared in minutes.

Indiana Jones Epic Stunt Spectacular—Scenes inspired by the *Indiana Jones* film series are re-enacted by stunt actors in this live-action theater show. Indy outruns a giant boulder, dances between spears, goes toe-to-toe with a rather large opponent, and (spoiler alert) ultimately saves Marion. The entire adventure is presented as if it's being shot as a film, with the director and camera operators taking part in the presentation. Audience members can volunteer to play extras.

Duration: 25 minutes.

Loads: Quickly. The theater can hold 2,000 people.

The Straight Dope *Rumors persist that this attraction will close soon. At press time, however, Indy remains alive and well—though often in quite a bit of peril.*

Streets of America

Wander just a bit further clockwise, and find yourself in the Streets of America section of the park. Forced perspective architecture and Imagineering ingenuity work to make this thoroughfare resemble urban streets in New York and San Francisco.

Here are the attractions you'll find around Streets of America:

Lights, Motors, Action! Extreme Stunt Show—Fast cars, running gun battles, motorcycle jumps, a guy falling off the top of a building, another one running around on fire, and explosions. That's a good afternoon at the Studios.

This show—presented as if it's being filmed, much like the Indiana Jones Stunt Spectacular—takes place in a six-acre set designed to look like a Mediterranean village square. Stunt drivers push cars to their limits as a storyline about an ongoing chase unfolds. Imported from Disneyland Paris, the show is exciting, funny, and holds a few surprises that I'll not spoil here.

Duration: 35 minutes.

Loads: Quickly. The stadium holds 5,000 people.

⭐ **Awesome/Stupid Disney Idea** *The title of Countdown to Extinction at Disney's Animal Kingdom was shortened to Dinosaur. Why not shorten Lights, Motors, Action! Extreme Stunt Show to something you can say in one breath? I've never been in Disney's Hollywood Studios with anyone who referred to it by its full name, anyway. It's always, "Hey, let's go see Ready, Set, Car! or whatever it's called."*

And now, a one-act play entitled, "Who has time for this?"

Sarah: "Say, would you like to go see Lights, Motors, Action! Extreme Stunt Show?"

Adam: "No, I don't want to see Lights, Motors, Action! Extreme Stunt Show. I would like to do something else, and then maybe see Lights, Motors, Action! Extreme Stunt Show."

Sarah: "Perhaps we could eat lunch and then see Lights, Motors, Action! Extreme Stunt Show."

Adam: "Yes, that would be a better time to see Lights, Motors, Action! Extreme Stunt Show. I like Lights, Motors, Action! Extreme Stunt Show. Lights, Motors, Action! Extreme Stunt Show is an exciting show that features lights, motors and action. And it is extreme."

And... Scene.

I've heard it referred to as "the car thing," "car show," "the stunt cars," and "that thing where the *Golden Girls* house used to be." Why not just paint some eyes on the windshields and call it "Cars"?

Studio Backlot Tour—This is a combination of a walking tour and a tram tour of the Studio's backlot area. The first part of the tour, "Harbor Attack," shows how special effects are used to create an exciting action scene. Guest volunteers help act-out the "attack." The tram portion of the tour takes guests past The Boneyard, featuring a number of vehicles that have seen screen time. The big finish comes as the tram travels through Catastrophe Canyon, where there's a potentially catastrophic (thus the name) wall of water that narrowly misses your tram. And fire. There's fire and explosions. Again, you can't really go wrong if there are explosions involved.

Duration: 35 minutes.

Loads: Quickly.

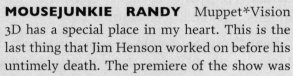

MOUSEJUNKIE RANDY Muppet*Vision 3D has a special place in my heart. This is the last thing that Jim Henson worked on before his untimely death. The premiere of the show was delayed until legal issues between Disney and the surviving family were resolved. This show just never gets old and really exhibits the genius of Jim Henson.

Muppet*Vision 3D—This is a 3D film featuring classic humor from the Muppets. They're all here—Kermit, Miss Piggy, Gonzo, the Swedish Chef, Beaker, and pretty much any other Muppet you can think of.

New, more advanced 3D technology dates this attraction a bit. *Mickey's Philharmagic* and *It's Tough to Be a Bug* look better, never mind big-budget advances like *Avatar*. But none of those films have the Muppets—beloved creations that allow Jim Henson's heart and soul to shine through.

Duration: 20 minutes.

Loads: Quickly. But get there early for the pre-show. It's loaded with Muppet humor and terrible, hilarious puns.

Animation Courtyard

Cut back across the front of the Sorcerer's Hat and you'll find yourself facing the Animation Courtyard.

Here are the attractions that are located in and around the Animation Courtyard:

Voyage of the Little Mermaid—This stage show, which uses a combination of live action, film clips, lasers, lighting effects, and unique and innovative puppetry, re-tells the story of the Disney film, *The Little Mermaid.*

Duration: 20 minutes.

Loads: Quickly: Theater empties, next group files in.

Disney Junior—Live On Stage!—This show brings your kids' favorite Disney Junior characters to life using puppetry and special effects. A recent refurb brings Doc McStuffins, Sofia the First, Mickey Mouse Clubhouse and Jake and the Neverland Pirates to the stage—all hosted by the only live cast member in the show, Casey.

Duration: 20 minutes.

Loads: Quickly. Theater empties, next group files in. However, I recommend getting in as early as you can. There are benches located along the back and sides of the open room. I send Amy and Katie up front, while I kick back on these incredibly convenient and comfortable benches. I can watch the show, see my wife and daughter, and park my butt for twenty blissful minutes.

Walt Disney: One Man's Dream—This walking, self-guided tour is essentially a museum dedicated to Walt Disney. It contains some great artifacts from his life and work, and features miniature models of some of Disney theme parks'

MOUSEJUNKIE KATIE It surprises me, but every time I watch the film at the end of One Man's Dream, I get very emotional. To see what Walt Disney accomplished during his lifetime is amazing, and it's a little sad to know that he's gone now and never got to see it completed. The film ends to the tune of "When You Wish Upon a Star," and it makes me feel incredibly sentimental. It's a touching film that should not be skipped.

instantly recognizable icons. It ends with a short film detailing the life and legacy of Walt Disney.

Duration: The film at the end of the attraction runs 15 minutes.

Loads: Quickly. Well, as quickly as you can walk in.

The Straight Dope *There's a trivia quiz that goes along with this attraction. Are you Mousejunkie enough to take it? Just ask a cast member about it.*

The Magic of Disney Animation—Why didn't I go on this tour for the first seventeen trips I took to Walt Disney World? Because I'm an idiot.

This is a fascinating, interactive look at Disney animation. Cast members host a short film/exhibition about animation. Guests can then show off their art skills at an animator's workspace in the Animation Academy, or move into a room full of interactive exhibits and character meet-and-greet spaces.

MOUSEJUNKIE KATIE One of my favorite things at Hollywood Studios is the Animation Academy. I love drawing there, no matter how messed up my drawings can be. My dad's drawings always make me laugh, because most of the time he changes it completely and makes it weird—like his drawing of Bolt, where he drew the Death Star in the background and Bolt wearing a shirt with a turkey leg on it. Another thing I love about the Animation Academy is that it's air-conditioned and very relaxing. After walking around the hot park the whole day, you finally can sit down in an air-conditioned room and draw Disney characters.

Mousejunkie Katie's "Bolt" from the Animation Academy.

The author's attempt at "Bolt."

MOUSEJUNKIE AMY Don't forget to actually put your paper on the light table. My mother kept complaining that her pencil wouldn't work. Finally we figured out she was trying to draw on the light table itself and not her paper. She was mortified, but it was pretty hilarious and we still laugh about it.

Duration: The initial film is 10 minutes long. The Animation Academy is 15 minutes long.

Loads: Quickly.

Mousejunkie Choice *Drawing a Disney character, under the tutelage of an actual Disney artist at Animation Academy is an absolute blast. Yet again, it's something every member of the family can do together. It's one of the more underrated attractions in the park, and should never be missed.*

The first time I experienced the Animation Academy was on a daddy/daughter trip one spring. Katie expressed a little interest in trying it, so I agreed. We skipped lunch and went back through five times in a row. We laughed hysterically and enjoyed every moment. Plus, at the end, you get a unique piece of art to take home.

Pixar Place

The final themed area in Disney's Hollywood Studio's is Pixar Place, home to the fantastic, addictive, superlative, nearly-perfect dark ride/game, **Toy Story Midway Mania**.

Guests who have been "shrunk" down to toy size wind their way through a queue designed to look like Andy's room from the Disney/Pixar *Toy Story* films. An audio animatronic Mr. Potato Head (Don Rickles) entertains, guests pick up their 3D glasses, twist up some stairs, over the attraction itself, and then down to the load area. Guests then jump aboard the ride vehicle, where they are whipped through a series of carnival midway-type games. A firing controller hurls eggs, darts, and pies at various targets.

Much like Buzz Lightyear's Space Ranger Spin at the Magic Kingdom, players shoot for high score, allowing for some good-natured trash talk when it's all over.

The attraction is colorful, exciting, and unique. The music is fantastic, the theming is perfect, and even the queue is fun. I've lost track of how many times I've heard people point to an oversized game or toy and say, "I had that," while waiting in the always-long line.

Duration: Six minutes.

Loads: Slowly. If you're not interested in experiencing Toy Story Midway Mania, you have problems, and Gatorland is fifteen miles down the I-4. Otherwise, head straight for Pixar Place as soon as the rope drops.

MOUSEJUNKIE JENNA Bottom line—you're going to want to ride this and you're going to want to do it more than once. This is doubly true if you have kids, love the *Toy Story* movies, or enjoy playing video games. TSMM also has some of the most insane wait times of any ride at Disney World. So without further ado, here is my no-fail strategy: Go straight to TSMM. Do not stop in for coffee at Starring Rolls. Do not stop to watch hilarious police officers "just for a minute." It's go time, people!

A day at Disney's Hollywood Studios should always end with a performance of Fantasmic!. However, since the show's schedule has been reduced to just a couple nights a week, be sure to check your park maps so you'll know when it's showing.

It's always crowded, and planning to sit in the center of the theater requires arriving at least an hour before show time. The Hollywood Hills Amphitheatre features metal benches that surround the performance area in a semi-circle. Your early arrival may get you a good, centrally located seat, but it's also going to guarantee you a numb rear end.

Avoid numb-butt by booking a Fantasmic! dinner package. This allows you to dine at specific times, and then arrive just before show time in a reserved seating area. (The reserved area is off to either the left or right side, but since the show is visible from any seat in the theater, that's not usually a problem.)

The Hollywood Hills Amphitheatre seats nearly ten thousand people. And when show is over, everyone leaves at once. The entire crowd is funneled into a single walkway, which is then split into to main exits. Being near the exit when the show ends can save a lot of time and aggravation.

The Straight Dope *Many people will advise you to line up for Fantasmic extremely early. Here's why they're wrong: If its ten minutes until the show starts and they're still letting people in, then by all means take a seat. The later you get there, the more likely it is that you will able to sit near the back and to the right. This is important for two reasons: You can see fine from anywhere, and—more importantly— you'll be near the exit.*

Full disclosure: I put this practice to the test on a recent trip. We arrived late on purpose and ended up in the standing-room-only section behind the seating area. Other than my legs being a bit tired from a day at the park, it wasn't a bad experience. We could see fine, my daughter made a new little friend, and we were half-way home to our resort before the last person had left the theater. If a seat up front or in the middle is important, this approach may not work for you. If you want to see the show and leave without going gray, it might be just the thing.

10 Mousejunkies Recreate

Kids are great, aren't they?

The magic in their eyes when they first catch a glimpse of Cinderella Castle or wrap their arms around Mickey Mouse is unforgettable.

Equally as unforgettable is when they throw up in line on a 100-degree day and it splashes all over your shoes. Or someone's doughy, moist, sticky-fingered cherub pushes by you in a queue, leaving behind great swaths of his DNA and God-knows-what disease on your leg. Or when they stand behind you in line and kick away at your calf until it feels like they may have fractured your tibia.

Yeah, kids are great. But occasionally it becomes time to get very, very far away from them, lest the karate skills come into play and you end up in the most magical holding cell in Orange County.

(Editor's note: Mousejunkies does not condone the karate-ing of children. Usually.)

Walt Disney World has plenty of places where adults can put some distance between themselves and the theme parks.

Water skiing, boating, golf, parasailing, fine dining, and my favorite, fishing, are all part of a Walt Disney World vacation.

Plus, you'll likely avoid being thrown up on unless you're recreating with a particularly odd adult.

Everyone rides It's a Small World and Space Mountain when they visit Walt Disney World, but there's a whole roster of activities that has nothing to do with long lines, FastPasses, parade times, or little kids. Here's a look at some of the things that'll get you out of line at the theme parks:

Downtown Disney

This outdoor dining/shopping/entertainment district has long been a favorite place to visit when it's time to get out of the theme parks. Packed with places to spend and relax, this location is easily accessible via Disney's bus system—which is the best way to get there, because the amount of construction going on has made parking more difficult than ever. Downtown Disney is home to the massive World of Disney store, an ever-changing roster of street entertainers, Cirque du Soleil, DisneyQuest and scores of other recreational options. It's a walkable, waterfront spot that is also useful as a bus transfer location if you're trying to get from one resort to another.

First things first, however. There's a lot going on right now at Downtown Disney—or whatever it's going to morph into.

What's New at Downtown Disney

The outdoor shopping, dining and entertainment district is undergoing a major change.

Walt Disney World has begun to move forward on a completely revamped Downtown Disney, giving it a new look and even a new name. The project, called Disney Springs, will turn the area into a re-creation of a turn-of-the-century lakeside community divided into four outdoor neighborhoods:

- ➤ **Town Center**, a mix of shopping and dining with a waterfront promenade.
- ➤ **The Landing**, a commercial district.
- ➤ **Marketplace**, which will feature an over-the-water pedestrian causeway and an expanded World of Disney store.
- ➤ **West Side**, which will have live entertainment and elevated spaces providing both shade and a great people-watching perch.

The whole area will be watched over by a signature water tower and grand entry. The new development will double the number of shops and restaurants to 150 establishments. Most will be third-party businesses, though Disney will have several of its own spots. That detail isn't much of a departure from the current arrangement (see, for example, the T-Rex Cafe, the House of Blues, the Lego Imagination Center and the Harley-Davidson shop, among others).

Downtown Disney had been made up of three sections: The Marketplace, Pleasure Island and the West Side—home to the Cirque du Soleil theater. Much of Pleasure Island, which once housed several nightclubs ranging from a comedy club and country music venue to a dance club and even a onetime wildly popular themed nightspot/theater experience called The Adventurer's Club, has been shuttered for some time. Disney initially announced completely different plans three years ago to make-over the district as a location called Hyperion Wharf—named for the address of the old Walt Disney Studios complex at 2719 Hyperion Ave. in Hollywood. While the initial announcement of Hyperion Wharf made a big splash, follow-up was strangely quiet. When Walt Disney Co. Chairman of Parks and Resorts Tom Staggs shared details of the recently-rumored (and now confirmed) Disney Springs project, he said the Hyperion Wharf plans were simply shelved because they thought they could do better.

The new Disney Springs will look dramatically different from its Downtown Disney/Pleasure Island state, drawing inspiration from old central Florida lakefront towns—think flowing springs and fountains in and around the sprawling facilities.

Disney Springs will also address ongoing problems that have made a trip to Downtown Disney problematic at times in recent years. Internal resort buses take guests to Downtown Disney as they do to the four theme parks. But heavy traffic along Buena Vista Drive made it a rather long trip at times. For those taking their own cars, parking could be an issue.

Endless looping around the parking lot often resulted in frustration, and other times entire sections of the lot were closed because they were simply full.

Disney reportedly hopes to construct a ramp from Interstate-4 that will bring guests over Buena Vista Drive. An additional two parking garages are also being added, allowing for a dramatic increase in parking availability.

In the meantime, Disney is working to make the transition as smooth as possible. The project is certainly ambitious, and comes on the heels of the New Fantasyland expansion at the Magic Kingdom. While building out that project—the largest in the theme park's history—the company went about its business with little-to-no disruption to guests. Likewise in the case of Disney Springs, a Disney spokesman said that efforts will be made to minimize any impact to cast, guests and operating participants during construction.

Disney Springs will open in phases until it is completed in 2016. Retail and dining vendors have not yet been announced or officially confirmed. Disney officials said they will share details about new tenants in the future, and that they are working with current tenants individually to determine how this will impact them.

The last major name change at Walt Disney World came in 2008 when the former MGM Studios theme park was rebranded as Disney's Hollywood Studios—a change that seemed to go smoothly, with visitors picking up on the new moniker quickly. The Disney Springs name won't come into use until construction is complete, so as you stand in line outside your on-site resort to catch a ride, expect to see that

Downtown Disney title on the front of your bus marquee for at least another three years.

Splitsville Luxury Lanes

A new upscale, retro-style bowling venue at Downtown Disney/Disney Springs/Whatever we're going to call it, gives visitors almost 50,000 square feet of bowling, billiards and bars. There are 30 lanes in the two-level venue, and food offerings are more than what you'd normally find at most bowling alleys. Sushi, salads and sliders are among the fare designed to keep customers going. The Downtown Disney location is the chain's fifth and largest site.

What's New Outside the Theme Parks

Exotic Driving Experience

Get behind the wheel of one of the world's most expensive cars in this new, adrenaline-charged experience at the Walt Disney World Speedway. Guests can ride-along or drive themselves in one of several high-performance machines: a Porsche 977S, an Audi R8, a Lamborghini Gallardo LP560-4, a Lamborghini Gallardo LP570-4 Superleggera or a Ferrari 458 Italia—a supercar valued at more than $280,000. Disney has also added new cars, including a Nissan GT-R and a Ferrari F430. Prices for each car are different and range from $179 to $414 for a six lap package. The experience includes a short orientation, instruction, a driver's meeting, driving and a closing ceremony. Ride-along participants must be fourteen-years-old, and anyone who wants to take the wheel must be at least eighteen-years-old and have a valid driver's license. To book this experience, call 855-822-0149.

The Richard Petty Driving Experience is available for for those who dream of driving like the King. There are six different programs: The Ride-Along ($109), where guests ride shotgun on a simulated three-lap qualifying run at more than 150 m.p.h.; the Rookie Experience ($449), which puts you in the driver's seat for eight laps; the King Experience ($849), two separate driving sessions of eighteen laps total that include training and feedback from the Pit Road instructor; and the Experience of a Lifetime ($1,299)—any motorhead's dream. This half-day experience includes training, thirty laps of pulse-pounding speed split into three segments, feedback from the Pit Road instructor; The SPEEDWAY Challenge ($2,099), a fifty-lap driving experience; and the Racing Experience, also fifty laps during a half-day of living your NASCAR dreams. The Rookie, King, Experience of a Lifetime, SPEEDWAY Challenge and Racing Experience packages all include a graduation packet with a time sheet that breaks down each lap; To book one of these pulse-pounding, high-speed experiences, call 407-WDW-PLAY.

Piston Cup Junior Ride-Along

Two characters from the Academy Award-nominated 2006 animated feature film *Cars*—Aiken Axler and Sage VanDerSpin can now take youngsters for a spin around the track at Walt Disney World Resort.

These two full-size custom character cars have become part of the Richard Petty Driving Experience at Walt Disney World Speedway.

As with everything Disney, there's a story: VanDerSpin races for team Gask-its and is the youngest winner of the Junior Piston cup Pro Series. Axler is the Nitroade racer who took the Vitoline rookie-of-the-year honors during his first season of Cup competition.

Special window wraps bring the cars to life, adding the identifiable, oversized eyes to each vehicle. Fans on the sideline can see the personality created by the wraps, while the driver and guests inside the car can see the entire track clearly. Both cars have custom-designed racing seats specifically created to ensure the safety of smaller racers. The full-containment racing seats, designed by the Joie of Seating, feature shoulder and head protection and a five-point safety harness—the same design used by NASCAR drivers.

For $59, the Junior Ride-Along program gives children ages six to thirteen (and at least forty-eight inches tall) the chance to experience real-life racing excitement as they ride shotgun with a professional driving instructor for three thrilling laps in a specially equipped Piston Cup race car. The Junior Ride-Alongs do not require reservations. (I'll stop for a moment while we all take that in—a Disney attraction that doesn't require reservations six months in advance.) It's all operated on a first-come, first-served basis. To get involved, visit Drivepetty.com or call 800-237-3889.

Guided Fishing Excursions

The placid, glass-like surface of Bay Lake explodes into churning, splashing foam as a largemouth bass dances across the top of the water. The rod dips, the drag sings and there isn't a churro or Mickey Mouse balloon in sight. Wet a line in one of Walt Disney World's many lakes, canals and waterways and you may just land a renowned Florida lunker during a guided fishing excursion. A healthy and carefully managed fishery has resulted in world-class angling in the shadow of Cinderella Castle. Excursions leave from several resort marinas, including the Grand Floridian, Contemporary, Saratoga Springs, the BoardWalk Inn and Downtown Disney. A single angler can book a two-hour excursion for $170. A two-hour excursion with two to five people is $270, and a four-hour trip is $455. All fishing equipment, bait and cold drinks are provided. Reservations are required. To book, call 407-939-7529.

Parasailing Over Bay Lake

Hook in to a multicolored, billowing parachute, let go and make like Tinker Bell. Tethered to a boat cutting back and forth across Bay Lake behind the Contemporary Resort, guests are unreeled into the sky high above Walt Disney World. The hum of the motorboat starts to fade away until it's just you, the blue sky and an unmatched view of the entire property. Taking flight over the resort provides unmatched sightlines of all four theme parks, Downtown Disney and straight into downtown Orlando. You'll know you've reached cruising altitude when the birds are circling below you. A single flight—10 minutes at 450 feet—is $95; a deluxe single—12 minutes at 600 feet—is $130. Tandem flights are $170 and $195 respectively. To book, call the Sammy Duvall Watersports Centre at Disney's Contemporary Resort at 407-939-0754.

Scuba Dive at Epcot

Epcot DiveQuest plunges guests into the 5.7-million gallon saltwater tank at the park's The Seas With Nemo and Friends pavilion. Scuba-certified guests can sign up for a three-hour experience that puts them among sea turtles, dolphins and even sharks. Crystal clear waters, absolutely no currents and a look at the adjoining Coral Reef restaurant from the other side of the glass makes this adventure a memorable way to spend the day at Epcot. A tour, instruction and forty minutes underwater is $175 per-person, ages ten and up. To book Epcot DiveQuest, call 407-939-8687.

Learn to Surf

Hang ten at Disney's Typhoon Lagoon water park. Guests can catch a wave in the park's 2.75-million gallon wave pool, guided by the pros who actually now what phrases like "shoot the curl" and "where are your pants?" actually mean. There are several options for would-be surfers: Private sessions are available for $1,100 during morning sessions and $1,200 for evening sessions. If you're only hanging, say, seven, at the end of your three-to-four hour lesson and you're got your heart set on ten, you can purchase more time/waves at $1,500 for an additional 125 waves, or $1,800 for 150 more waves. The fee covers your private event and a maximum of 25 guests. Expect to bring your own board and towels.

Beginners can Learn to Surf Like a Pro on select days prior to the water park opening. Classes are taught by pros and start from scratch. It all begins with dry-land instruction and then heads to the water on a soft-sided surfboard, and waves as high as six feet tall. Lessons are $165 per-person. To book, call 407-939-7529.

Spa-ing Partners

There isn't a better way to rejuvenate after a long day at the theme parks than taking advantage of Walt Disney World's top-notch spa treatments. Full-service spas provide much-needed pampering for tired guests. There was a time when there were just two spas welcomed tired guests. However, there are now an abundance of options. Reservations are recommended.

Spa	Location	To book
La Vida Health Club	Disney's Coronado Springs Resort	407-939-7727
Muscles and Bustles Health Club	Disney's BoardWalk Villas	407-939-7727
Olympiad Fitness Center	Disney's Contemporary Resort	407-939-7727

Spa	Location	To book
Senses— a Disney Spa	Grand Floridian Resort	407-939-7727
Senses Spa	Disney's Saratoga Springs Resort	407-939-7727
Ship Shape Massage Salon	Disney's Yacht Club Resort	407-939-7727
Sturdy Branches Health Club	The Villas at Disney's Wilderness Lodge	407-939-7727
Survival of the Fittest Fitness Center	Disney's Animal Kingdom Villas/ Kidani Village	407-939-7727
Zahanti Massage and Fitness Center	Disney's Animal Kingdom Lodge	407-939-7727
Mandara Spa	The Dolphin Hotel	407-934-4772

★ **Awesome/Stupid Disney Idea** *Funnel cake aromatherapy.*

Treatments at the Saratoga Springs Spa, for example, range from the standard manicure/pedicure to the more interesting Adirondack Stone Therapy, in which heated stones and oils are used to loosen stress points and knots. With nary a youngster in sight, the searing heat and daunting queues at the Disney World attractions couldn't seem farther away.

MOUSEJUNKIE WALT For years I wanted to try a massage but I just never did. Finally I got over my hesitance and tried it. Now I'm addicted. There's nothing better than relaxing and letting yourself be pampered. You get up feeling great.

I tried the spa at the Grand Floridian. It was just starting to rain the day of my appointment, so it was a perfect time to get inside and relax. I signed in and was brought into a room where everything was sparkling clean. Soft music was playing and I immediately started to unwind.

The facilities are beautiful and I enjoyed going over all the different options available. I chose a Swedish massage, which is what you think of when you hear "massage." My therapist asked what kind of pressure I was interested in, and I told her medium.

Another great thing is that once your massage is over, you have full access to the spa's facilities. I felt totally loose and fantastic, so I jumped in the Jacuzzi for a little while to complete the perfect hour-long appointment.

Would I do it again? Oh yeah. I'd like to give the spa at Saratoga Springs a try sometime.

MOUSEJUNKIE JENNA I took advantage of discounts offered to Disney Vacation Club members and booked a fifty-minute Swedish massage and a peppermint pedicure for the day I arrived at Walt Disney World. It seemed like an excellent way to dive into vacation relaxation.

Saratoga Springs is a very calm and quiet resort in the first place, but the spa there is so far removed from Mickey Mouse, popcorn, and FastPasses that it's almost spooky. It's a place of barely audible instrumental music, cotton waffle-weave robes, and pitchers of ice water served in a lounge where everyone whispers. It's a very relaxing atmosphere, but not somewhere to get excited about a Disney trip.

My first appointment was the Swedish massage. My massage therapist asked me some questions about allergies and trouble spots, and went to work on all those airplane coach seat knots. I think fifty minutes is just enough massage to relax without feeling ridiculous, though the spa offers shorter and longer massage times. Unfortunately, I am a bit chatty, so I never took the opportunity to just tune out. Afterward, I had a ten-minute break in the lounge. It seems to me that it has some special name like Quiet Lounge or Meditation Room, which gives you a hint to its sole purpose. You are supposed to sit in this quiet room with its dimmed lights, drink ice water and not talk.

Soon, I was called by the technician who would be doing my pedicure, and fled the quiet room. I was

(Continued on next page)

fortunate enough to travel to Walt Disney World while the spa at Saratoga Springs was offering its Peppermint Pedicure. The Peppermint Pedicure is named after a candy famous in Saratoga Springs, (and sold in the Artist's Palette gift shop): the Peppermint Pig. The hand-and-foot treatment room has two pedicure chairs and two manicure tables. Additionally, they can set up a portable manicure station so guests getting a mani-pedi can get their fingers polished while their tootsies are soaking. The Peppermint Pedicure includes a soak in the foot spa, a massage with a tingly and fresh-smelling peppermint lotion, and the usual trim and polish. At fifty minutes, the pedicure lasted as long as the Swedish massage and I think I enjoyed it more. When I was done, my spa technician sent me off with all of the emory boards, buffing blocks, and toe separators she used on me, and tucked a nice-sized sample of the peppermint lotion for good measure.

It was a very relaxing visit to the spa, but I don't know that I can fully recommend it as a first-day treat. This was the second time that I have spent my first day at Walt Disney World at the spa. It was also the second time that I have left the spa worried that my luggage wouldn't be waiting in my new hotel room (it wasn't the first time) and that I'd show up late for dinner with massage oil in my hair and in the same tired clothes I flew down in.

If you want the relaxation of a spa visit to last, my advice is to schedule it in the middle of your vacation on a day when you have no concrete plans.

Duffing at Disney

Golfers have four options at Walt Disney World, at courses that have all been certified by Audubon International as Cooperative Wildlife Sanctuaries.

The Straight Dope *If you're staying on-property, Disney will provide complimentary transportation to the golf course. Just talk to bell services the night before your tee time and let them know where you'll be playing. You'll get a voucher for cab fare, and the car will be waiting to take you right to the course you'll be playing.*

Disney's Lake Buena Vista Golf Course is a classic country-club course that has hosted the PGA Tour, the LPGA Tour and USGA events. Elevated bunker greens make your approach shots especially important, and an island green on seventh could give you fits.

Disney's Magnolia Golf Course is a Tour-style championship course and is the longest of all the Disney courses. You'll be tempted to grip it and rip it through the wide fairways, but there are water hazards on eleven of eighteen holes and 97 bunkers could make you regret flexing.

Disney's Palm Golf Course is tucked within the trees and lakes that best illustrate the natural beauty of the area. Beginners and pros (and self-proclaimed pros) will all feel at home on this course, which boasts nine water hazards and 94 bunkers.

Golf carts are included in the greens fees for all three of these courses. Greens fees range from $39 to $165.

Disney's Oak Trail Golf Course is a nine-hole, par-36 walking course great for younger players and those who want to spend some time on the fairways with them. Greens fees range from $20 to $38.

Rental clubs are available at the Magnolia, Palm and Oak Trail pro shops, and guests who bring their own clubs can store them and transfer them from one Disney club to the next each day for free. All of Disney's golf courses are run by Arnold Palmer Golf Management.

The Straight Dope   *This is Florida. If your ball goes in the water hazard, leave it there. Alligators and snakes are among the native residents, and they're not always known to be gracious hosts.*

Walt Disney World resort guests can book a tee time ninety days in advance, while non-resort guests can book sixty days in advance. To reserve a tee time, call 407-939-4653.

Date Night at Disney

There are literally scores of adult dining choices at Disney, but for the best views this side of Cinderella's Castle, head to the California Grill, located atop the Contemporary Hotel.

Guests also can enjoy an evening without the kids at Citricos at Disney's Grand Floridian Resort and Spa; Jiko—The

Cooking Place at Disney's Animal Kingdom Lodge; Artist Point at Disney's Wilderness Lodge; Todd English's bluezoo at Walt Disney World Dolphin; and The Dining Room at Wolfgang Puck's in Downtown Disney.

Visitors wishing to truly upgrade their dining can opt to splurge at Victoria and Albert's at the Grand Floridian—a special-occasion restaurant designed to cater to the most discriminating culinary tastes. A customized seven-course gourmet meal is served each night in the intimate sixty-five-seat dining room. The wine cellar, with more than 700 selections on the menu and 4,200 in the cellar, has been recognized by *Wine Spectator* magazine with an Award of Excellence.

Of course, this being Disney, each waitress answers to Victoria, every waiter is known as Albert, and diners are presented with a personalized menu at the end of the meal. Dinner is $135 per person, $200 with a wine pairing. The coveted Chef's Table is $210 per person, $315 with a wine pairing. This is the one establishment on Disney property where you really can't let your hair down. Jackets are required for men and evening wear for women.

Dashing at Disney: runDisney

I've run a race at Disney. It went from the bus stop at the Magic Kingdom to the buffet at the Crystal Palace. I didn't get a medal, though.

There is a special breed of guest, however, that runs through Disney with a much higher purpose. These are the runDisney people. runDisney stages a number of running

Who Needs Theme Parks?
Resort Recreation

MOUSEJUNKIE CAROL Each Disney resort has its own hidden secrets. When checking-in, take a look at the package of information that they give you. Each has activities planned throughout the day. Almost every pool on property has dance parties for the kids and games poolside around 3 P.M. The adults can lounge with a nice, refreshing drink the kids can be entertained by the Disney staff.

One day during an April vacation I was walking to my room at the Animal Kingdom Lodge when I noticed several televisions set up with life guards nearby ready for some gaming action. At the Animal Kingdom Lodge's Kidani Village resort, the Lifeguards had set up some Wii stations ready to battle guests on the latest games. This time it happened to be a Wii game called "Just Dance." With some practice under my belt, I accepted the challenge and battled for the win. I forgot that the lifeguards are there daily and have many more hours of practice than I, but good times were had.

Most resorts play Disney movies outside after dark. My favorite resort to go to for this is the Beach and Yacht Club resorts. They set up the theater right on the beach and have a fire for roasting marshmallows and making s'mores.

Location is everything: After enjoying the movie I head over to the BoardWalk where the evening entertainment of jugglers and magicians take over for the perfect ending to an exhausting day.

events through the year that sends runners through the Disney theme parks and across the property along courses that can only be a Mousejunkies wildest dream. Runners get a chance to see the theme parks in a completely unique way, enjoy Disney entertainment along the way and they even earn a fantastic piece of memorabilia in their race medal. The races range from a 5k family fun run to a full-on marathon. First-timers can take on the shorter events, while elite athletes can tackle the 26.2-mile course. Completely insane people (committed, healthy, admirable athletes) can even attempt the Dopey Challenge—running every race over Disney's Marathon Weekend, resulting in a journey of 48.6 miles. There are races in January, October, November, May and other times throughout the year.

Here's a look at what it's like to participate in a runDisney event by radio personality and sworn Mousejunkie, Heather Bishop-Dumka:

"Let's just say I am not overly fit. I do the Gallaway method, which is to walk, run, then walk in intervals. It's a great way to run a race for us normal people. I will say this— Disney races are races. Don't think they are just walks in the parks.

We usually go to Walt Disney World in February around the time they stage the Disney Princess Half Marathon, so I made it a goal to run one.

Registration: Research each race and find one that is right for you, and know that they are adding new races all the time. The race really starts at registration because these races are selling out the day registration opens. Make sure you don't get sticker shock when signing up. My Disney Princess Half cost more than $160 just to register. And in true Disney style, you can pre-order the commemorative necklace, pin, purse and retreat. Cha-ching. And that's before you add in travel and tickets.

Training: runDisney is fabulous about training. Check out the web site (runDisney.com) for detailed training schedules and YouTube channel for tips and tricks. Remember, this is Disney, so you will also want to wear a costume during your race. Do a few training runs in the costume. I saw so many people with amazing costumes just throw them to the ground within a mile or two from the starting line.

Travel: I highly recommend staying on-site. You need to be up at 2 A.M. the day of the race. And most have buses to and from the race. Plan on getting to the race expo early because if you want to buy commemorative items that you didn't pre-order, they get bought up quickly. It can be a madhouse. Remember that you want to play a very low-key day on the day before your race. I was stupid and we did Hollywood Studios the day before my race. By 2 P.M. my legs hurt and I was starting to freak out about the race the next day. Plus I was stopping at every bathroom because I was hydrating prior to the run. Another side note: If you are from someplace like the northeast, remember that the humidity in Orlando, even in February, can be horrible. I trained during one of the worst winters in memory, so the unexpected humidity knocked me on my butt. Get there early, relax, hydrate and go to bed early. I know it's Disney and everyone wants to see the fireworks, but you can do that later in the trip.

Pre-race: After attempting to sleep, race day arrives very early. Get up, get your costume on and get to the bus early. I had a friend who stayed off-site and almost missed it all because of the traffic. There's a lot of entertainment before the race, and there are great backdrops for photos and even food vendors. Bring some cash and get breakfast before the run. Hit the restrooms before you enter the corrals, which are a full mile from the drop-off location. There are a few on the way to the corrals. Ever wonder why they're called corrals? Because they pack you in to these metal gated cubes like cattle. If you're claustrophobic you will have issues. Even at this point there are huge video screens and great hosts to entertain you while you wait. Each corral gets its own start, meaning you may not start running for up to a full hour before the first group leaves. However, each corral also gets its own countdown and fireworks send-off.

The race: It's finally here—the moment you've been waiting for. Chances are it's still dark, but there are lights on the course, and entertainment along the way ranging from large kites up in the sky to DJs, Disney characters or giant banners. One warning: Do not get sucked into the character trap. You'll run about a mile before you see your first character (for us it was Captain Jack Sparrow.) The characters you see in that first stretch will also be available on the say back.

Pick and choose which ones you want to stop for. Lines to see the characters along the route can be ridiculous, so keep in mind that you've got a race to run. You must maintain a sixteen-minute mile from when the last person crosses the start line. People have not finished. They will pull you from the course and put you on a bus if you cannot keep up. Disney needs to open the parks to guests, so everyone has to be finished by a certain time.

There are first aid stations all along the route, and can help with bio-freeze, Tylenol and other things you might need along the way. Every mile has a great sign to let you know just where you are.

The parks: No one can explain the joy of running through the Magic Kingdom auto entrance on World Drive. Seeing landmarks you love as you run toward them will give you goosebumps. Seeing the bus stop lights in the fog as I ran toward the Magic Kingdom was amazing. You run in the backstage area into the Magic Kingdom and up a very crowded Main Street USA—it was a dream come true. You run up to the Hub into Tomorrowland and then right around through Cinderella Castle. From there it's onto Liberty Square and out through the backstage area. The tough part follows, as you head back to Epcot. This is when I hit the majority of the characters. You enter through the backstage area and then up to Spaceship Earth, over to the International Gateway and into the final stretch. There are people cheering throughout the Epcot part of the run. It really helps you get past that twelve-mile point and push on to the finish.

After: You did it! You're greeted with water and a cold towel and then your medal. There are many exits where you can have your photo taken in front of a backdrop. You can grab a food box or stop by one of the many booths where you can buy food, champagne, get your medal engraved or get a massage. I went straight to my bus. There's a lot to see and do, but I wanted to get to the Magic Kingdom with my family.

My takeaway? It's an amazing thing and I'm glad I did it, but I won't do it again. It's magical, amazing, you get to see parts of Disney you never get to see otherwise, you get to meet characters who are never around and you get to walk around the rest of the week with that medal around your neck. But there are too many people, it's too crowded certain areas, it's too expensive and it can cause you pain for the rest of your vacation. However, if you're a park regular or a hardcore runner or if you want to check it off your bucket list, then go for it."

Disney Recreation Checklist

- ❑ Golf reservations: (407) WDW-GOLF (4653)
- ❑ For group outings: (407) 938-3870
- ❑ To book a spa treatment: (407) 939-7727
- ❑ To book a parasailing excursion: (407) 939-0754
- ❑ Horseback riding at Fort Wilderness: (407) WDW-PLAY (939-7529)
- ❑ Richard Petty Driving Experience: (800) BE-PETTY (237-3889)

- ❑ SCUBA diving and SCUBA-assisted snorkeling: (407) WDW-TOUR (939-8687)
- ❑ Surfing lessons at Typhoon Lagoon: (407) WDW-PLAY (939-7529)
- ❑ Water skiing on Bay Lake: (407) 939-0754
- ❑ runDisney information: (407) 939-iRun (4786)

Mousejunkies Procreate

AT FIRST I COULDN'T TELL what had awakened me. All I knew was that one moment I was unconscious, and the next I was sitting up, staring into the darkness of our room at the Saratoga Springs resort.

In the span of about half a second, I did a rapid check of what was going on around me:

1. No light coming in the window. Not time to get biscuits and gravy yet—check.
2. I'm awake in a hotel room at Walt Disney World, yet Stacey isn't on the TV—that's odd, but check.
3. Air conditioner is on. Room remains freezing cold—check.
4. There's some little kid next to me and she's throwing up all over the bed—check. Wait, what?

I was starting to shake the cobwebs out of my head. Things were coming into focus.

"Oh, right, I have a daughter," I remembered. "That must be her."

Then it all came flooding back: We were on a Christmas season trip with family with whom we were sharing a two-bedroom suite at Saratoga Springs. Katie, Amy and I were sharing a king-size bed. Which is what put me in the spray zone.

Amy bolted out of bed and hit the light switch, because evidently it's better to be able to see what's happening instead of lying back down and willing it to go away. Which is usually my approach. She's always a lot quicker to react to these kinds of things than I am. I think it's a mother's skill. Dads are supposed to fumble around as they come out of a deep sleep, while moms spring into action. I was playing my role perfectly.

As the room became instantly illuminated and my eyeballs tried to dig a hole in the back of my head, an image was burned into my retinas just before I squeezed my eyes shut. It was of a little girl—my daughter Katie—reminding me that we had deep-fried Oreos for dessert at Boma earlier in the night.

How was she reminding me? She was showing them to me. And the sheets. And the bedspread. And the pillows.

Now I was fully awake.

Amy grabbed Katie and raced her into the bathroom. It was too late, however. There was a huge mess all over the bed. And since she was tending to the child, it was going to be my duty to begin the cleansing process.

But first, a thought crossed my mind that defined the entire incident: So this is what it's like when you come to Walt Disney World with kids.

I stripped the bed and did the best I could to scrub everything. After a quick bath and a few minutes to catch her breath, it appeared as if Katie was recovering nicely. She sat in a chair while Stacey babysat her from the television. Her mother and I started to put the room back together with clean bedding.

MOUSEJUNKIE KATIE "Sorry."

It's certainly part of traveling to Walt Disney World with kids, but of course it's not all 2 A.M. vomiting surprises. There are countless moments when an unforgettable memory is created and framed in the vacation slide deck of your mind.

I'm just saying that along with holding her hand as we walked up Main Street USA and seeing her meet her favorite princess for the first time, this would also be among those everlasting images. It's part of being a parent, and part of being a parent who goes to Walt Disney World frequently.

Our Disney habits had changed dramatically since Katie came into the world four years earlier. Where once we'd jump from park to park, doing whatever we felt like at the speed our legs would carry us, we now were forced to slow down considerably and factor-in the needs and best interests of a youngster.

Kidless, we would skip carelessly past exhausted looking parents who were trying to calm their red-faced, usually crying, and equally exhausted children. When we'd hear a young one throwing a fit somewhere nearby, we'd even be so cavalier as to jokingly say, "That kid hates Disney."

We thought it was funny then. Now I empathize with those parents. Having a child and bringing them along for the first time changes your Disney skill-set entirely. There are dozens of things to think about that had never crossed our minds previously. Do we need a stroller? Did she get enough sleep? Will she be scared of certain characters or attractions? Is she hydrated enough? Why did she just throw up deep-fried Oreos at 2 A.M.? ("Because you fed her deep fried Oreos, goofball," would be your answer. And you'd be right.)

But these were things we never had to consider previously. We were now among those who we once stepped around to get to our next destination.

The Straight Dope *When it comes to character encounters, be patient. See how your child reacts the first time they see a character. If they act frightened, don't force it. Our little one was a little nervous as we were approaching Mickey in the Judge's Tent in Toontown, but the look of sheer joy on her face when she finally came around the corner and saw him was worth the gamble.*

Let's Nap-It-Out, Stitch

A little crankiness comes hand-in-hand with a Walt Disney World vacation. It's just a fact. It's usually hot, crowded, and often times you wake up early and stay out until very late. For a young kid a schedule like that can be taxing. Heck, for a forty(mumble)-year-old it can be taxing.

It can be difficult to deal with, because a Walt Disney World vacation isn't the cheapest way to spend a week. But sometimes trying to talk sense to a slightly dehydrated, sleep-deprived toddler can be the wrong way to go. It gets especially tough when you see dollar signs floating away because your kid insists on going back to the pool instead of using your rather expensive park passes to stay in the theme park. On every trip I see far too many parents trying to berate their kids into having fun, which almost always results in a general meltdown.

Consider the nap: A midday respite, spent huddled under the covers in complete darkness. (It might be 112 degrees outside, but I keep our room's air conditioning frigid at all times.) I know it can seem like a waste of time. While you're lying in a darkened room back at the resort, the rest of the World is going on just minutes away. Parades, character meet-and-greets, shows—everything you want to get done on your vacation is still happening. But you're prone and motionless as the daylight hours tick away.

A much-needed nap, however, can save an entire day. It's impossible to scream a kid into a good mood, so rather than battle back-and-forth in the heat and the crowds, pack-it-in and grab some down time. A recharge of the batteries and a splash of water on the face can do wonders for a little one's mood. And her mom's.

I am often the butt of some pointed Mousejunkie barbs because of my nap routine. But I swear by it.

An ode to the nap, as expressed through ancient art of haiku:

> Bus back to the room
> Ice-cold air conditioning
> No one is crying

A Lack of Character Is
Not Such a Bad Thing

The next thing we learned is not to base our vacation around Disney's colorful and conveniently available characters. They certainly are part of the Walt Disney World experience, but standing in long lines to get a picture with a character is not an efficient use of time. We haven't put a number on how many character interactions of photos are enough, it's just a matter of getting a feel for how the day is going.

When I look back at my old trip photos, or someone else's, the least-interesting ones are the posed character pictures. It looks like everyone is lined up for execution at dawn, and there's usually very little emotion outside of a wave and a smile.

I took a picture of Cinderella Castle in 1981. I took another one in 1998, and yet another in 2010. Guess what? It hasn't really changed. The people standing in front if it, however, have changed. And that's what it's all about, in the end. I put more value in photos of my daughter's reactions to unexpected events or resting in her mother's arms after a long day. If you still feel like you need your character interaction, and don't misunderstand me—it's still a great part of a Walt Disney World vacation—let them come to you.

And yet there are others for whom the character interaction makes the entire trip.

The Straight Dope *Book a couple of character meals. The characters come to you. It's much easier and it all takes place inside—so it's air-conditioned. Plus, food.*

MOUSEJUNKIE RYAN Alice is my obsession, and during my last trip, I made meeting her my number one priority. I scheduled my days and coordinated my outfits around meeting my favorite Wonderland chick (the best shirts to show of my Alice tattoos, of course), and I was not disappointed. I met her three times in one trip, and twice it was the same girl and she recognized me immediately. Our interactions by far were the most magical moments of the trip, from her excitement at remembering me and my tattoos, to her declarations to onlookers that we were special friends. Meeting your favorite character can be just as magical as meeting a celebrity or your idol. Don't pass up the opportunity.

Strollers Are Your Friend

If you think your child might need a stroller, bring it. You can pack your own or rent one at the parks. Stroller rentals are available at all four theme parks: $15 per day, or $31 for a double-stroller per day. We always brought our own, and I'm very happy we did. While it can be a pain to get it on and off the Disney buses, it looks different from the vast fleet of hard plastic rental strollers that converge in alarming numbers in Fantasyland, and is therefore easier to find after exiting an attraction.

It's also more common for the Disney rental strollers to be stolen. You can't tell them apart, so it'd be hard to identify it as yours.

The Straight Dope *Having your stroller stolen is a hazard every parent must face, but here's a unique strategy that may lessen the chances of this happening. It's simple: Take a diaper, put it in a see-through freezer bag, pour some root beer into the bag and hang it from your stroller's handle. Voila—the "soiled diaper gambit" keeps your property safer from stroller poachers.*

I get totally wiped out walking around all day, so the last thing I want to do is carry my daughter around all night. Putting her in the stroller conserved her energy, it helped us keep track of where she was all the time, and it gave us a place to put stuff—cameras, souvenirs, and so forth. Not to mention it preserved her dad's back for a few more years

The Straight Dope *Mark your stroller with something that's easy to spot. We use a neon-orange Mickey-shaped luggage tag. It makes your stroller much easier to locate after riding an attraction, especially if it was moved from where you parked it on the way in.*

Stroller parking areas are located throughout the parks. Just because you left your stroller in a certain place when you went into an attraction, doesn't mean it'll be in that same spot when you come out. It doesn't necessarily mean someone took it, however. Cast members often have to relocate strollers to make room for others or to clear a pedestrian area.

On a related note, don't leave anything of value in the stroller when you park it and walk away. Take any digital cameras, park passes, or pocketbooks with you.

Stroller Rental Locations

The Magic Kingdom: The first level of the Main Street Railroad station.

Epcot: At the main entrance—just to the right. International Gateway—on the left before the turnstiles.

Animal Kingdom: Go through the turnstiles and they'll be on the right.

Disney's Hollywood Studios: At Oscar's Super Service— just look for the gas station on the right after you walk through the turnstiles.

A length-of-stay stroller rental is also available. Guests make a one-time payment for as many days as will be needed at a rate of $13 a day (saving $2 a day), and double strollers for $27 a day (saving $4 a day.) Just show your receipt at the stroller rental location and you'll be on your way.

Tackling the Magic Kingdom

The Magic Kingdom is the Holy Grail for the younger set. It is the iconic park and it has the most attractions appropriate for children.

The Straight Dope   *If your child shows fear or starts to cry while in line at an attraction, consider skipping it. It's not worth the frustration involved as you attempt to calm an upset child while adding up the cost of the trip in your head.*

When we first took our daughter to Walt Disney World, she was three years old. She was afraid of the dark rides—primarily because we'd get into a ride vehicle and be taken into a dark tunnel. Yet she loved any of the attractions that were located outside.

When I asked her to review Magic Kingdom attractions after that first trip, most of her comments contained the phrases, "no," "scary," and "never again."

But that was years ago. She's braver now, and generally wants to ride anything she's tall enough to get on, which brings with it its own set of restrictions.

A list of Magic Kingdom attractions with height restrictions:

Land	Attraction	Height restriction
Tomorrowland	Space Mountain	44 inches
Tomorrowland	Stitch's Great Escape	40 inches
Tomorrowland	Tomorrowland Speedway	32 inches to ride, 54 inches to drive
Frontierland	Big Thunder Mountain Railroad	40 inches
Frontierland	Splash Mountain	40 inches

The Straight Dope *Use the "baby swap" to experi-*
ence any attractions you might want to, but your child does
not (or is too short for). It works like this: Parents and child
queue up together. Parent A rides first, while parent B stands
to one side with the child. Once the ride is over, the parents
trade places and parent B gets to ride the attraction without
waiting through the entire line again.

Approaching the Magic Kingdom with Kids

Be at the park early. You'll get to see the opening show, and
you'll get a jump on all those other people who are still abed
while you're storming the Castle.

Attack **Fantasyland** first. It's tailor-made for kids, but the
beauty of it is that parents can ride-along on every attraction
without feeling awkward or outsized. If you've got youngsters
along, get Fantasyland out of the way as soon as possible. I'm
not saying to run from attraction to attraction, but focusing on
the slower-loading kid magnets early will save you from unnec-
essary stress later in the day. Specifically target Dumbo, Peter
Pan's Flight, The Many Adventures of Winnie the Pooh, The
Mad Tea Party, Under the Sea—Journey of the Little Mermaid
(and working toward Tomorrowland) the Tomorrowland
Speedway. Lines can form quickly at these attractions in particular, and it's best to get to them as early as you can.

If the kids are older, follow the crowds to the **Seven
Dwarfs Mine Train, Splash Mountain** and/or **Big Thunder
Mountain Railroad. Space Mountain** also packs them in
early, so prioritize and execute.

★ **The Straight Dope**   *Use a FastPass+ to meet Anna and Elsa. The lines get insanely long. Waiting in lines like that can eat up valuable park time.*

If the 3 P.M. parade is kicking off and you're stuck in the back of the crowd near Main Street, consider relocating to Frontierland near the bridge at Splash Mountain. The crowds are usually much thinner there and little ones will have a better chance to see what's happening.

Need some room to breathe by midday? Raft over to Tom Sawyer's Island, hop on the WDW railroad for a few loops, grab a seat in the Hall of Presidents or catch the Country Bear Jamboree to power-down with the kids.

If your kids will sit still long enough and you'd like a front-row seat to the evening parade and Wishes, pull up a curb on Main Street or the Hub in front of Cinderella Castle about at least an hour before show time.

One of our favorite viewing spots for Main Street Electric Parade and Wishes is from the second floor of the Main Street train station facing the Castle. If you want to catch everything from there, plan on arriving a couple hours early.

Epcot with Kids

At first glance, Epcot has less to offer the little ones than the Magic Kingdom—what with the learning and lectures and such. Beyond the initial impression, however, there lies a full day of things to do for parents and children.

Here's what we've found works best when touring Epcot with youngsters:

You've heard it before, but it works: Arrive at the park before it opens. When the ropes drop and everyone makes a mad dash to get their FastPass+ for Soarin', head straight for the Character Connection (located near the Fountainview Café) for some (normally) easy access to characters.

Activity areas spread throughout Future World and the World Showcase—Kidcot Fun Stops—are a great way for kids to feel involved in the park, and to accidentally learn something. The Kidcot Fun Stops are designated on park maps with a big "K" in a red square. There are sixteen of them located throughout Futureworld and the World Showcase. Children are given a cutout mask which they can color and decorate as they stop at each of the locations. Cast members will also stamp the mask at each country or Kidcot Fun Stop. The activity areas are staffed by cast members native to the specific country, who will stamp the child's mask and quite often write something in their native language. Kids can also purchase an Epcot passport, which cast members will stamp at each country they visit.

The Kidcot Fun Stops are free, and if you don't point it out, they may not notice that they can also be educational. It forces you to seek out the activity tables, drawing you deeper into the World Showcase pavilions. It provides a better opportunity to uncover details and interact with cast members. In Future World the Kidcot Fun Stops are located in The Land, Test Track, Innoventions East and West, and The Seas

With Nemo and Friends. They're also located in each country of the World Showcase.

The Living Seas With Nemo and Friends, based on the Disney/Pixar film, *Finding Nemo*, is a natural when traveling with children, and getting there is half the fun. After winding through an imaginatively designed queue area, guests board appropriately themed "clamobiles" where they'll travel along with Marlin and Dory in search of Nemo, who has gone missing again. A little further along, guests encounter Mr. Ray instructing his students, and then come into a school of jellyfish. An anglerfish pierces the darkness—one of the only moments that may spook skittish children—leading to Bruce the Great White and Chum the Mako.

The clamobiles are then swept into the undersea current with Nemo (found), Crush and Squirt. "In the Big Blue World," a song written for the Animal Kingdom's Finding Nemo: the Musical, rounds it all out.

During the adventure, visitors glide by displays that use new animation techniques that project characters from the film into tanks of actual aquatic creatures.

Headlining the pavilion proper is the interactive Turtle Talk With Crush. Crush, the stoner/surfer character from *Finding Nemo* treats guests to ten-minute shows where he interacts with, talks to, and messes with the audience. No two shows are alike, and it's a clever, customized attraction perfect for kids.

The entire complex is tucked into a series of tanks that make up a 5.7-million-gallon marine environment—one of the largest of its kind anywhere. Kids can take their time watching scores of different types of aquatic life from a myriad of viewing areas.

The World Showcase has several experiences that target youngsters in particular. A hedge maze in the United Kingdom is just the right size for younger children. Kids can join the fife and drum corps outside the American Experience as they recite the Pledge of Allegiance. A miniature train display next to the Germany pavilion can keep kids entertained for a few minutes. A stand of hand drums at the African village is very likely to keep youngsters attention for a bit longer. They can bang away for as long as they like. Dancing and making a God-awful cacophony is not only O.K. here, it's encouraged.

A list of attractions at Epcot with height restrictions:

Land	Attraction	Height restriction
Future World	Mission: Space	44 inches
Future World	Soarin'	40 inches
Future World	Test Track	40 inches

Strollers in the Studios

Disney's Hollywood Studios is the home of Disney Junior— Live On Stage! That, alone, is enough of a reason to point the stroller at this theme park and begin marching. Characters from a number of The Disney Channel's shows take the stage live, in a singing, dancing and storytelling performance that urges the tykes to get up and take part. The show is geared toward preschool-aged audiences, and is located in the Animation Courtyard.

Stage shows, including Beauty and the Beast, located on Sunset Boulevard just before the Twilight Zone Tower of Terror, and Voyage of the Little Mermaid, located in the Animation Courtyard, are both musical, entertaining shows not to be missed.

Beauty and the Beast is a Broadway-style spectacle, while Voyage of the Little Mermaid combines live actors, animation, laser displays and some incredibly innovative puppeteers to tell Ariel's story. This seventeen-minute production often draws crowds, but the theater can hold a substantial number of people so the wait time (the queue is covered, protecting little ones from direct sun and rain) tends to be reasonable.

If there's a wait at Muppet*Vision 3D, consider yourself lucky. The pre-show contains dozens of puns and jokes— particular to the Muppets' sense of humor—that will entertain parents, and keep youngsters occupied.

The show is very similar in execution to Mickey's Philharmagic in the Magic Kingdom, and It's Tough to be a Bug in Disney's Animal Kingdom. Where Bug might frighten children, Muppet Vision 3-D is mild and funny enough to keep everyone in the family happy.

Disney's Imagineers are constantly pushing the envelope, coming up with inventive ways to entertain guests, and using the latest technologies to wow visitors. So what do younger kids find the most fun? Water fountains and playgrounds. Just like the ones they could've played at down the street for a lot less money and effort. Regardless, there are several scattered throughout the Studios, and in every theme park, and they can be a fantastic way to cool off and get off our feet for a few.

For slightly older kids, the Great Movie Ride can be fun. It's in the reproduction of Mann's Chinese Theater at the end of Hollywood Boulevard. (Walk toward the Sorcerer Mickey hat and keep going.) Just because there aren't any people waiting outside the theater doesn't mean a queue hasn't formed. This attraction can hold a great many people inside.

The twenty-minute guided tour through movie history is entertaining, but easily-spooked youngsters may find the *Alien* portion of the attraction a bit unsettling.

A list of attractions at Disney's Hollywood Studios with height restrictions:

Area	Attraction	Heigh restriction
Sunset Blvd.	Rock'n'Roller Coaster	48 inches
Echo Lake	Star Tours	40 inches
Sunset Blvd.	Tower of Terror	40 inches

Animal Kingdom with Kids

Thrill rides, learning experiences, and stage shows now make this park a must-do for anyone spending time at Walt Disney World. Activities for children abound:

The Festival of the Lion King is, hands down, the single best stage show on Disney property, and appropriate for all

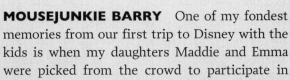

MOUSEJUNKIE BARRY   One of my fondest memories from our first trip to Disney with the kids is when my daughters Maddie and Emma were picked from the crowd to participate in "Festival of the Lion King" show at Disney's Animal Kingdom. The smiles on their faces could not have been any broader as they marched around with their maracas and danced. They both have acted in local theater since that visit, and I wouldn't be surprised if that first little taste of the spotlight lit the fire for them.

ages. A Broadway-caliber show based on the film, this production features live singing performances, acrobatic displays, wire acts, dancing and audience participation.

The Straight Dope   *Try to sit as close to the front as possible if you bring a child to Festival of the Lion King. Near the end of the performance, cast members pull children up from the audience to take part in the finale.*

Head to the opposite end of the park for Finding Nemo: The Musical. Brightly costumed cast members manipulate puppets across a massive stage. The music is catchy and the cast of characters is extensive. This performance is fine for all ages, but may do best with younger children.

Kilimanjaro Safaris remains a must-do attraction for all ages, providing an amazing experience for adults as well as children. Guests board a large safari truck and are taken on a guided tour of a 100-acre east African savanna that serves as home to dozens of species of animals. Guests have a chance to catch an extreme close-up view of elephants, giraffes, antelope, lions, hippos, cheetahs, and rhinos, among other beasts. This nearly twenty-minute ride through a small re-creation of Africa is an enthralling experience for all ages.

Youngsters can spend hours playing in the Boneyard, and meeting Disney characters at the various character greeting trails.

Flights of Wonder, a stage show featuring trained birds, would be easy to pass off as a simple parrot showcase. But deeper conservation themes, surprisingly funny cast members, and breathtaking stunts by trained hawks, cranes, owls, and other fowl make this show one of the strongest in the entire park. Youngsters love the up-close encounters and their parents will enjoy the quick-witted host, Guano Joe. There are audience-participation opportunities for brave youngsters.

While there are plenty of activities and attractions that parents and children can take part in together, there are a few the skittish should avoid. Obviously, the more thrilling attractions like Expedition Everest would not be a wise choice for little ones. But there is one attraction that draws kids like flies (you'll get that clever turn of phrase in a moment) and one parents should think twice about.

The Straight Dope *Avoid taking easily scared tykes to see It's Tough to be a Bug—a 3-D experience located inside the lower portion of the Tree of Life. While the 3-D bug glasses may seem silly, the show always seems to frighten youngsters in the audience.*

Every performance of It's Tough to Be a Bug I've attended has resulted in at least one absolute freak-out by a startled child. Large spiders descend from the ceiling, and several tactile surprises jar little ones unexpectedly. However, older children may love the show.

A list of attractions at Disney's Animal Kingdom with height restrictions:

Land	Attraction	Height restriction
DinoLand U.S.A.	Dinosaur	40 inches
Anandapur	Expedition Everest	44 inches
Asia	Kali River Rapids	38 inches
DinoLand U.S.A.	Primeval Whirl	48 inches

Mousejunkies Expectorate

The Voyage of the S.S. *Regurgitation*

The boat was pitching. There was regret. There was sickness. This was not how I thought the first night of our Walt Disney World vacation would go. It was the voyage of the *S.S. Regurgitation*.

Yet there it was, spread out before us in great and terrible detail. Through this unexpected adventure, Katie sat sympathetic to her poor mom's travails. Her calmness in the face of yuck was rather remarkable.

Let me explain by backing everything up a few hours...

Amy, Katie and I were meeting a large group of people for dinner at the Whispering Canyon Cafe, which is located just off the lobby of the Wilderness Lodge over near the Magic Kingdom. We caught a bus from our hotel—the Animal Kingdom Lodge—and then caught a water shuttle over to the Wilderness Lodge.

Everything seemed fine. At first. In retrospect it probably wasn't the meat-mountain we scaled at the Whispering Canyon that caused Amy to show everyone on our shuttle boat what she had for dinner. As an artist, Amy described, in vivid technicolor, what we had just eaten. Her medium of choice was fluids.

She had complained about feeling a little odd as we waited in the cavernous lobby of the Wilderness Lodge Resort prior to our dinner. I shrugged it off as moodiness as our Advanced Dining Reservation was moved back first an hour, and then a bit more. It wasn't Disney's fault—we had a large group so we had to wait for everyone to arrive.

Note: If for some reason you find yourself married to Amy, just make sure she's well-fed. If that task is taken care of, you're all set. Should you find your own Amy in need of foodstuffs, get thee to a beefery. Which is exactly where we found ourselves late one autumn night at Walt Disney World.

Whispering Canyon Cafe deals in large food. At dinner you order a skillet—made up of three types of meat—described as "all you care to enjoy." Let's just call it what it is: Bring it until I'm angry at myself. If I've got the meat-sweats, I've had just about enough.

That night our group agreed that our skillet would consist of ribs, beef loin and chicken. Great heaps of it was carted to our table and everyone dug in. I didn't really notice that Amy wasn't eating much, since I was engaged in my own hand-to-rib combat with this wall of protein. As it turns out, she wasn't really partaking with the same gusto the rest of us were. I made the mistake of finishing my soda quickly, which resulted in a two-liter-sized glass of Coke being thrust in front of me—it's one of the funny charms of this particular restaurant. I attacked it as if it was a challenge. Meanwhile, Amy sipped at her water and gingerly nibbled on some greens.

We wrapped up our dinner, 22 out of the 23 of our group stuffed, and headed to the water shuttle that would take us back to our respective resorts. The first hints that this would not be a normal trip back to the room began to manifest themselves on the dock. Clouds of tiny bugs swarmed the warm lights illuminating the wooden pier that jutted out into Bay Lake, as Amy clutched the woven rope railing unsteadily.

"I don't feel so good," she said.

But she said that a lot. So I just shrugged and figured she'd be fine after a night's sleep. After all, it was late. A short time later the boat pulled in to haul us all over to the Magic Kingdom, where we'd disperse via the motor coaches there. The boat itself was a closed-cabin style—comfortable and more than up to the task. We filed in and sat in the second row—Amy at the window, me in the middle and Katie on the aisle. As the captain pulled the vessel out into the lake itself and we began to bob up and down slightly, Amy looked right at me and said: "I really don't feel good. I feel like I'm going to throw up."

I still didn't take her seriously. I looked over my shoulder to the right, and then turned back to tell her something. Instead of speaking at her face, I found myself staring out the window at the water going by us. Amy, meanwhile, was bent over at the waist, shouting what little she had eaten into a white bag of Katie's leftovers she had brought to re-heat in our room.

She sat up and looked at me. She hadn't been exaggerating.

"I don't think I'm done yet," she said.

Now I knew she was serious. Our friends in the seat in front of us tried to help, but about thirty seconds later Amy went back for round two. She held the bag in front of her and disgorged as discreetly as possible.

Before I describe what happened next, I'll ask this trivia question: Did you know Disney uses biodegradable bags? We didn't know that, but we certainly learned that over the course of the next minute.

I looked to the front of the boat—starboard or aft or port side or whatever—and saw there was a trash barrel at the foot of a set of stairs leading up to the captain's perch. I took Katie and jumped over to the row across from us so Amy could make her way to it. Only Amy couldn't really stand up to do that. So instead of looking like I was being helpful it just looked like I was running away from my sick wife. Instead she leaned into the big, white bag and hurled into it for a third time.

The bag had done its job valiantly up to this point, but it had been pushed too far. It seemed to hang on as tightly as possible until the last second, when it could do no more. It disintegrated completely and exploded outward in a shower of the most magical offal this side of Mission: Space.

Our friends Christopher and Maureen, who had been sitting just in front of us, sprang into action. Napkins appeared out of nowhere and even a motion-sickness patch was offered. They tended to Amy while I recoiled across the aisle. The captain of the ill-fated S.S. *Regurgitate* appeared and took a look at what was going on.

"She threw up," I said, pointing out the obvious.

"Is it on the floor?" he asked.

"It's all over the floor. And some on the walls."

I felt bad for the guy, but there wasn't much we could do about it. I only assumed they were equipped for such an occurrence. It seemed like the type of environment that could be hosed down.

We hustled Amy off the boat so as to not ruin the poor captain's night any more and headed for our bus.

Katie was sympathetic, but also grossed out. We eventually got poor mom home and tucked in. Katie and I spent the rest of our evening watching the in-room resort channel as Amy jumped up every few minutes to run into the bathroom.

In the end, Amy was sick for a good portion of our week at Walt Disney World. We moved hotels to Bay Lake Tower, located just outside the Magic Kingdom. There it was—just yards away, and we had a violently ill family member unable to even leave the room. It was certainly unfortunate, but these things happen.

When you travel to Walt Disney World often, it's bound to occur. It's just a matter of odds, really. I've been struck down while on Disney property twice previously. One time I was fighting off a flu-like malady when I was self-quarantined to my room. In a haze at one point I got up, determined to get myself together and meet my fellow travelers out in the parks. I got about three minutes into my effort when I said—and I want to quote this accurately: "Bleeauurrrgggghmagical." I wasn't going anywhere.

For a Mousejunkie, there could be no worse torture. So I decided to soak up what I could—mainly antihistamines. If a little would help, maybe a lot would get me on my feet so I could join my friends the next day.

It's something I've learned over many trips to central Florida: Sometimes people get sick. And sometimes people get sick at Walt Disney World. And nearly overdosing on cold medicine isn't going to help. The epilogue of that particular episode was that I forced myself to get out of bed the next day and walked in forty-foot jaunts before I had to stop for a rest. It took forever to get where I was going, but I did get to bask in the Magic Kingdom before heading home. I wasn't going to allow a collapsed lung to get between me and another ride on Big Thunder Mountain. Basically, if you can die from stubbornness, I probably will.

Unfortunately I've had a few occasions to hone my "getting sick at Disney" skills. It all seemed to clear up on one trip when I visited the concierge, who suggested I call my doctor back home and have him call in a prescription to Turner Drug—a pharmacy nearby that delivers to Walt Disney World resorts.

I made a few calls, spoke with Turner Drug, and heard these magic words: "We'll be there within an hour."

They were, and I began the process of getting back to my park-touring weight. It took longer than I would have liked, but I firmly believe I was saved from dropping further into sickness by the kindness of that concierge, and the existence of Turner Drug.

We don't usually have a car, so when a pharmaceutical need became necessary I never really considered what to do. I normally just figured I'd get through the rest of the trip and visit the doctor when I got back home. However, Turner Drug delivering to Disney resorts can be an invaluable resource should you be stricken by an ill-timed malady.

To contact Turner Drug: 407-828-8125.

Avoiding Epcrotch

It's no secret that there's a lot of walking involved during a Walt Disney World vacation. And everyone knows the central Florida climate approximates a blast furnace for nine months out of the year.

Combine those two and you've got something that could potentially turn an enjoyable vacation at Walt Disney World into a remarkably painful death march.

Of course, I speak of the worst possible sentence that can be passed on an unprepared park visitor: Epcrotch.

Epcrotch is the chafing that occurs only in the confines of Walt Disney World. Heat plus extensive walking plus ill-fitting underclothes equals a pain only Disney guests know.

This isn't the normal chafing associated with long-distance runners or triathletes. Those guys have it easy. They don't have to get from the Main Street train station to the Crystal Palace during the Main Street Electrical Parade with their inner thighs aflame with the heat of a thousand suns.

Epcrotch is an aggressive, flesh-searing strain of chafing that strikes at the least convenient time. Because no matter when it starts to peel away layers of skin and rub raw, you've got days of walking ahead of you. Once it sets in, there's not a lot you can do. It's already too late. On a vacation built around walking, it can interrupt even the best-laid plans.

No one is immune to Epcrotch. This objectionable condition isn't relegated to the overweight or those who wear their shorts too tight (though, don't do that.) It can strike anyone in the Florida heat.

There is only one way to protect oneself from this debilitating and mentally-scarring pain and its closely-related
cousin, blisters—and that is proper preparation.

There may be other options, but I have come across an
extremely successful manner of banishing Epcrotch from my
vacations: Bodyglide anti-chafing balm.

Bodyglide comes in a stick resembling deodorant. It is
applied in a similar manner to any area that may experience
chafing or blisters. Through repeated research, I've found
that it completely prevents chafing and blisters. It works. It's
your friend.

Slather it on first thing in the morning before leaving your
resort. One application is enough to keep the thigh fires at
bay. It can literally save a vacation.

Health and Well-Being Checklist

- ❑ Aspirin packed
- ❑ Antacid packed
- ❑ CPAP machine packed (for sleep apnea patients)
- ❑ Bodyglide packed
- ❑ Prescription drugs packed
- ❑ Turner Drug (will deliver to Walt Disney World resorts):
  407-828-8125
- ❑ Celebration Health—hospital in Celebration, Florida:
  (407) 303-4000

13 **Mousejunkies Marry**

Disney Vacation Club

It's a miracle that I belong to Disney Vacation Club.

Right now you're saying to yourself, "You're a sick man with an unhealthy attachment to Disney. Why wouldn't you belong to Disney Vacation Club?"

Because I am married to Mousejunkie Amy—the reluctant Mousejunkie. She is a fun person who loves the magic as much as anyone I know. It's just that she cares about our family's financial health as well.

She's the smart one. I'm the fun one.

So when we took the Disney Vacation Club tour in 2005 (initially just to score the $100 promised by the marketing department), I was a little more than shocked when she said the whole deal made sense. Hey, if she says so, I'm on board.

We've since spent many nights in one of the several DVC resorts scattered around the property. We've used points, borrowed points, banked points, rented points and yearned for more points. The point? We're happy with our decision. In the long run, it'll save us money. In the short run (or, the way I see things,) it'll allow us to return to Walt Disney World twice a year for pretty much the rest of my life. (Assuming I live to be a healthy 80-something-year-old Mousejunkie.)

Here's a basic rundown of how it works:

Disney Vacation Club is a timeshare-like operation, allowing members to buy a real estate interest through a one-time purchase of "vacation points." Members use points to pay for accommodations at one of the DVC resorts. Members can use the points, bank them for future use, borrow from future use years, or transfer them in or out of their account. The points renew every year. When making a reservation, members are charged points. The number of points depends on what kind of room, what resort, and what time of year the reservations are for. Members can book a reservation at their "home resort" up to twelve months in advance, or at any other resort up to seven months in advance.

MOUSEJUNKIE DEB   Although I've enjoyed every trip, our first time staying on WDW property was when I really started to love the whole theming immersion and realized we'd be coming back often. We stayed at Port Orleans Riverside (Dixie Landings at the time) and have never stayed off property since, buying into Disney Vacation Club and into a lifetime of memories. We vacation at many other places and always will, but DVC's "home away from home" mantra is a reality for us. People have beach houses on the Jersey Shore, time shares in Cabo, points and comps in Vegas, and we have our DVC.

MOUSEJUNKIE CAROL It's probably the easiest way to spend around $20,000 that I have ever experienced. Randy (my husband) had gone on the DVC tour a few times. He was having a tough time convincing me that it was the way to go, so eventually he got me to go on a tour. (I will admit the free $100 in Disney dollars for taking the tour was my real enticement). At the end of the tour, our salesman, Marshal (how many people fondly remember the name of the guy who convinced them to buy a timeshare), worked with us and talked about the different number of points we might want to buy. A quick 220 points later and we were out of there. It's the best in that we do save money in hotels every time we visit. It's the worst, because, well, let's say that we tend to go more than our allotted 220 points will allow. So what do we do? We are now in a network where we will buy someone else's unused points for the year, transfer into our accounts and we're good to go one more time. DVC has really just been an instrument to bring us to Disney at least three times a year and if we can do so, four to five times a year.

Members can use their points at one of several Disney Vacation Club resorts around the property, and a few off-property. The resorts range from quite nice to extravagant.

The DVC Resorts

Old Key West: A sprawling resort inspired by the architecture and spirit of the Florida Keys, Old Key West was the first Disney Vacation Club resort to be constructed. It costs the fewest amount of points of all the DVC resorts, yet offers the largest rooms.

Old Key West has one table-service restaurant, Olivia's, and the Gurgling Suitcase bar. Guests can rent boats or catch a water ferry down the Sassagoula River to Downtown Disney.

Old Key West still represents a fantastic value if measured by points used to the quality of the resort.

Beach Club Villas: Designed to look and feel like a New England seaside resort, the driveway into the Beach Club is a toll road, each guest gets a copy of the Herald and a scratch ticket. Concierge cast members are required to end every sentence with "Sox rule."

O.K., not really. But that'd make it pretty authentic.

The Beach Club Villas are a top-notch DVC option. The Beach Club shares the best hotel pool on property, Stormalong Bay, with its sister resort, the Yacht Club.

The most important amenity at the Beach Club is its location: just a short walk to Epcot's International Gateway, and a quick boat ride to Disney's Hollywood Studios.

The Villas at Wilderness Lodge: Tall trees and thick woodlands surround this majestic resort, which is themed to look like a National Park Service lodge. The DVC villas are integrated into the resort, attached to the main lobby by a short walkway. A massive lobby welcomes guests, with rough-hewn exposed logs and an eighty-foot-tall fireplace dominating the space.

The Iron Spike Room boasts an impressive collection of Walt Disney's train memorabilia and deep, luxurious leather chairs in which to contemplate said collection. If you go at Christmas time, the lobby of this resort is worth a visit whether or not you are a guest there. A massive Christmas tree shoots up into the cavernous entryway, an impressive and festive display.

BoardWalk Villas: A favorite to almost anyone who stays there, the BoardWalk is a true showpiece among Disney's resorts. Designed in the image of a turn-of-the-century Atlantic seashore hotel, the stately yet whimsical BoardWalk is among the most picturesque of all Disney's resorts.

If location is important—the BoardWalk is for you. If perfect theming is something you look for—the BoardWalk is for you. Want to feel pampered and be right in the middle of everything? You want to stay at the BoardWalk Villas. The BoardWalk boasts its own entertainment district, with musicians, magicians, and showmen roaming the boardwalk (lower case "b") throughout the night, passing by one of the several restaurants and snack bars that dot the lakefront space.

While much of the after-dark hubbub that goes on out in front of the guest rooms is filtered out, visitors will not be able to ignore the nightly fireworks at the adjoining Epcot theme park. Any thoughts of turning in early to get some rest will be sharply interrupted by the sound of IllumiNations going off nightly at 9 P.M.

Saratoga Springs Resort and Spa: The upstate New York horse racing destination has been faithfully recreated at the site of the former Disney Institute. A massive complex, Saratoga Springs Resort and Spa features themed pools, Victorian architecture, various springs, and fantastic views of Downtown Disney—which is located just across the lake. A short walk or ferry ride and you're right in the middle of the shopping, dining or people-watching action.

Not surprisingly, Saratoga Springs is a beautiful resort. The grounds are immaculate, the lobby is bright and clean, the main themed pool feels like a natural lake amidst large rock formations, and horse racing themes abound. It is a pleasure to stay at this resort.

Saratoga Springs is a large resort. Plan to leave plenty of travel time when heading out for any scheduled plans. We usually end up breaking one of our cardinal rules if we stay at Saratoga Springs: We rent a car. I normally would never consider it, but being able to come and go when we want makes for a more convenient experience when the alternative is standing at a bus stop for forty minutes as the advanced dining reservation you made 180 days ago goes by.

Saratoga Springs is broken up into five areas:

The Grandstand—Across a parking lot from the main lobby, this area features a barbecue grill area and the Backstretch pool bar.

The Paddock—The Paddock runs along Union Avenue and has two bus stops.

The Carousel—These rooms are the furthest from the Carriage House.

The Springs—The Springs are closest to the Carriage House lobby, the High Rock Spring theme pool, arcade, spa, and many of the resort's amenities.

Congress Park—Congress Park is the area of Saratoga Springs that sits closest Downtown Disney. The buildings closest to Buena Vista Drive offer easy walking access to Downtown Disney and its bus stops.

The Treehouses at Saratoga Springs: Every one of these elevated vacation homes was constructed off-site, and then trucked-in to replace the old octagonal treehouses that stood on the same spot.

Disney calls them "cabin casual." These three bedroom, two bath Treehouses stand ten feet off the ground and feature flat-screen TVs and granite countertops.

Animal Kingdom Villas: The Animal Kingdom Lodge villas are located both in the existing Animal Kingdom Lodge and in the newer Kidani Village. The new units more than double the current size of the resort and include a children's water play area, a restaurant—Sanaa—and its own savanna.

Staying at the Animal Kingdom Lodge is everything it's purported to be. A savanna-view room allows guests to start the day with a stunning view of animals in their natural

MOUSEJUNKIE J   The Treehouses have their benefits and drawbacks.

The good:
➤ Two-bedroom points for a three-bedroom unit.
➤ Brand new—nicely decorated, vaulted ceilings
➤ Detached units—No neighbors banging on the ceilings, walls, floors, etc.

The not-so-good:

➤ Location, Location, Location—It's not a bad spot if you like Downtown Disney and spend time there. We lucked out and got the primo location so it was manageable. We never took the internal bus because it was a short walk to the Grandstand bus station at Saratoga Springs from our villa. But people at the other end of the Treehouses would have a long walk. The internal bus was running on time but it is still another bus that you have to transfer to. We avoided it. The boat was O.K. if you wanted to go to Downtown Disney. It was always on time and dropped you off at Pleasure Island near the old Rockin' Roll Beach Club.
➤ It's really not a nice place to just hang out. The deck is nice but the bugs are out in the wooded areas.
➤ It's not like sitting on the balcony at BoardWalk. You can't people watch at all.

I would not stay in them again. I would choose a two bedroom at Old Key West first.

habitat. Sunrises and sunsets explode through the Jambo House lobby, bathing the authentic African art in a golden glow. One end of the massive, six-story lobby is glass-enclosed, providing a bright, naturally lit atmosphere.

Kidani Village, located just next door to the Animal Kingdom Lodge, has a similar, yet much smaller lobby. It lends the resort a more intimate feel. Disney calls the Vacation Club resorts "home away from home." Kidani Village lives up to this description more than any other. It feels like home.

Bay Lake Tower: Ultramodern (read: a little cold, according to some), Bay Lake Tower sits just outside the Magic Kingdom and on top of what used to be the Contemporary Resort's north garden wing. A coveted Magic Kingdom-view is part of the new tower, making it a much sought-after booking.

The interior features abstract Disney art, and bright, clean lines and colors. A sixteenth-floor Top of the World Lounge provides amazing views of the property, and of the Magic Kingdom, in particular. Only guests staying on points are provided access to the Top of the World Lounge.

Christopher Lamb and Maureen Strong, a couple from Forked River, N.J., were curious about all of the DVC resorts, so they approached it with an analytical eye: They booked a vacation where they spent one night in each of Walt Disney World's DVC resorts. Every day meant a new resort (and more tipping, since cast members would forward their luggage to the next destination each day.)

"It's not something I really want to do again," Maureen said of the couple's sampler getaway. "But we got to try all the resorts. Instead of spending years trying them out and

MOUSEJUNKIE AMY Bay Lake Tower feels like a hospital, to me. It's very sterile. It could have been great, but they went beige.

possibly making a mistake by staying at a resort you didn't like for a week, we saw them all in about 10 days."

In each of the DVC resorts, guests can choose from one of four room types:

➤ A studio room is essentially a standard hotel room that can sleep four people.

➤ A one-bedroom vacation home has a master suite, living room, kitchen and a patio. The one-bedroom unit can sleep up to five people.

➤ A two-bedroom vacation home, also referred to as a two-bedroom lock-off, consists of a one bedroom unit and a second bedroom attached. A two-bedroom unit can sleep up to eight people.

➤ The grand villa is the granddaddy of all DVC units. It is luxury, convenience and comfort all in one. The grand villa has three bedrooms, three baths, is a two-story unit and can sleep upwards of twelve people comfortably. While the BoardWalk grand villa is a one-story unit, and the Wilderness Lodge and the Beach Club do not offer grand villas, the top of the line unit at Old Key West is bigger than many private homes.

Renting the Secret

Disney Vacation Club counts more than 300,000 people among its members. Quite often, members end up with points they won't be able to use during a designated use-year. This glut is a bonus for visitors to Walt Disney World, who can rent points from members and stay at a deluxe resort for a fraction of the cost. The transaction, normally conducted completely online, requires a bit of trust, but it results in a much less expensive room rate.

The transaction works like this: The owner of the points—the DVC member—agrees to reserve a room in the renter's name in exchange for a cash payment. The trust element comes into play because the renter, assuming he or she is not a DVC member, has no control over the points. An unscrupulous DVC member could potentially play havoc with a trusting vacationer's plans and funds. While it has happened, it appears to be an uncommon occurrence. The average price-per-point rate ranges from $10 to $12, and sometimes slightly more.

The Straight Dope *Arrange to rent points at sites such as dvcrequest.com, disboards.com, mouseowners.com, or dvctrader.com.*

In addition to reduced rates at deluxe-level, there are members-only perks. DVC members enjoy discounts while shopping, dining, and booking entertainment and recreation options. The most valuable perk, however, is the reduced rate on an Annual Pass. Annual Passholders enjoy entrance to all four theme parks for one calendar year, access to special "Passholder-only" events, and occasional discounts on rooms, merchandise, and dining.

 MOUSEJUNKIE BARRY I am of the shameful branch of the Mousejunkies family tree that doesn't belong to Disney Vacation Club. This, however, hasn't prevented me from enjoying the spoils of a greatly discounted resort room.

A recent visit to Disney found me back at the Wilderness Lodge Resort, where my family stayed during our first trip. Since we were to be traveling with another family, we figured that it made sense to book one of the Wilderness Lodge Villas. After a bit of research, I discovered that there are some DVCers out there with such an abundance of points that they have been known to rent those points to others. They benefit because they don't waste the points and I benefit because I wind up: a) staying at a DVC resort and b) saving quite a bit of cash that I can later spend on bottomless milkshakes and ribs. Actually, I could probably afford to buy a fancy monocle and top hat to wear while I gorge myself on those ribs.

All told, I ended up paying considerably less for the Villa than I did in staying in a regular room in the Lodge some fourteen months prior. Renting points *is* on the honor system, but the overwhelming majority of folks reporting online on their experiences with these transactions have only positive things to say. Why pay full price when you can pocket the extra hundreds—maybe thousands—of dollars. It just makes sense.

14 Mousejunkies Confess

I INITIALLY FELL IN LOVE WITH Walt Disney World in a nondescript hallway during a preshow to a now-defunct attraction. But the moment when I was absolutely convinced I was helpless in the face of Walt Disney World came on our second trip.

The Lightning Bolt Moment

We were walking through the World Showcase at Epcot, when an announcement was made that a parade would be starting soon. Knowing this would likely slow our walk to a crawl, we found a bench just to the side of the Germany pavilion, cuddled up with a pint of Beck's and waited for the undoubtedly garish display to get out of our way so we could continue on to the next country.

But a funny thing happened on the way to parking my butt. I sat down an enthusiast, but when I stood twenty minutes later my transformation into absolute Disney freak had taken place. I surrendered.

The Tapestry of Nations parade took its colorful, theatrical beauty and smashed me in the mind. It left me woozy (though it could've been the Beck's) and shockingly, touched.

The first time I experienced this parade I had no idea what to expect or what was going on. A majestic, towering figure in a flowing robe trimmed with gold alchemy symbols came walking out of a gate directly in front of me. That got my attention rather quickly. He gave a monologue about world peace; (delivered via one of 416 speakers cleverly hidden around the World Showcase) took a left and disappeared. He was trailed by a line of inventive, completely unique flowing puppets that would interact with guests and dance in time to a rhythmic, hypnotic soundtrack. The music had no discernible lyrics, but it spoke to me. It swelled and grew quiet. It exploded again majestically as drummers on giant wheels rolled by, beating out the pulse of this otherworldly performance. I was speechless as the dramatic procession played out in front of me. I had fallen in love with Walt Disney World about a year earlier, but this was the moment that would cement the obsession.

For each Mousejunkie, without exception, there is a similar experience.

Sharman Merrill, Methuen, Mass.: Two years ago we went on what I thought would be our "last" trip for a long time. My older son, Nathan, had graduated from high school, and we thought a big, extravagant trip would be the perfect way to celebrate. The trip was great. Fast forward to now, when my "baby" is eighteen, and all he wants is to go back to Walt

Disney World. We're booked for next month and (God willing) once a year indefinitely. Why? Because, to quote my kids, "Disney is where it's O.K. to dance in the street, be six-foot, three-inches tall and still hold hands with your mom, ride Dumbo with your Dad, admit you know all the words to the Tiki Room song, tear up at The American Adventure, and get excited because you got reservations at Le Cellier."

Carol Hanken, South Hiram, Maine: A few years ago my son Jason and his girlfriend Laci went to Walt Disney World with her parents for a week during March. As a family we are all Mousejunkies. We started taking the kids in 1988 and have been many times since then. As soon as the kids were old enough to vacation on their own, they often chose Walt Disney World as their vacation destination. About midway through their vacation Jason texted me a close-up photo of Laci holding a Splash Mountain FastPass+. I was at work at the time but checked my messages often, always hoping for an updated report on how their week was going, what they were doing or where they were eating. I was so excited to see that they had gotten FastPasses for Laci's favorite ride. It was several minutes later that I realized she was wearing an engagement ring! It was their way of announcing their engagement to us. He had proposed as they exited the ride to a round of applause from cast members and guests.

Postscript: *They later got married on Disney property—on the walkway near the launches to the resorts in front of the Magic Kingdom. It was not an official Disney wedding, instead, it was*

*a bit undercover. The family had shirts made that said "What
Wedding?" and they wore those as they celebrated around the
World Showcase at Epcot.*

Karen Goldfine, Rochester, N.Y.: We were at one of my
favorite Disney restaurants one night and I was telling the
server about how much I loved Walt Disney World pens—
the white-and-black ones they leave in your hotel room. We
had been to Disney the year before and I had brought back
a few and it was all I used to write notes with during college lectures. I told him I was excited to be back because my
pen from the year before had run out of ink. Before dinner
was over the server stopped by the table and went to sneeze.
When he "sneezed" a bunch of those pens fell from his hands
all over the table. I used a Disney pen for everything the rest
of my college career.

Dr. Michele Pakula, Merrick, N.Y.: As a psychologist and
a mom of two boys, ages eleven and thirteen, I have a few
stories about WDW that show how it's so much more than
an amusement park. First of all, from a psychological stand-
point, Walt Disney World brings so much to my family's
psychological and emotional well-being. I am always telling others about the psychological benefits of a trip to Walt
Disney World, from the planning stages to the trip itself as
well as the family memories that cannot be matched (most
think I'm crazy but who cares.) On a personal note we were
significantly effected by Hurricane Sandy and our upcoming trip to Walt Disney World was just a few months after

Sandy. It's what got us through. After having a significant part of our home destroyed, no electricity, heat or hot water for months and then seeing my children run to their favorite rides, enjoy wonderful meals and shows and finally relax and enjoy themselves, forgetting about all the stress at home, was truly magical. There is nowhere else in the world in my opinion that you can travel to and escape completely. We were euphoric on our trip, even though we knew we were coming home to crazy construction and expenses. We let ourselves be immersed in the magic—as we always do, but this time it was even more powerful. And the cast members were so kind and listened to our stories if we wanted to tell them. And I was able to do laundry while we were there which I could not do at home! I think that trip in particular was so good for my family's mental health. People kept asking how we were coping so well under the circumstances and my response was: "Because we're going to Walt Disney World!"

Amy vanSwol, Manteno, Ill.: My son Caden has Tourette's Syndrome and has facial tics that make him sometimes look like he is making strange facial expressions. Disney has always been wonderful about this, and this trip was no exception. We were at Star Wars Weekends and all Caden could talk about was meeting Mace Windu. He has always been a fan. I wasn't sure of that possibility actually happening, so I told him we would just have to see. During the Motorcade, I watched as Mace Windu came down the street, nodding to people. Then, he came over and took Caden's hands in his and said, "May the Force be with You." He didn't do this to anyone else that I could see. Caden turned around in shock and said, "Did you just see that?" while jumping up and down with joy. We thought that was the end of the story. However, later on in the day we were exited out of the Little Mermaid show due to a fire that occurred and we were a bit bummed. We decided to wander over to the Streets of America and see what was going on there. We saw a line, so we got in it, not knowing who was on the other side. My husband poked his head around the corner and came back and said, "It's Mace!" Caden was super excited at this news. Just as we got up to the front the cast member asked who we were waiting to see and we told her. She said she was just getting ready to trade him out, but she'd ask him if he would wait for one more. He agreed. As Caden came around the corner, Mace said, "I remember you!" Caden quickly told him he was his favorite and I thanked him for giving him some special attention. Mace then bent down to his level and had a conversation with him. I have no idea what they talked about, but what I do know is that Caden was having a lot of tics brought on by his excitement and they didn't even phase Mace at all. They had a special picture with just the two of them. It touched my heart.

Nancy Layton, Bedford, N.H.: Six years ago I learned I had skin cancer on my forehead. It was bad. The little irritated spot turned out to be like an iceberg that covered my whole upper forehead down to the bone. I had four surgeries in three months trying to piece my upper forehead back together. The one thing that kept me from falling apart was a trip to Walt Disney World coming later that year. My daughter and I were splurging and staying at the Contemporary in a Magic Kingdom-view room. I dreamed of it and it kept me going through a terrible time. I broke down on the phone with the cast member who booked our room. She was so sweet, kind and positive. Everything went as well as the surgeon could manage with the surgeries, and finally there was no more cancer. I was left with extensive scarring and a dent in my forehead that looked like I got hit hard with a hammer (I cover it with bangs.) Cut to check-in at the Contemporary six months later—we were told that we were being upgraded to the twelfth-floor concierge level and were met with balloons, candy, flowers and our own private cast member to take us up to the room! I broke down and asked why they were doing this? The woman behind the desk said, "Because you deserve it after what you went through and we are thankful that you are here with us today!" I got a hug from both of them and there were tears all around. Every day something special was sent to our room: More flowers, balloons, candy, special desserts, front-row seats at the Spirit of Aloha dinner show at the Polynesian Resort and so much kindness and support from the staff. It was the trip of a lifetime. I remember going out on the balcony after my daughter was asleep to take it all in. I got to see Cinderella's Castle "goodnight kiss" (magical twinkling lights) for the first time. I felt such joy and relief. Disney had reached out to me and gone above and beyond with kindness. I am forever grateful. I try to go to Walt Disney World at least every year. It never loses the magic. It is a special place where your dreams really do come true.

Melissa Martin, Philadelphia, Penn.: One of my fondest memories is when my then two-year-old was eating dinner with her father and I at 1900 Park Fare for the Cinderella dinner. She was decked out in her Cinderella gown and tiara, and even had on her glass slippers. All the characters came and went, taking pictures and exchanging jokes and posing tips with her. She was ecstatic. At the end of the dinner, Cinderella and Prince Charming shared a dance in the middle of the dining hall, so we went up to watch since we were seated in the back. As we watched my daughter asked me if she could dance with Prince Charming too, and I replied yes. She waltzed right on up to the dancing royals, tapped Cinderella and asked if she could dance with the prince, too. Cinderella stepped aside and being a good sport with great Disney spirit, the Prince sure enough obliged and twirled my little girl, all decked out in her Cinderella gear, all around the dance floor when he was supposed to be putting on a show for the diners. It was so fantastic and so overwhelming to see. Even all the diners were taking pictures of them together, twirling all over the dance floor. I almost kicked myself for not taking video, but it just never occurred to me and it happened so fast. Once the crowd started clapping, she got embarrassed and ran to me. But she still remembers the day she stole a dance from Cinderella with Prince Charming. For the rest of the week, random people would come up to us asking if she was the little girl who danced with the prince.

Clair Williamson, Dawsonville, Georgia: Walt Disney World is somewhat new to me, but at the same time, I feel like I have always loved Disney. I had never been to the world as a child, and when my husband and I were planning a honeymoon, his mother actually offered to pay for us to honeymoon at Walt Disney World. I brushed her off thinking I wouldn't want to spend my honeymoon with a bunch of kids. We wound up going to Daytona Beach, which isn't too far from Orlando, and my husband insisted on bringing me to Disney World for just one day. We arrived at the Ticket and Transportation Center and I wasn't impressed. Then my husband pulled me toward the ferry boat and I saw the Castle. Like most people who see the Castle for the first time, I was speechless, followed by excited and giddy. We couldn't get across the lake fast enough. I finally made it past the turnstiles and was awestruck. This place was magic—you could feel it in your bones. After watching me drink it all in, my husband finally dragged me off and we started riding rides. Each one was a journey into my childhood, movies I had loved, books I had read, characters that were real! It felt like each turn we took we were getting to know each other more and more deeply and falling more and more in love. We didn't have any money since we had spent it all on the wedding, but we shared a turkey leg for dinner and my one souvenir was a pen with Eeyore on it. Whenever we go back to Disney, I relive all those feelings: That closeness with my husband, the thrill of childhood coming to life in front of my eyes and the excitement when you see the castle for the first time. I wished for our son during Wishes, and two years later, we brought him to see it for himself. I cried that time too. Disney is home. It is happy, it is magical.

Christopher Hicks, Xenia, Ohio: Back in 2006 my wife and I returned to Walt Disney World for our tenth wedding anniversary. It was the last day of our trip. We had dinner at 'Ohana (where they announced our anniversary and made us dance the hula) and then headed back to Magic Kingdom for Wishes. Somehow, with only a few minutes to spare, we made it all the way up to the hub around the Partners statue just before the show started. So I stood there, next to Uncle Walt and Mickey, my arms around my wife, ten years to the day we were married and listened to a song tell me that wishes do come true. I couldn't help it. I cried like a baby. It felt perfectly normal to me to be that emotional there. Not too far away a dad was hugging his little girl as overcome with emotion as I was. It was, well, perfect. Not only is it my best Disney World memory, it is one of my best memories period.

Dana Wiggins, Summerville, S.C.: My son, who is now nine, is a huge Indiana Jones fan. My husband Ronnie and daughter Kaitlyn had gone off together to ride Tower of Terror and the Aerosmith Rock 'n' Roller Coaster so I could take Harryson to see the Indiana Jones Stunt Show. After the show we stayed so we could meet Indy and take pictures. I had made Harryson's autograph book for this trip and the cover was Indiana Jones. Indy liked it a lot! He got down on one knee so he was eye-level with my son and began to ask him a series of questions. Indy asked Harryson if he had the hat, whip, and jacket to which he replied, "Yes!" Then he asked him if he had the gloves and Harryson looked up at me and then shook his head no. The cast member playing Indy began to take off the gloves he was wearing, gave them to my son and told him: "Now you do!" Harryson was speechless and I was almost in tears. The gloves were worn and even had duct tape in places, but to my son they were priceless. Dreams really do come true at Disney.

Kristi Grady, Amarillo, Texas: In 2012, we took our then four-year-old to Walt Disney World for the Halloween Party and to enjoy our favorite spot in the universe. We had no idea that our attorney would call to tell us that my partner and I got to adopt our daughter the night of the Halloween Party. My wife and daughter were on the new Dumbo ride. I usually wait while they ride anything that goes in a circle, so I got the call that we had been waiting four years for. My daughter could legally be adopted! You can imagine my shock. There I was, in the Magic Kingdom, dressed in a full-length costume with matching cap with tears streaming down my face. When my wife and daughter got off the ride they found me next to the stroller, just sobbing. My wife thought someone had died, but no, a miracle happened—right there in the New Fantasyland. We were going to finally get to be a family. Our next stop after Fantasyland was Tomorrowland. We were shopping at Merchants of Venus when the cast members noticed that I was still teary. They immediately asked what was wrong, and I got to tell them how it wasn't wrong, it was right. They were so excited for us. They made buttons that said "Celebrating Rylee!" and "Congratulations Walker Family!" It still makes me tear up. I don't know if those two cast members will ever know how much that night meant to us. Their reaction made the night even better. It was Magical.

Chrissy Spakoski, Pembroke, Mass.: In 2007 I was lucky enough to go on a Magical Gathering with my family—there were eleven of us, my grandparents, aunts, uncles, cousins and me. My grandparents had only recently retired from the restaurant business, and this trip was to celebrate my grandmother's seventieth birthday and an aunt's fortieth birthday. This was the first vacation any of my aunts had ever gone on with my grandfather as he had never been willing to leave his restaurant. At the age of seventy-four he was meeting Mickey Mouse at breakfast at Chef Mickey's and I still get a little lump in my throat thinking about the genuine joy on his face as he held out his strong Italian hand to shake Mickey's, and then went on to tell Mickey all about how when he was a child he had Mickey's face all over his bedroom wallpaper. It was as if he was talking to an old friend. I feel so lucky and so blessed to have been able to experience that with him. Disney's magic knows no bounds, there are no age limits on who it touches, and I feel as touched by that memory today as I did seven years ago.

Why We Go

Something happens when the blazing Florida sun dips below the horizon and darkness begins to settle-in.

Twinkling lights blink to life, illuminating the too-perfect surroundings in a way that makes everything even more magical. Main Street USA takes on a new, golden glow. Tiny lights resembling fireflies flicker in the trees. Cinderella Castle is bathed in ever-changing colors, dressed in her evening best.

It makes even the most jaded adult stop for a moment to take in the wonder. That perfect hour between dusk and when the stars seem to paint a backdrop specifically for your own personal moment is something that can't be explained to the uninitiated.

Try to explain that when the lights blink on and the park puts on an entirely new face, the dream-like environment combines with hypnotic music to create a euphoric feeling.

Try to explain to someone that when you walk under the train station on your way out of the Magic Kingdom for the last time, it's usually in silence. What can you say when you turn your back on a world built from the blueprints of your childhood dreams and walk away?

Try to explain to someone who's never experienced Walt Disney World that you actually feel sadness when the end arrives. I tend to try to fight it off as long as I can by clinging to everything around me. But when the Magical Express bus passes under the Walt Disney World sign and we turn onto the interstate on our way to the airport, it all seems to disappear.

It's never fun when a vacation comes to an end. But a Walt Disney World vacation finale is different. Packing up and heading home also means leaving behind unforgettable experiences and unexpected feelings. Because somehow, the cast members and Imagineers have created a world where guests—even repeat guests—can be surprised by sometimes subtle, sometimes profound moments that leave them breathless.

When I'm preparing for a Walt Disney World vacation, I get the same questions: "You're going again?" "Doesn't it get boring?" "Are you going to wear pants this time?"

Anyone who wears the title of Mousejunkie faces similar questions. Unless someone has touched, or has been touched by a small piece of Walt Disney's imagination, it's difficult to explain. Perhaps that's why I love going on vacation with someone who has never been to Walt Disney World before. It's an incredible experience to introduce someone the Castle for the first time; to watch them stand in awe of the Tree of Life; to walk the streets of old Hollywood; or to actually feel the concussions of Illuminations: Reflections of Earth as it displays a future of hope and light.

I go back for the chance to feel like a kid again. And to see the look on my daughter's face as she sees her dreams literally come to life.

The park's heart pulses through those twinkling lights that bathe the central Florida night in an ethereal wash. Stirring music flits up and around, alternately playful and profoundly moving, as I wonder what Walt Disney would have thought had he lived long enough to see his creation come to life.

Could he have seen the Florida Project blossom into a massive resort offering dreams-come-true to anyone who crossed into the playground of his imagination? Is Epcot what he imagined it might be one day? Would he recognize the glitz of Hollywood Boulevard or could he have foreseen the virtual veldt that is now home to the scores of animals who played such an important role in Disney's world?

He may not have survived to see the resort named in his honor completed, but his fingerprints are all over that wonderful world.

There's a quote attributed to Walt Disney that goes like this: "It is my wish to delight all members of the family, young and old, parent and child."

Dozens of trips. Thousands of memories made with my wife, my daughter, family members, and some of my closest friends. I've seen grandfathers sitting alongside grandsons and great-grandsons on the same attraction. On more than one occasion I've stood by as a young man drops to one knee and proposes to his fiancée in the shadow of the Partners statue in the Magic Kingdom. But maybe most profoundly I've seen families with young children fighting terrible diseases treated like royalty by Disney cast members. And for that brief time it's as if they don't have a care in the world.

Memo to Walt: Mission accomplished.

Personally, I found my answer. It may have taken years and cost me more than I'd like to admit, but I got it.

There's a week at the end of each summer where the hockey camps are over, the town rec program has ended for the year and there's nothing to do but sit around and wait for the final days to pass before school begins. Those few days scream to be filled with Disney.

From the time my daughter was five years old, she and I have run away to Walt Disney World for a quick daddy/daughter getaway during those final summer days. Mousejunkie

Amy can't usually break free around then, so it's just me, the kid and the Mouse. It was on one of those trips that I learned a very valuable lesson.

I've spent years thinking about why the place means so much to me. People ask why I continue to devote so much time, money and effort to visiting there. I always felt there was a deeper motivation to my obsession, but other than the obvious answers, the reasons have remained elusive. Until now.

It was on our last trip there together that I discovered why a place like Walt Disney World is so important. I finally have my answer.

My daughter, Mousejunkie Katie, is twelve now. I have no idea how it happened, but all of a sudden she's on the verge of becoming a teenager. When she was five, she'd throw her little arms around my neck and give me a hug and we'd talk about Mickey Mouse and Santa and dream about all the adventures we'd have. We've been lucky, in that we've been able to go on some of those adventures. But now they're in the past—gone. And if you're not careful, the magic starts to wear off, too. It's a very slow process at first, but soon it, too, can disappear. I noticed it one day recently. She had a little worry about her that never used to be there. She was just a little more serious and thoughtful and I even got my first eye-roll this year. Can't say I blame her.

The end of the summer came, and again we planned another daddy/daughter Disney trip. The day arrived and we flew to our favorite vacation destination. On our first full day, we arrived quite early at the gates of the Magic Kingdom. It had been a while since our last visit, so we wanted to stake out a spot for the opening show and take in every sight, smell and sensation that we could. There was music, dancing, the traditional opening and soon we were walking under the Main Street train station and into the park itself.

It was at that moment that any question about why I return to Walt Disney World so often was answered. She reached for my hand and we stepped on to Main Street together. I held on tightly as we rounded the corner and Cinderella Castle came into view. The little girl holding my hand was no longer twelve, anxious or serious. She was five years old and her world was full of magic. Her eyes grew big and a huge smile crossed her face. Disney, at that very second, became a fountain of youth. Everyday life imposes pressures and time eats entire pages of the calendar before we even notice. Yet here we were, transported back to a point where nothing else mattered. The years fell away and we were lost in time. We talked and laughed and she asked me questions and goofed around. I was "daddy" and not "dad." And the whole time she held my hand. We were completely immersed in the magic without a care in the world. I could see her, much younger, running toward the Castle in a tiny blue and white Cinderella dress. I would have given anything to go back to that day. Suddenly, I was there.

I became aware that our walk up Main Street USA was coming to an end because as we approached the Partners statue we had to make a choice: Head straight and explore New Fantasyland, or take a right and head into Tomorrowland. After that, we'd be judging standby lines, timing FastPasses and moving to the end of the row. We'd be among crowds for a good part of the rest of the day. Not that we wouldn't be enjoying ourselves, but these moments of perfection—when there's nothing but possibilities and wonder—would pass.

I started to walk more slowly. There had to be a way to make time slow down. Couldn't she stay little for a while longer? What if I let go of her hand and those years returned? I didn't care if we made it to the Seven Dwarfs Mine Train. I didn't care if we got in line at Be Our Guest in time for lunch. I just wanted our walk up Main Street to go on for as long as possible.

That's when I realized what I've been doing all these years. Every time I make that short trek, I'm going back to an idealized time where responsibilities are on the other side of those gates, where we're all younger and healthy and happy and where I get to hold on to my daughter's hand just a little longer. She is little and I am strong and I put her up on my shoulders and together we plunge into a dream world where everything exceeds your wildest expectations.

I don't think I'm quite done with Walt Disney World yet.

Resources

Finding Others of Our Kind

Four theme parks, twenty-two resorts, scores of restaurants, five championship golf courses, dozens of recreation opportunities and endless shopping spread across forty-seven square miles.

This is what you're attempting to get your arms around when you book a trip to Walt Disney World. It can leave even the hardiest vacationer beaten. I've seen them. They pay full price for everything, they spend too much time standing in line and their chafed and blistered bodies are strewn from one end of Fantasyland to the other. You can identify them by the tell-tale stroller tire marks across their backs. They leave tired, frustrated and broke.

I know because all of these things have happened to me at some point in my Disney addiction. I'm not free of its grip, but I have gotten a little better at navigating Walt Disney World.

It can be daunting, but there are some great resources to help ensure you don't become a casualty.

➤ **Mousejunkies.com:** Let's just get this out of the way—I write a supplemental blog attached to the *Mousejunkies* books. It has words like "mayhem," "splurge" and "droppings," which, in context can be quite amusing. (Mousejunkies.com)

There exists a community of online Disney journalists, and they are special people who are friendly, helpful and are an endless font of valuable information. The following are the kings of online Disney information:

➤ **WDWToday:** Mike Scopa, Matt Hochberg, Mike Newell and Len Testa lead an interactive webcast/podcast that airs new episodes three times a week. They are funny, smart, and a can't-miss. Their collective experience is invaluable when planning a Disney vacation. Listen in a few times and you'll be considering them friends. Every time I fly to Walt Disney World, I load up my MP3 player with episodes of the WDWToday podcast to pass the time. It's a great way to get into the proper mindset for the upcoming trip. (WDWToday.com)

➤ **WDWRadio:** Lou Mongello is the iron man of online Disney information. The hardest working man in WebDizBiz, Lou has won multiple awards for Best Travel Podcast. He's branched out to video reports, live broadcasts and in-park meet-and-greets. Do yourself a favor and dive into WDWRadio.com.

➤ **JimHillMedia.com:** Who has better sources than Jim Hill? No one. Jim gives his view on all doings at Walt Disney World, and the Disney company as a whole. His dogged reporting has got to have Disney execs scratching their heads and wondering how he keeps breaking news. (JimHillMedia.com)

➤ **Mickeyxtreme.com:** Great info, another great online personality, and the most up to date collection of Walt Disney World News. Julian's news section is like a Drudge Report of Disney news. I visit this site daily. (Mickeyxtreme.com)

There are a million online Disney forums, but the granddaddy of them all is the DISBoards. It is the largest, most expansive online Disney community on earth. Need to find out about theme park strategies? Dining information? Renting Disney Vacation Club points? You can find it all here. If you have a question about planning a vacation, search the forums here. (Disboards.com)

And of course there's the official Walt Disney World site, which is really good at getting you to throw caution to the wind and your money down the rabbit hole. And I wouldn't have it any other way. (WaltDisneyWorld.com)

Important and Useful Phone Numbers

General Information

Walt Disney World: (407) W-DISNEY

Annual Passholder information: (407) 560-PASS

Disney College Program, U.S. students: (407) 828-3091

Disney College Program, outside the U.S.: (407) 828-2850

Cirque du Soleil—La Nouba: (407) 939-7600

Walt Disney World golf: (407) WDW-GOLF

Disney guest relations: (407) 824-4321

Fireworks cruises: (407) WDW-PLAY

Lost and found: (407) 824-4245

Walt Disney World tours: (407) WDW-TOUR

Walt Disney World Resorts

All Star Movies: (407) 939-7000

All Star Sports: (407) 939-5000

All Star Music: (407) 939-6000

Animal Kingdom Lodge: (407) 938-3000

Beach Club: (407) 934-8000

BoardWalk Inn: (407) 939-5100

BoardWalk Villas: (407) 939-5100

Caribbean Beach: (407) 934-3400

Contemporary: (407) 824-1000

Coronado Springs: (407) 939-1000

Fort Wilderness: (407) 824-2900

Grand Floridian: (407) 824-3000

Old Key West: (407) 827-7700

Polynesian: (407) 824-2000
Pop Century: (407) 938-4000
Port Orleans French Quarter: (407) 934-5000
Port Orleans Riverside: (407) 934-6000
Saratoga Springs Resort and Spa (407) 827-1100
Shades of Green: (407) 824-3600
Walt Disney World Swan: (407) 934-3000
Walt Disney World Dolphin: (407) 934-4000
Wilderness Lodge: (407) 824-3200
Wilderness Lodge Villas: (407) 938-4300
Yacht Club: (407) 934-7000

Walt Disney World Dining

Dining Reservations: (407) WDW-DINE
Disney Dinning Experience: (407) 566-5858
Same-day Advanced Dining Reservations, on-site guests:
55 from hotel
Same-day Advanced Dining Reservations, off-site guests:
(407) 824-2858

Glossary

Mousejunkies—people who are obsessed with all things Walt Disney World—can sometimes seem to have their own language. Acronyms, nicknames, and shortened versions of longer titles pepper their conversations. Venture onto any Disney-related online community and you'll be overwhelmed by Mousejunkie-speak.

To help readers navigate the pixie dust-clouded waters of Disney lingo, here is a glossary of some of the more common terms and acronyms found in this book and often used in online Walt Disney World correspondence:

AA: The American Adventure, an attraction at Epcot.

AA: Audio Animatronics, lifelike figures of animals or humans used throughout the parks.

ADR: Advanced Dining Reservations. Guests who call to reserve a dinner reservation are actually making an Advanced Dining Reservation. To make an ADR, call 1-407-WDW-DINE.

AK: Disney's Animal Kingdom theme park. See also, DAK

All-Star Resorts: The term "All Stars" refers to three of Disney's value level resorts—All-Star Music, All-Star Sports, and All-Star Movies. The three resorts are located next to one another near Disney's Animal Kingdom theme park.

Animal Kingdom Lodge: A deluxe level resort that opened in 2001, the Animal Kingdom Lodge (AKL) is situated around a savannah where giraffes, zebras and other wild animals graze.

AP: Annual Pass

Bay Lake: A lake located to the east of the Magic Kingdom and just behind the Contemporary Resort. It connects to the nearby Seven Seas Lagoon. Fishing excursions, parasailing and boating activities are offered on Bay Lake.

Beach Club: The Beach Club Resort (**BC**) is a deluxe level resort located near the Epcot theme park. It is themed to look like turn-of-the-century seaside Atlantic cottages.

BoardWalk Resort: The BoardWalk Resort (often shortened to **BW**, **BWI** for BoardWalk Inn, or **BWV** for BoardWalk Villa), is a deluxe level resort designed to look like a 1920s Atlantic boardwalk.

Candlelight Processional: A massed-choir and orchestral performance of the Christmas story performed at Epcot during the holiday season.

Caribbean Beach Resort: A moderate level resort opened in 1988, the Caribbean Beach Resort (**CBR**) is located near Epcot, and features a Caribbean theme throughout. The buildings encircle a small lake called Barefoot Bay.

Cast Member: An employee of Walt Disney World. Often shortened to **CM**.

Character Meal: A dining option where Disney characters make their way around the room for photo and interaction opportunities with diners.

Contemporary Resort: One of the original resorts at the Walt Disney World resort, the Contemporary (**CR**) was built using modular construction. Pre-built rooms were placed into the building's frame by a crane. A bit of trivia: President Richard Nixon gave his "I'm not a crook" speech at the Contemporary Resort in 1973.

Coronado Springs Resort: Opened in 1997, this moderate level resort has a southwestern theme and features a pool in the shadow of a Mayan pyramid. Coronado Springs Resort (**CSR**) has a large convention center and often hosts trade shows.

Disney's Animal Kingdom: The fourth theme park built at the Walt Disney World resort, Animal Kingdom (**AK** or **DAK**) opened in 1997.

Disney's Hollywood Studios: The third theme park built at the Walt Disney World resort, it was opened as Disney-MGM Studios in 1989. The name was changed to Disney's Hollywood Studios (**DHS**) in January of 2007.

Disney's Magical Express: Guests staying at a Walt Disney World resort can use Disney's Magical Express buses (**DME**) to travel from Orlando International Airport to their resort for free.

Disney Vacation Club: Often referred to simply as "**DVC**," Disney Vacation Club is essentially a vacation timeshare, allowing people to purchase a real estate interest in one of the DVC resorts. Members purchase points which are used to make reservations at a DVC resort. The points are renewed annually.

Dolphin: The Walt Disney World Dolphin hotel is located in the BoardWalk resort area. It is operated by Starwood Hotels and Resorts Worldwide under the Sheraton Hotels brand. It is decorated in "Floribbean" style, using nautical themes in varying shades of pink and coral. It is adjacent to the similarly-themed Walt Disney World Swan hotel.

Downtown Disney: An outdoor shopping, dining, and entertainment complex at the Walt Disney World resort. It features several themed and chain restaurants like the Rainforest Café, House of Blues, and Planet Hollywood, as well as the Cirque du Soleil theater where *La Nouba* is performed. Downtown Disney (**DTD**) is divided into three sections: the Marketplace, Pleasure Island and the West Side.

ECV: Electric Convenience Vehicle—the scooters those with mobility issues can take advantage of.

Epcot: The second theme park built at the Walt Disney World resort, Epcot opened in 1982. Originally named Epcot Center, its name was shortened to Epcot in 1994.

Epcrotch: The chafing that occurs while vacationing at Walt Disney World.

Extra Magic Hours: One of the Walt Disney World theme parks opens early or stays open after regular park closing hours every day. Guests staying at a Walt Disney World resort can take advantage of Extra Magic Hours (**EMH**), enjoying, in theory, shorter wait times and lighter crowds.

Expedition Everest: An expertly-themed roller coaster at Disney's Animal Kingdom. Expedition Everest (**EE**) was built to resemble Mount Everest—complete with snowy peaks and jagged rock formations.

FastPass+: Disney's FastPass+ (**FP**) is a virtual queuing system wherein guests insert their park tickets into a kiosk that then distributes a small ticket with a return time stamped on it. Guests return to that specific attraction at the prescribed time, thus bypassing the sometimes lengthy standby line. Guests are allowed to have only one FastPass+ per park ticket at one time.

Festival of the Lion King: A can't-miss musical performance at Disney's Animal Kingdom.

Fort Wilderness: A resort with campsites that allow guests to tent, use their own camper or recreation vehicle, or stay in a cabin. Fort Wilderness (**FW**) opened just weeks after the Magic Kingdom in 1971.

Friendship Launch: These are the boats that shuttle guests around the Epcot theme park and resort area. The Friendships travel from one side of the World Showcase Lagoon to the other, and from the BoardWalk area resorts—including the BoardWalk, Yacht Club, Beach Club, the Swan and Dolphin hotels—to Epcot and Disney's Hollywood Studios theme park.

Future World: An area of Epcot located adjacent to the World Showcase. Spaceship Earth, Soarin', Test Track, and Mission: Space are among the more prominent attractions located in Future World (**FW**).

Grand Floridian: Disney's Grand Floridian Resort and Spa (**GF**) is a deluxe level resort across the Seven Seas Lagoon from the Magic Kingdom. Its look was inspired by the beach resorts of Florida's East Coast.

Great Movie Ride: This attraction (**GMR**) takes guests on a tour through memorable films throughout Hollywood history.

Hidden Mickey: A cleverly disguised shape in the form of Mickey Mouse's head. Disney's Imagineers sometimes work them into attractions or theming as a way of "signing" their work.

Hoop-Dee-Doo Musical Review: A dinner show held at Pioneer Hall on the grounds of Fort Wilderness, the Hoop-Dee-Doo Musical Review (**HDDMR**) is a Wild West vaude-ville review. The shows run approximately two hours.

International Gateway: A "back door" entrance to the Epcot theme park, the International Gateway is accessible through the BoardWalk area resorts. Entering through the International Gateway puts visitors into the United Kingdom pavilion in the World Showcase.

It's a Small World: Classic attraction at the Magic Kingdom, sometimes shortened to **IaSW**.

Kidcot Fun Stops: There are sixteen Kidcot Fun Stops located in the Epcot theme park throughout Futureworld and the World Showcase. Children are given a cutout mask that they can color and decorate as they stop at each of the locations throughout the park. Cast members will also stamp the mask at each country or Kidcot Fun Stop.

Magic Kingdom: The Magic Kingdom (**MK**), which opened in 1971, was the first theme park at the Walt Disney World resort.

Magic Your Way: What Disney calls its theme park tickets. Guests can buy the base Magic Your Way ticket, or add several options, such as Park Hopping or No Expiration.

MCO: Orlando International Airport.

MNSSHP: Mickey's Not So Scary Halloween Party—a hard-ticket, after-hours event at the Magic Kingdom celebrating the Halloween season.

Mousejunkie: Anyone interested in or obsessed with Walt Disney World. Someone of high standards, great knowledge, a sense of humor, a yearning for fun, and is normally extremely attractive and intelligent.

MVMCP: Mickey's Very Merry Christmas Party—an after hours, hard-ticket event at the Magic Kingdom celebrating the holiday season.

Old Key West: The original Disney Vacation Club resort, Old Key West (**OKW**) opened in 1991 and evokes a Key West theme.

Park Hopping: The act of leaving one Walt Disney World theme park and going to another in a single day is called Park Hopping. Guests must have the Park Hopper option in order to move between two or more theme parks in one day.

Pop Century: A value resort, Pop Century has 2,880 rooms in ten separate, themed buildings.

Polynesian: Disney's Polynesian Resort (often referred to in the shorthand, "the Poly"), opened in 1971 on the shores of the Seven Seas Lagoon. It reflects a Hawaiian theme, and is one of the original Magic Kingdom area resorts.

Port Orleans French Quarter/Riverside: A moderate level resort, the French Quarter (**POFQ**) and Riverside (**POR**) were once two separate resorts. They were combined in 2001.

Reedy Creek Improvement District: Sometimes shortened to **RCID**, it is the governmental structure overseeing the property of Walt Disney World.

Saratoga Springs: The Saratoga Springs Resort and Spa (**SSR**) is located across the Lake Buena Vista Lagoon from Downtown Disney, and was built to look like the upstate New York spa and horseracing town. It is the largest of the Disney Vacation Club resorts.

Seven Seas Lagoon: The man-made body of water located in front of the Magic Kingdom.

Spaceship Earth: The geodesic sphere (the giant golfball) that functions as the Epcot theme park's icon, Spaceship Earth (**SE**) stands 18-stories tall and houses a 13-minute dark ride that takes guests through the history of human communication.

Swan: The Walt Disney World Swan hotel is located in the BoardWalk resort area. It is operated by Starwood Hotels and Resorts Worldwide under the Sheraton Hotels brand. It is decorated in "Floribbean" style, using nautical themes in varying shades of pink and coral. It is adjacent to the similarly-themed Walt Disney World Dolphin hotel.

Tree of Life: A 14-story artificial tree that acts as Disney's Animal Kingdom's park icon. Images of more than 325 animals are carved into its trunk, and the structure houses a 3-D movie, *It's Tough To Be a Bug.*

TTC: The Ticket and Transportation Center is located between the Magic Kingdom parking area and the Seven Seas Lagoon. At the TTC you can board a monorail to Epcot or the Magic Kingdom, or a ferry boat to the Magic Kingdom. The Magic Kingdom Kennels are also located there.

Wilderness Lodge: Disney's Wilderness Lodge Resort (**WL**) is a deluxe level resort on the shores of Bay Lake. It look was inspired by the great lodges of the Pacific Northwest.

World Showcase Lagoon: The body of water around which Epcot's World Showcase is situated. Epcot's IllumiNations: Reflections of Earth show is displayed over the World Showcase Lagoon nightly. The World Showcase Lagoon has a perimeter of 1.2 miles.

Yacht Club: Designed to look like a New England seaside retreat, the Yacht Club (**YC**) is located in the boardwalk area near the Epcot theme park.

Index

Acknowledgments

The following people have been extremely important in helping bring this all together: Amy and Katie Burke, Randy and Carol Houle, J and Deb Cote, Jenna Petroskey, Ryan Elizabeth Foley, Walter Pomerleau, Barry Kane, Judy and Stephen Demeritt, Christopher Strong and Maureen Lamb, Heather Bishop-Dumka, Donald Chang, Kelly Koch, Bart Scott, Arthur Lyons, Charles Stovall, Rose Monahan, Patrick LaKemper, Julian Pupo, Kevin Linn, Adam and Sarah Powers, and God.

About the Author

Bill Burke is a veteran newspaper reporter and editor. He is also a columnist at *Parenting N.H. Magazine* where he has been named a three-time consecutive winner of Best Humor Column by the Parenting Media Association.

He has traveled to Walt Disney World countless times over the years. During his twenty-one-year journalism career, he has covered marathons and murders, and written everything from business features to comic book scripts. Bill has been traveling to and writing about Walt Disney World for the past seventeen years.

A dyed-in-the-wool New Englander who recently came to the conclusion he hates the cold weather but can't live without good fried clams, Bill spent portions of his childhood living in different parts of the country and traveling throughout the United States. Now he flees to the warm embrace of central Florida whenever time and finances allow. Or even if they won't.

After trying out a number of different career options ranging from installing concrete foundations and digging ditches to working as a bouncer at an oceanfront nightclub and selling sci-fi collectibles, he stumbled across journalism.

He lives in southern New Hampshire with his wife, Amy, twelve-year-old daughter, Katie and their psychotic dog, Figgy.